GOD'S BANKER

The Life and Death of Roberto Calvi

Rupert Cornwell

The death in London by hanging of one of Italy's leading bankers, Roberto Calvi, focused the world's attention upon the affairs of the Banco Ambrosiano, a bank closely involved in Vatican finance. This bank, which Calvi had devoted his career to building up, was under heavy investigation at the time of his death, and Calvi himself had been charged with fraud and the illegal transfer, or misappropriation, of funds running into millions.

Following Calvi's macabre downfall, the Banco Ambrosiano collapsed, exposing the darker face of Italy, its financial and political intrigue, sinister secret societies, intimidation, blackmail and murder. The Ambrosiano affair shook the international banking system. It helped to expose years of reckless financial behaviour by the Vatican, calling into question the judgement of the Pope himself. Aspects of the affair have still not been explained: some probably never will be. But the broad outline of what happened is now clear.

After intensive research, including interviews with leading figures in the Italian financial world, with Cavi's family and associates in the United States and with bankers in the capitals of Europe, Rupert Cornwell, the *Financial Times* Rome correspondent, has been able to unravel the complex story of Roberto Calvi and his world, and to piece together this amazing chronicle of financial malpractice in high places.

For this *Counterpoint* edition he has up-dated and expanded the final chapters to take account of the latest developments in this extraordinary story.

D1634734

Epimenides the Cretan said: all Cretans are liars.
Was he telling the truth or a lie?

Euboulides, Greek Philospher, 4th Century B.C.

. . . Fare che diventasse per sempre – non più una
burla, no; ma una realtà, la realtà di una vera
pazzia: qua, tutti mascherati, e la sala del trono,
e questi quattro miei consiglieri; segreti, e –
s'intende – traditori.
(. . . So that it might be no longer a joke; but a
reality for ever, the reality of true madness. Here,
in the throne room, with everyone masked; and
these four secret advisors of mine – naturally
traitors all.)

Pirandello, *Henry IV*.

GOD'S BANKER

Rupert Cornwell

The Life and Death of
ROBERTO CALVI

COUNTERPOINT

London
UNWIN PAPERBACKS
Boston   Sydney

First published in Great Britain by Victor Gollancz Ltd 1983

First published in Unwin Paperbacks 1984
Reprinted 1984

UNWIN PAPERBACKS
40 Museum Street, London WC1A 1LU, UK

Unwin Paperbacks
Park Lane, Hemel Hempstead, Herts HP2 4TE, UK

George Allen & Unwin Australia Pty Ltd.,
8 Napier Street, North Sydney, NSW 2060, Australia

To Angela

ISBN 0 04 332099 6

Printed and bound in Great Britain by
Cox & Wyman Ltd, Reading

ACKNOWLEDGEMENTS

This book is drawn from three main sources: my own experiences and recollections as correspondent of the *Financial Times* in Italy, during the events described in the last two thirds of it; the work of colleagues in the Italian and foreign press—an irreplaceable support for the journalist everywhere; and direct interviews with and documentary assistance from many of those involved with the story of Roberto Calvi and Banco Ambrosiano. Numerous people have given their time to help with the book's preparation. I am deeply grateful to all of them, especially those who would have preferred not to discuss a subject they would best like to forget. Many of them too have specifically asked not to be mentioned; and obviously I must respect their confidence. For that reason I will mention none of them, as a partial list of thanks might only be misleading.

Those to whom I can express gratitude include my paper for allowing me to take a sabbatical at the ideal moment, as well as friends on its staff who gave hospitality and help. They include Duncan Campbell-Smith in London, Reggie Dale in Washington, Paul Betts in New York and Nikki Kelly in the Bahamas. In Italy, I would take the opportunity of acknowledging my debt to the excellent book already published on the Ambrosiano affair, *Il Banco Paga*, by Leo Sisti and Gianfranco Modolo. Some of the other published works from which I have drawn are referred to in footnotes. Then I must thank Professor Luigi Spaventa, who kindly read the manuscript and made valuable suggestions and caught potentially embarrassing mistakes. Similar thanks, for similar reasons, go to Mary Venturini, my colleague in Rome, James Buxton, and to George Armstrong. A special affectionate word must be kept for Nicoletta Rosati, our secretary in the *Financial Times* Office in Rome. She not only typed out two thirds of the manuscript, but also produced some precious and, she will not mind my saying, very Roman insights into an uncommonly complicated tale.

This book is an effort to provide a reconstruction that is at least understandable. Inevitably however, I will have made errors. I apologize for them in advance, offering in my defence only the observation that the book has been written in good faith—not the most conspicuous quality in the Calvi story.

Finally a brief note about the currencies referred to throughout the book. To avoid unmanageable strings of noughts, I have used the American billion in preference to thousands of millions, where the Italian lira is concerned. Between 1970 and 1982, the value of the pound varied between a low of around 1,400 lire and a peak of about 2,400 lire. The simplest, if rather rough, average conversion rate would perhaps be 2,000 lire. The lira/dollar rate has risen even more sharply. Between 1970 and 1975 the dollar stayed within the range of 580 to 680 lire. In 1976 it jumped at one stage to 900 lire. Over the next three years the rate declined to 780 lire. But from 1980, the dollar began an ascent which was showing no sign of abating during the time of writing. By early June 1983, it had passed the 1,500 lire mark.

Rupert Cornwell

CONTENTS

Some of The Cast

Andreatta, Beniamino: Born 1928. Professor of Economy at Bologna University. Since 1976 a senator for the Christian Democrat party. Named Budget Minister August 1979. Between October 1980 and November 1982 Minister of the Treasury. He ordered the liquidation of Banco Ambrosiano.

Andreotti, Giulio: Born 1919. A Christian Democrat member of Parliament since Italy became a Republic. Many times Minister, including five terms as Prime Minister, in 1972 and 1973, and from July 1976 to August 1979. One of Italy's most experienced politicians, and famous for the aphorism *Il potere logora chi non ce l'ha*—"Power wears out those who don't have it."

Baffi, Paolo: Born 1911. Entered Bank of Italy in 1936. Head of Research department, then general manager, and Governor between 1975 and September 1979. He ordered the inspection of Banco Ambrosiano in 1978.

Bagnasco, Orazio: Born 1927. Financier active in property-based mutual funds. Since 1980 owner of the CIGA chain of luxury hotels. Deputy chairman of Banco Ambrosiano from January 1982 until the end.

Bazoli, Giovanni: Born 1932. Deputy chairman of Banca San Paolo di Brescia. In August 1982 named the first chairman of Nuovo Banco Ambrosiano, which took over the Italian parts of the old Banco Ambrosiano group.

14

Bonomi, Carlo: Born 1940. Financier, chairman of Invest Spa, the family holding company. The Bonomi group, then headed by Anna Bonomi Bolchini, mother of Carlo, was between 1973 and 1975 associated with some of the dealings of Roberto Calvi.

Botta, Giacomo: Senior official in the foreign department of Banco Ambrosiano. Until 1981 director of Banco Ambrosiano Andino in Lima. Since 1981 in charge of foreign business at head office in Milan.

Calvi, Roberto: Born 1920, died 1982, after career of some 35 years at Banco Ambrosiano. Named general manager in 1971, deputy chairman and managing director from 1974, and chairman from November 1975 until his death. Chairman of La Centrale since 1976. Chairman of Banco Ambrosiano Holding Luxembourg and of Banco Ambrosiano Overseas, Nassau. He was a member of the P-2 freemasons' lodge from 1975 or 1976, or perhaps earlier.

Canesi, Carlo: Died 1981. Chairman of Banco Ambrosiano from 1965 until 1971. He took on Calvi at the bank, and helped shape his early career.

Carboni, Flavio: Sardinian property contractor, with a wide variety of contacts. Met Calvi in August 1981. Influential on Calvi during the last ten months of his life, and organized the flight to London in June 1982.

Carli, Guido: Born 1914. Governor of the Bank of Italy 1960 to 1975. He was instrumental in the downfall of Sindona. Chairman of Confindustria, Italian employers association between 1976 and 1980.

Ciampi, Carlo: Born 1920. Spent career entirely within Bank of Italy. Deputy general manager 1976, general manager 1978. Appointed Governor of the Bank of Italy in September 1979. His intensifying pressure led to the exposure of Calvi's fraud in 1982.

Craxi, Bettino: Born 1934. Since 1968 member of parliament representing Italian Socialist Party. Since 1976, leader of the party.

Cuccia, Enrico: Managing director of Mediobanca in Milan from 1946 until his retirement in 1982. A determined enemy of both Sindona and Calvi.

De Benedetti, Carlo: Born 1934. Since 1978 deputy chairman and chief executive of Olivetti. Between November 1981 and January 1982 deputy chairman of Banco Ambrosiano, and a fierce critic of the methods of Roberto Calvi during his brief stay at the bank.

Di Donna, Leonardo: Born 1932. Between 1976 and 1982 a director of ENI, the Italian state-owned energy group. Together with Florio Fiorini, for part of the period finance director of ENI, he arranged substantial loans for the foreign subsidiaries of Banco Ambrosiano between 1978 and 1981. Listed as a member of the P-2 freemasons' lodge.

Gelli, Licio: Born 1919. Grandmaster of the P-2 freemasons' lodge until its discovery and dissolution in 1981. A powerful influence on Calvi in the later stages of his career. Arrested in Geneva, September 1982.

La Malfa, Ugo: Died 1979. A founder of the modern Italian republic and leader of the Italian Republican party until his death. Many times Minister, Treasury Minister in 1973 and 1974, and a fierce opponent of both Sindona and Calvi.

Leemans, Michel: Born 1938. A Belgian, with wide international financial experience. Since 1974 at La Centrale, the holding company for the Italian interests of the Ambrosiano group, and until August 1982 its managing director. He conducted the final talks with the IOR, the Vatican bank, to try and save Ambrosiano in June 1982.

Leoni, Filippo: Born 1940. In charge of foreign division of Banco Ambrosiano for much of the period before the bank's collapse in 1982. Between 1979 and 1981 chairman of Banco Andino. A director of Banco Ambrosiano Holding of Luxembourg, and from 1981 joint general manager of Banco Ambrosiano, Milan.

Marcinkus, Paul: Born 1922 at Chicago, Illinois. Left to study canon law in Rome, 1950. Chairman of the Istituto per le Opere di Religione (IOR), the Vatican bank, since 1971. Pro-President, or "mayor", of the Vatican City State since 1981.

Mennini, Luigi: Born 1911. Managing director of the IOR. His son, Alessandro, was an executive in the foreign department of Banco Ambrosiano.

Milan Magistrates: Giuliano Turone, Gherardo Colombo, Luca Mucci, Gerardo d'Ambrosio, Pierluigi dell'Osso and others. They conducted the frequently overlapping investigations of the bankruptcies of first Michele Sindona and then Calvi.

Ortolani, Umberto: Perhaps Gelli's closest associate in the P-2. Instrumental in bringing the Rizzoli publishing group within the orbit of the secret lodge. Proprietor of Banco Financeiro Sudamericano (Bafisud) in Uruguay, in which Ambrosiano Overseas of Nassau held an interest.

Pazienza, Francesco: Born 1946. Business consultant, with links to Italy's former secret services, certain politicians, and figures in US public life. Closely involved with Calvi from 1981. He tried to form the consortium which would rescue Banco Ambrosiano.

Pesenti, Carlo: Born 1907. Financier of long-standing Catholic connections. He also had a close business relationship with the Ambrosiano group. In March 1982 he became Banco Ambrosiano's largest declared shareholder, and was appointed a director.

Rizzoli, Angelo: Born 1943. Since 1978 chairman of Rizzoli publishing group, which bought the *Corriere della Sera* newspaper in 1974. From 1975 his companies were heavily reliant on loans from Banco Ambrosiano. He was named as a member of the P-2 in 1981.

Rosone, Roberto: Born 1928. Spent his entire career at Banco Ambrosiano, mostly on the domestic side. From 1981, general manager and deputy chairman. He proposed placing the bank in the hands of the Bank of Italy in June 1982.

Rossi, Guido: Born 1931. Named as chairman of the Consob, the Milan stock market regulatory authority in 1981. He forced Banco Ambrosiano to be quoted on the main market. Resigned from the Consob in August 1982.

Sarcinelli, Mario: Born 1934. Entered Bank of Italy in 1957. In 1976 he was appointed a deputy general manager, in which capacity he superintended the inspection of Banco·Ambrosiano in 1978. Briefly imprisoned during the "Bank of Italy affair" in 1979. All charges against him were dismissed and he was reinstated in 1980. Since 1982 director general of the Italian Treasury Ministry.

Siegenthaler, Pierre: A Swiss citizen, he was president of Banco Ambrosiano Overseas of Nassau from its inception in 1971, and as such closely involved with the foreign operations of Calvi.

Sindona, Michele: Born 1920. A financier, and an early mentor of Calvi, then partner with him in many deals. Declared bankrupt in 1974 and convicted of fraud and perjury in 1980 by a Manhattan Court. Currently in jail in the US. His name appeared in the membership lists of the P-2.

Tassan Din, Bruno: Born 1942. Entered the Rizzoli group in the early 1970s, to become general manager and then managing director. The financial strategist of Rizzoli, he negotiated with Calvi the sale of 40 per cent of Rizzoli to La Centrale in 1981. His name featured on the lists of P-2 members found in March 1981.

CHAPTER ONE

Introduction

WAR, SPORT AND scandal. Italy's general public hardly knew which way to turn in the summer of 1982. Down on the edge of the world in the South Atlantic, Britain was recapturing the Falklands capital of Port Stanley, to put an end to a conflict which had divided and discomforted Italy. The country had been torn between a natural sense of obligation to support an old European friend whose sovereign rights were being challenged, and its instinctive sympathies for Argentina, nearly half of whose population is of Italian extraction. Much closer to home, in Vigo in North-Western Spain, the national football team was unimpressively beginning its own campaign, that would culminate in world cup victory just four weeks later.

But something else was stealing up on Italy, which in the months ahead would overshadow memories of the battlefields of the South Atlantic and the playing fields of Spain.

On the evening of Saturday June 12, the main television news bulletins gave prominence to a most curious occurrence: two days earlier Roberto Calvi, chairman of Banco Ambrosiano, Italy's most important privately owned bank, had disappeared without word from his flat in central Rome. In most instances the temporary absence of a leading financier or industrialist, even if unexplained, would hardly be a matter of immense public concern. Roberto Calvi was, however, no ordinary financier, nor his bank an ordinary bank. For several years, and despite an outward appearance of soundness, Banco Ambrosiano and its chairman had been the object of suspicion and dark rumours.

Since the previous summer he had been without a passport after conviction and sentence to a four-year prison term for serious breaches of currency law. Calvi only remained at liberty pending an oft-postponed appeal, but due at last to be heard on June 21. Magistrates in Rome and his home city of Milan were investigating others of his turbid financial involvements.

Calvi had emerged as a member of the sinister P-2 freemasons' lodge, discovered in 1981 and swiftly outlawed as a threat to the security of the State. Nor was that all. By the time of Calvi's disappearance, many in authority in Rome, and in the know in Milan, were well aware that the court cases, the P-2 and the gossip were but symptoms of a deeper illness at Ambrosiano.

Small wonder that the Italian government was watching the affair intently, and that on that June Saturday Giovanni Spadolini, the Prime Minister, observed publicly that the vanishing act was "an extremely serious event". Just how serious, however, not even he can have imagined.

Within a week of those words, Calvi was dead; and perhaps the most disastrous bank collapse anywhere since the Second World War had been set in motion. In the absence of the newspapers, halted for a strike, it was left to the radio to make known the scarcely credible; Calvi, carrying a falsified passport, his pockets stuffed with foreign banknotes and weighed down with stones, had been found hanging under a bridge, far away in London.

While British police and Italian magistrates were trying to piece together the truth of the last days and hours of Calvi's existence, other facts were coming to light at home, stretching the limits of credulity further. Far from being basically solid, Ambrosiano had buckled beneath the weight of $1,300 million of loans, extended by subsidiary banks in Latin America, and which now could not be recovered. The recipients of such largesse were a handful of Panamanian and Liechtenstein shell companies. And who owned them? The answer was none other than the Vatican itself.

As the unusually hot summer of 1982 wore on, the investigators tried to establish precisely how the money had been lost. In the process they began to uncover the history of a decade of inglorious partnership between Calvi's Ambrosiano and the Istituto per le Opere di Religione (IOR), literally "the Institute for Religious Works", but more prosaically, the Vatican bank. Half, maybe more, of the missing money had been used to buy shares in Ambrosiano and other companies controlled by Calvi. The destination of the rest constituted perhaps the greatest financial mystery of the early 1980s.

Some, it has been suggested, was channelled to Italian political parties, some went to finance the nefarious activities of the P-2, and much, in the closing stages, to buy help from any quarter to stave off gathering calamity. There is some evidence that towards the end Ambrosiano may have been linked with international arms trading; other rumours were that the bank's complex network *could* have served as a channel for financing Solidarity, the independent Polish trade union, close to the heart of a Polish Pope, and which was outlawed in December 1981.

What is clear is that for the last year of his life and more, Calvi, reputed to be one of Italy's most powerful men, was no longer master of his destiny. The predator had become a prey, fit only to be exploited, blackmailed, threatened and finally abandoned.

On June 7 his last redoubt fell, when the Ambrosiano board, previously accommodating of his every whim, voted him down for the first and only time. Then flight, death in London, and the discovery that only the Vatican, if it agreed to repay some at least of the money lent to companies that it had sponsored, could prevent complete ruin. But the Vatican refused, and on August 6 the old Ambrosiano, once known as the "priests' bank", was no more, ordered into compulsory liquidation by the Italian Government. A year later, the echo of the scandal was still reverberating both inside and outside Italy.

By the extravagant standards of the international banking crisis of the summer of 1982, the Ambrosiano affair was modest. A good part of the missing money was made good by the Bank of Italy, and creditors would recover some at least of the rest. In any case $1,300 million was of small account when measured against the $84,000 million on which the sovereign state of Mexico all but defaulted that August, and the huge debt repayment difficulties faced by countries like Poland, Brazil and Argentina. If the world's banking system found itself under unprecedented strain at that time, Banco Ambrosiano was only one of the smaller reasons.

But the fascinations of the story of Roberto Calvi are enormous. They lie in the length and method of his swindle, its geographical extent, and its backcloth of the enduring division between "lay" and

Catholic in Italian society. Then there is the cast of characters which peoples it. They range from a golfing archbishop in the Vatican to a jailed Sicilian financier, from eminent central bank governors to small-time hustlers and big-time criminals, from a dynasty of publishers to the venerable grandmaster of a secret freemasons' lodge.

If Italy is notoriously riddled with scandals, the Ambrosiano affair presents no few novelties. Above all, perhaps, the pattern was different. Italian scandals usually start with sensational disclosures, more often than not carefully orchestrated to further a cause in a given political or financial feud. Generally they move from the complicated to the virtually incomprehensible, and the outside world, and most Italians, give up even trying to understand. Banco Ambrosiano and Roberto Calvi are the reverse. Their scandal started with innuendo and rumour, persisting for a long period. Then the explosion, leading not to obscurity but greater clarity, allowing many apparently unrelated events of the past to be understood as part of a single plot.

In other respects, however, the disaster of Roberto Calvi is only too familiar. Ambrosiano is but the last of a series of banking scandals which have peppered the 123 years since the modern Italian state was founded. Back in 1922 a prominent newspaper began an editorial with the words that "Italy is a fertile breeding ground for bankruptcies and banking scandals".

That observation was in the immediate wake of the Banca di Sconto (literally "Discount Bank") affair, a contorted tale of how Government credits, originally intended for financing wartime production, were used for speculation and ill-judged expansion both in Italy and abroad. Some thirty years before that, Italy's political establishment had been agitated and discredited by an earlier crop of bank failures—most notably that of the Banca Romana.

One of six regional issuing banks then authorized in the country, the Banca Romana lavishly financed not only the construction boom which accompanied the choice of Rome as Italy's permanent capital, but politicians and their parties as well. The misbehaviour extended to the printing of false banknotes, and led to the trial of Bernardo Tanlongo, the Banca Romana's Governor. The scandal even contributed to the resignation of the Government headed by Giovanni Giolitti, the dominant Liberal politician of his time. But an inquiry afterwards cleared him of any suggestion of personal enrichment; as with most politicians brushed by later bank scandals, including Ambrosiano, Giolitti lived to fight another day.

Recent decades have witnessed no let-up in the pace. The sequence has varied relatively little; the unscrupulous financier who helps meet the need for funds of the political parties, in exchange for protection, which at a certain point can be extended no longer. The most striking recent example, at least until Calvi's own contribution to Western financial history, was Michele Sindona, a Sicilian tax lawyer who in the 1960s and early 1970s constructed from Milan an empire which spanned the Atlantic. He had the unusual distinction of seeing his Italian and American banks go under virtually simultaneously. Sindona, as we shall discover, plays no small part in the history of Calvi, first as teacher, then partner, and finally as avenging tormentor.

The similarities with the Banca Romana scandal are glaring, but should not be surprising. For the ground rules of the system which provides such periodic abuses have remained much the same, for all the changes that have overtaken Italy in more than a century. The country has passed from liberal monarchy through two decades under Fascism to democratic parliamentary republic, from a heavy dependence on agriculture, to emergence as the world's seventh industrial power and a founder member of the Common Market. But for all the depth and breadth of the transformation, Italy has not acquired an efficient and transparent financial market of comparable depth and breadth.

The stock market where Calvi and Sindona flourished remains tiny, the natural home of speculators and insider trading, despite all recent efforts to improve its appeal. The banks remain the pivot of Italy's financial system. Risk capital, normally provided by the share market, is conspicuous mainly by its absence; to raise money in Italy is to secure a loan from a bank. The banks, however, can in turn be heavily conditioned by the politicians. Even before the Ambrosiano affair, some three-quarters of the Italian banking system were owned by the State. And in many cases the senior posts are politically conditioned appointments, the accepted spoils of power.

In the early postwar years, matters were comparatively simple, as the electoral domination of the Christian Democrat party, much influenced by the Vatican, was assured. On the left, the Socialists and Communists were weakened by the ripples of the cold war beyond Italy's frontiers, and their own differences within them. But from the mid-1950s on a subtle change took place. Although the Communists, despite a gradual climb in their vote, remained disqualified from power, pressures for a change in the formula by which the country was governed steadily grew. For the first time the Christian Democrats began to feel that their hitherto complete sway was threatened. The party moved to increase its control of the banking system and of the constellation of public sector corporations which had contributed much to Italy's postwar "economic miracle". Inevitably, temptations multiplied to use bank funds for mistaken industrial ventures, conceived in good part for reasons of patronage or vote winning.

By the early 1960s, Italy was moving leftward unmistakably. The trend was reflected both in the birth of the "centre-left" formula of government, bringing the Socialists into the arena of power—and in the intensifying struggle for top public sector jobs. The process, as might be expected, reduced the capacity of the State to act as an independent ringmaster. Sometimes it would seem little more than the sum of the various interest groups as they jostled for position. The same jostling also produced the succession of short-lived Governments and frequent "crises", for which Italian politics is best known abroad.

And yet, despite this illusion of instability, the system was, and remains, largely static. The Communists rarely strayed from the sidelines of national power, apart from the three years up to 1979 when, on the strength of their 34 per cent vote in the 1976 general election, they could not be denied a place in the ruling majority, if not in Government itself. Those were the years of "national solidarity", to be brought to an end by a decline in the Communist vote and an increase in East–West tensions abroad.

The governance of Italy returned to a series of brittle alliances between Christian Democrats and Socialists, condemned to the role of *frères ennemis*; obliged to co-operate, yet the keenest of rivals. Genuine political alternation, as in Britain and now France, where today's opposition may be tomorrow's Government, still requires that the Communists, the largest party of the Left, be recognized as an acceptable partner in Government.

Thus the threat of a spring-clean by one's political opponent, that most potent of checks and balances, does not obtain in Italy. The system has grown in upon itself, with little prospect that abuses will be rooted out. The Christian Democrats and Socialists, safe in the knowledge that their position in Government will be undisturbed, have split into factions competing as much against each other as against the theoretical Communist opposition. These factions and cliques, the natural descendants of the city states, communes, duchies and kingdoms which fought through much of Italy's earlier history, have found their new battleground in the banks and other appendages of the State.

Ambrosiano was the ultimate example of what could go wrong with the system at large. It was a mutant child of an imperfect financial structure, of the political parties' unquenchable thirst for money, of the secret ramifications and connivances of a distorted state, of the unresolved relations between Italy and the tiny sovereign state of the Vatican, planted in the heart of its capital.

But the Ambrosiano affair was more than a monumental swindle. In its way, and for at least two reasons, it was a tragedy. The first consists of the remorselessness with which events unfolded, and the powerlessness of those in authority to prevent, or even mitigate, final disaster. The second element of tragedy is the central character himself. The Roberto Calvi who emerges from these pages is not the conventional stereotype of the financial rogue; urbane, sophisticated and charming. True, Calvi was a skilled and unprincipled manipulator, able to exert a spell over many who should have known better. But if his fraud was on an epic scale, he himself appears to have been in many respects a most ordinary and unimpressive man.

It is in some ways a secondary consideration whether Calvi was murdered or whether he committed suicide. The gods had been satisfied, and vengeance was complete. One of those with whom the author spoke argued that the full truth would never come out—or that if it were to, at least half a dozen trained investigators, with money and time without limit, should be assigned to the task. That, obviously, has been impossible. But what follows is an imperfect attempt to tell this remarkable, but happily far from representative, Italian tale.

CHAPTER TWO

The Beginning

IT ALL STARTED, as it would end 86 years afterwards, with the priests. Or rather *a* priest. Little is known of Monsignor Giuseppe Tovini, other than the considerable imprint he has left on the Italian banking system. But whatever his spiritual qualities, he was surely a most resourceful and enterprising figure.

In the late 1880s he led a group of Catholics to set up Banca San Paolo in Brescia, the industrial city today just an hour's drive east by motorway from Milan. Indeed, to this day Brescia remains the strongest "provincial" rival of Milan within the prosperous region of Lombardy, the heart of industrial and commercial Northern Italy. Then, in 1896, Tovini transferred his financial ambitions westward to the metropolis itself.

There, on August 27 of that year, and with the blessing of Cardinal Andrea Ferrari, archbishop of Milan since 1894, he founded Banco Ambrosiano. Tovini persuaded more than 150 devout Catholics of the city to put up the 1 million lire which constituted the initial capital of Ambrosiano. He himself would be its first chairman. Curiously— yet with deliberate point—the man chosen in another August 86 years later to be the first chairman of the Nuovo Banco Ambrosiano was to be the deputy head of San Paolo di Brescia. The province had had its revenge at last. But that, of course, is to put the end of the story almost before its beginning.

Tovini's reason for founding both banks was the same, to provide a counter-weight to the great "lay", or non-Catholic, banks which had emerged along with the Italian nation three decades earlier. Such distinctions and antagonisms may seem odd to the non-Italian. But they are a constant of the country's history, of a land over much of which for centuries the Church *was* the State, and a dominant

27

temporal power in the peninsula. Guelf had fought Ghibelline, the Reformation ran into the Counter-Reformation. The divide, though less evident, still exists today, 113 years after Italian troops had burst through Rome's walls at the Porta Pia to annex the citadel of Catholicism for the country's capital. But in Tovini's time, feelings ran much stronger.

For their part, the "lay" banks were held to be strongholds of freemasonry, the movement which contributed greatly to the unification of Italy. Chief among them was the Banca Commerciale Italiana, whose newly scrubbed headquarters stand in Piazza della Scala barely a stone's throw away from Ambrosiano, nestling in the shadow of the great opera house.

Tovini had named his new bank after Saint Ambrose, the patron saint of Milan and its archbishop in the fourth century, who had fought throughout his life for the freedom of his church from secular interference. And a guiding purpose of Banco Ambrosiano was "to provide credit without offending the ethical principles of Christian teaching", an explicit rebuke to the aggressive "lay" banks. To ward off the unwanted attentions of outsiders, Ambrosiano's original statute prevented any individual from owning more than five per cent of its capital. Shareholders were required to produce a certificate of Catholic baptism, plus a voucher for their good character from the parish priest. Thus armed, they had to submit themselves for individual approval by the board. This *clausola di gradimento*, or "clause of consent", was not to disappear entirely from Ambrosiano's statute until what proved to be its last meeting of shareholders in April 1982, just two months before the end.

And there were other, even more tangible connections with the Church hierarchy of Lombardy. This century two of Milan's archbishops have become Pope. One was Achille Ratti, who took the name of Pius XI when he ascended St Peter's Throne in 1922. He was to sign the Concordat on the Vatican's behalf in 1929, and his nephew, Franco Ratti, was later to become a chairman of Banco Ambrosiano. The other was Giovanni Battista Montini, better known as Paul VI. His family, furthermore, still retains ties with Banca San Paolo di Brescia, so intimately concerned with both the foundation and re-foundation of Ambrosiano itself.

From the first, the new bank pursued its goal of "serving moral organizations, pious works, and religious bodies set up for charitable aims". A shareholder from start to finish was, for example, the Veneranda Fabbrica del Duomo, the corporation responsible for the building and upkeep of Milan Cathedral, that Gothic extravagance with 135 separate spires, emblem of the bourgeois mercantile confidence of the city. Today, from the room on Ambrosiano's fourth floor which once was Calvi's office, you can look through the bullet-proof glass window, across a terrace to the Cathedral's central spire, topped with its copper-gilt painted statue of the *Madonnina*, the traditional protectress of Milan. When disaster struck in 1982, the Fabbrica del Duomo possessed over 180,000 shares in Ambrosiano, worth 4.7 billion lire on the basis of the bank's last-ever stockmarket quotation, but subsequently all but valueless. Thirteen other organizations were listed as shareholders, including orphanages, missions and old people's homes, all run by the Church.

Not surprisingly, Ambrosiano became known as the "priests' bank". And in a quiet, conservative fashion it prospered, attracting as its customers the solid, righteous citizens of Milan. Often the depositors and borrowers would become shareholders too, creating that extraordinary trust in the bank which lasted until the end. Gradually Ambrosiano extended outward into the rich Milanese hinterland, and further into Lombardy. It became part of the fabric of the city, cautious, of impeccable reputation, but creating hardly a ripple in the world beyond. Not until 1937 did the bank open a branch in Rome, and for all its life it remained quintessentially Milanese, enmeshed with the city's aristocracy. Franco Ratti was a count and Tommaso Gallarati Scotti, chairman between 1953 and 1965, was a duke. Such a proliferation of titles must have weighed upon the mind of the young Roberto Calvi, as he embarked upon his own career at Ambrosiano in 1947.

Roberto Calvi came from what today would be called a normal white collar background. He was born in Milan on April 13 1920, the son of an employee in the legal department of Banca Commerciale. But his origins were partly from the Valtellina, a long Alpine valley just south of the Swiss border. There was something of the dour cunning of the mountain man in Calvi's own character. With little doubt the young Calvi saw from early on his future in banking or finance. After studying book-keeping, he enrolled in 1939 at the prestigious Bocconi university of Milan, in the faculty of economics and commerce. Friends at that time remember him as an assiduous student, but little more. His only extra-curricular activity seems to have been helping with the review published by the University's Fascist association.

But war prevented him from taking a degree, something which probably contributed to his later lack of self-confidence. In 1940 Mussolini brought Italy into the fighting, and by the summer of 1941 was promising Hitler the despatch of Italian soldiers to join the Germans on the Russian front. At the age of 22 Calvi enlisted. He chose, however, not the most popular Fascist destination of the Air Force, but the Novara lancers, the cavalry regiment with a traditionally aristocratic flavour. After a three month crash training course, Calvi that autumn left Verona as a second lieutenant on the long train journey for Russia.

The young man was quick to show himself a most competent soldier, thorough and dedicated. He was only just into his twenties, "but he seemed like a man ten years older", a fellow officer who encountered him at Verona would recall. Calvi was long in Russia and performed well. During the appalling conditions of the withdrawal, when supply lines were non-existent and the cavalrymen were forced to slaughter their horses to stay alive, Calvi earned much gratitude. On one occasion, he later recounted, he managed to trick some peasants out of horses of their own, by promising them large sums of money which never materialized. Probably he helped in this way to save Italian lives, but it was also an early example of financial fraud. More generally, in his quiet yet forceful way, he was displaying the self-control and resourcefulness in the face of adversity which were to remain such prominent qualities until almost the end of his life.

Long afterwards Calvi would talk at length about his Russian experiences, as if to escape the harsh present reality for a simpler past. In another small way, too, Russia left its mark. Calvi never drank much, but one of his favourite spirits was iced vodka.

By 1944 he was back in Italy—and in that ingenious way of his, Calvi was taking his precautions. Those were treacherous times, as the line of liberation moved gradually northward. Calvi would afterwards maintain that he went everywhere with two party membership cards. One was of what remained of the Fascist party; the other was one of the first issued by the Italian Socialist party as it regrouped after Mussolini's downfall. it bore the number 43. You never knew who you might run into.

Soon, though, the young ex-cavalryman had his first job. It was in his father's bank, the Banca Commerciale. But instead of Milan, Calvi joined its branch in the southern city of Bari. After a couple of years he left. Some have since claimed that he was advised to go after the discovery of an accounting irregularity, but there is no evidence to support this suggestion. Rather, as an ambitious and determined young man he seems to have decided that the prospects for rapid advancement in the enormous and state-controlled Banca Commerciale were dim. Calvi returned to a Milan that was starting to rebuild after the devastations of the war. Toscanini was back conducting at La Scala after a self-imposed exile under Fascism, providing the most vivid symbol of the city's desire for a fresh start.

Calvi's arrival at Banco Ambrosiano appears to have been fortuitous. The story goes that his father one day ran into Carlo Alessandro Canesi, a senior manager at the bank, who was on the lookout for promising young recruits. Roberto Calvi's name inevitably came up and he was quickly taken on. The support of Canesi, who in 1965 was to succeed Duke Tommaso Gallarati Scotti as Ambrosiano's chairman, was crucial to Calvi's rapid advancement thereafter. As Canesi rose, so did Calvi in his wake. He served variously in the foreign department, as Canesi's personal assistant, and in the loans department.

The two men were in some respects opposites. Canesi was outgoing and gregarious, with a profound feel for Milan and the Milanese. "Crafty, but a gentleman, who ended up knowing everyone and their secrets too", is how he has been described. Calvi, on the other hand, was already showing the secretiveness and shyness which ever marked him. But he was young, a hard worker, eager to learn and bright—and in the Ambrosiano of those years such a combination of qualities was uncommon.

Just how Calvi from his modest origins could have made his way to the very pinnacle of Ambrosiano has often been asked. The answer is probably simple—that he had precious few challengers. The bank was unadventurous, content enough with its status as a prosperous but middling Catholic institution; with few pretentions outside Milan, let alone internationally. In that sense it was wide open for one with Calvi's combination of ambition and discretion. Ambrosiano, moreover, was privately owned, belonging to but not dictated to by its shareholders, and given to promotion from within. This removed the risk of an appointee from outside, as might easily be the case, particularly in a public sector bank. For Calvi, the wholehearted backing of Canesi, clearly himself destined for the top, was in all likelihood enough. That he was never a seriously practising Catholic did not much matter.

Just when he began to conceive the projects that were to bring his downfall is not clear. It was Canesi, though, who set about broadening Ambrosiano's horizon, and his protégé needed no second bidding. In the mid-1950s Calvi had the then novel idea of Ambrosiano underwriting an issue of bonds by the Marelli industrial group. A little later he launched Inter Italia, the first Italian mutual fund. By the early 1960s, Ambrosiano was stretching its ambitions further. Canesi had become managing director, and the total of the bank's branches had risen to over 50. More important, Ambrosiano had made its first foreign acquisition, the Banca del Gottardo, just across the border in Lugano, Switzerland. At around that time too the bank joined an international consultancy arrangement with private banks from six other West European countries. Within Italy Ambrosiano and two other leading privately-owned banks, Banca Nazionale dell'Agricoltura and Banca d'America e d'Italia had set up a medium-term credit institute called Interbanca.

More and more, his was the guiding hand in these deals, all of which offer clues to his later design of creating a merchant bank or French-style *banque d'affaires*, along the lines of Paribas or Suez, which would not only take deposits but hold interests in industry and finance as well. In the meantime the rising young executive had in 1952 married a slight, attractive girl called Clara Canetti, whom he had met at the Adriatic resort of Rimini. The following year she bore him a son, and in 1959 a daughter. Throughout his life Calvi was devoted to his family; indeed, outside Ambrosiano they were almost his only interest.

By the mid-1950s Italy's postwar "economic miracle" was in full swing, and Milan was at its heart. Rome might be Italy's capital, but, as was often said, the title belonged morally to Milan. With membership of the Common Market, the tide of Italian affairs was running in favour of the North, by temperament and history closer to the European mainstream, and more receptive to ideas and trends from outside.

The city was completing the job of reconstruction, and money and creativity abounded. Even Milan's two football teams were doing their share to enhance its prestige, winning various European trophies. By present standards inflation scarcely existed, and as Italian exports multiplied the lira was proving itself one of the world's soundest currencies. In Rome, the Government felt sufficiently emboldened to allow banks greater freedom abroad, and capital restrictions were cautiously lifted. Italy was emerging from its chrysalis, and so was Ambrosiano.

In 1963 the bank established in Luxembourg a holding company called Compendium, which was in time to be rechristened Banco Ambrosiano Holding (BAH). Canesi duly became chairman, and at the age of 45 Roberto Calvi won key promotion to the rank of *direttore centrale*, in the command centre of the bank, and only a rung or two below the main board itself.

There was little doubt that he would climb still higher. Courteous and able, quick to grasp ideas and unfailingly discreet, Calvi was a skilled banker, by now determined to launch Banco Ambrosiano as a real force in international finance. His workload was considerable, yet still he found time to study French and English, two languages of which a working knowledge was essential if he was to project himself and his bank beyond Italy's frontiers. This on its own might have been enough to place him comfortably ahead of potential rivals within Ambrosiano. But Calvi had the ear of the chairman too. The combination seems to have been irresistible.

Nevertheless, certain traits in Calvi's character were already being noticed. People from outside the bank who had to deal with him would complain of his obsessive secrecy, the way he would claim to be familiar with something when quite plainly he wasn't. From early on, to lie was second nature for him. Then there was that hermetic barrier which Calvi would sometimes erect between himself and the world, *incomunicabilità* as the inelegant Italian word has it. Worse still, for all his endeavours and progress, Calvi had still failed to win acceptance by the Milanese banking community which really mattered. Human relations, as always, were his weak point. For Banca Commerciale or Credito Italiano, the other leading "lay" bank of the city, Calvi was and would remain an alien body, a pariah from the other side of the fence, an odd and suspect mixture of ambition and reticence. Bankers, like everyone else, are wary of potential rivals they cannot properly fathom. Just who was this man, who at no point in his career would ever genuinely enjoy the social occasions that sprinkle a banker's working life?

A sense of insecurity and inferiority is a recurring theme of recollections about the Calvi of those years. His comparatively modest origins, the failure to complete his degree course at the Bocconi were surely factors. In April 1982, at the last shareholders' meeting of Ambrosiano, he spoke with pride of the way he had risen to the top, unaided by connections of wealth or birth. Throughout his extraordinary career, shyness and secretiveness fought with the desire for social recognition. But if he would never dazzle in conversation in the *salotti* where the inbred Milanese financial world assembled to exchange gossip, then the bank, by the mid-1960s growing at between ten and twenty per cent a year, would speak for him. Its results would make up for any lack of sophistication on the part of the man himself.

From then on, moreover, Calvi would see the world as full of predators, from whom both he and the bank must be protected. Financial Milan has always been a mirror of political Italy, made up of competing interest groups, and complex and sometimes short-lived alliances, where today's friend might become tomorrow's foe. The possibility of an unwelcome foray against Ambrosiano had worried Canesi before Calvi, for the bank's fragmented structure of ownership made it peculiarly vulnerable to such a threat, whatever the cover given by the *clausola di gradimento*. One early precaution was an exchange of shareholdings with Kredietbank of Luxembourg, which would be Ambrosiano's second largest declared shareholder when the end came.

But a more determining influence on Calvi's future was a Sicilian tax lawyer who was making something of a reputation for himself in Milan. His name was Michele Sindona, and he seemed to have conveniently to hand the answers to some of Calvi's problems.

CHAPTER THREE

Sindona

"I WAS TEN years ahead of Calvi," Sindona will now boast to anyone coming to benefit from the stream of highly selective reminiscences he dispenses from the Federal prison of Otisville, two hours' drive upstate from New York city. As he talks, the still beautifully manicured hands expertly and abstractedly turn out piles of little paper boats, folded according to the ancient Japanese skill of *origami*. In fact, just eight years at the end were to separate the collapse of his own transatlantic financial card-castle from the débâcle of Banco Ambrosiano. But when his path first crossed with that of Calvi, in 1967 or 1968, Sindona was approaching the height of his powers.

The war experiences of the two, almost exact contemporaries, could hardly have differed more. While Calvi was performing with some distinction in the Russian snows, Sindona was still in his native Sicily, illegally trafficking in grain, with the benign acquiescence of the Allied Military Government on the island. During this period were born Sindona's links with the US. There too he gave his first proof of his innate skill in dealing with the Church, and learnt to become a formidable poker player. These disparate traits were to remain hallmarks of his career.

But Sindona's basic early training was in taxes; first at university and then, when the tide of war had shifted north in Italy, to work at a tax practice in Messina, the biggest city close to his birthplace at the small town of Patti, some 50 miles to the west. But for so clever and ambitious a young man, with the heady taste of wealth and real power imparted by contact with the occupying forces, Messina would never be enough.

Just after the War's end, Sindona trod the traditional migrant's path northwards to Milan, then as now the real financial centre of Italy. By coincidence, the young Calvi was at about the same time himself returning from Bari in the south to Milan. But if the latter's ascent at Ambrosiano was to be painstaking and at first little noticed, Sindona's progress was more eye-catching. His fortune was to be put in touch with Raoul Biasi, a mild-mannered accountant, but *ben introdotto*, "well introduced", as the Italians say, in some Milanese financial circles which mattered. Sindona so impressed Biasi that they became partners. Through Biasi, he met Ernesto Moizzi, owner of a small bank called Banca Privata Finanziaria. As its name would indicate, its merits for appreciative clients included an ability to conduct delicate financial transactions without asking too many questions. And one of these clients was Franco Marinotti, chairman of Snia Viscosa, then Italy's largest textile company.

Sindona swiftly earned the gratitude of both. Moizzi was impressed, if a trifle disconcerted, by how the accountant could nimbly resolve the tax difficulties of valued customers. Marinotti reaped the benefits of the American contacts Sindona had cultivated since his Sicilian days to sell some textile patents in the United States. In return, Marinotti helped Sindona achieve another crucial goal—that of winning the confidence of the Vatican, and its bank, the IOR.

Sindona made his move in 1958 when, with the help of an introduction from a distant relative and the recommendation of Marinotti, he arranged a meeting with a Roman aristocrat named Massimo Spada, then in charge of the IOR.

It was to prove one of the decisive turning points of this story. For from that encounter there gradually but directly developed first Sindona's own intimate relationship with the Vatican, and then that of his successor Roberto Calvi. Sindona was to establish himself as the indispensable standby as the Holy See embarked ten years later on a radical shift in its investments, out of Italian industry into financial shareholdings and assets, many of them outside the country. Through the Vatican also, the Sicilian would make the acquaintance of many who counted in the Rome of those times including, it would seem, various Christian Democrat politicians, traditionally close to the Church. Then there were other new friends, like Umberto Ortolani a typical creature of the Roman political undergrowth with excellent connections in the Vatican and Latin America; and his remarkable associate Licio Gelli, a most unusual freemason with ambitions equal to Sindona's own.

But it was in Milan where the powers of Sindona were most visible. A place on Snia's board marked the esteem in which Marinotti held him, while in 1961 he gained control of Moizzi's Banca Privata Finanziaria. The technique was one Sindona and Calvi were to employ throughout their careers. The vehicle for the acquisition was a shadowy front company called Cofina, his partners Marinotti, and the IOR.

At the same time, and if anything with still greater discretion, he was busy on behalf of Italo-American financiers, some of a distinct Mafia odour, keen to further their Italian interests. In fact, as early as 1967 the American police were seeking details of Sindona as a possible suspect in a drugs ring between Italy and the United States. The Italian authorities replied that they could unearth no evidence of that. But this is how Giuseppe Parlato, the Milan police commissioner of the day, described Sindona in early 1968. He was, wrote Parlato, "at the head of a network of specialist legal practices, backed up by teams of lawyers, accountants, trustees and technical experts". All that, and his own bank as well. By then Sindona had a Rome office at 94, Via Veneto, where he was—as Parlato drily noted—"keenly sought out by leading business figures and in particular by American citizens".

Even the alert, ambitious Calvi can hardly have been aware of these transatlantic exchanges. But quite clearly Sindona was someone worth knowing. And most fortunately a means of access was to hand, in the person of Giuliano Magnoni, whom Calvi knew from his university days at the Bocconi, and whose son in the meantime had married Sindona's daughter. Magnoni duly arranged a meeting, in 1967 or 1968.

Calvi can only have been enthralled by Sindona. The two had some characteristics in common. Their backgrounds were similarly modest. In the status-conscious Milan of the day, both had a fierce desire to overcome such limitations; and both had designs which stretched well beyond Italy. Already the Sicilian was weaving the tapestry of shell companies, foreign front operations and trusteeships which would further his attempt to build an unchallengeable conglomerate of finance. To the task he brought formidable talents which Calvi shared: a memory of steel, a swift imagination and the capacity to keep a secret—or *omertà*, to use the word the Sicilian Mafia has given to the world.

But Sindona combined these qualities with others that the introverted man from Ambrosiano knew he lacked: a gift for communicating, an electrical ability to charm and persuade people, a quicksilver sparkle and humour which even now survives the dull routine of an American prison. In those respects Calvi and Sindona were opposites; the closed man of the North and the hypnotically fluent Southerner. Only with the utmost difficulty would Sindona lure Calvi out of the fastness of Banco Ambrosiano for those plush lunches where Milanese bankers and financiers would exchange gossip and sketch their plans.

For both, however, the advantages of alliance were plain. Calvi would gain expert guidance in the use of the opportunities offered by the system, and a host of precious introductions. Truly, Sindona appeared ten years ahead. But he also took a liking to Calvi, recognizing a kindred spirit and a financier of undoubted skill. Nothing he controlled could match Ambrosiano for resources, nor its standing in Milan. The "priests' bank", moreover, was a natural complement to the relationship he was developing with the Vatican. Best of all it had no dominant shareholder, so that those who ran it had an unfettered hand. Thus far these unusual advantages had not been put to proper use, Sindona reasoned, but Calvi might be the man to do so. So why not give him a nudge towards the top?

For the next four years Sindona displayed to Calvi the repertoire of his skills. He lured potent foreign allies to his banner—Hambro's, the London merchant bank with ties to Italy dating back to Queen Victoria's reign, and Continental Illinois, one of the biggest US banks, whose chairman, David Kennedy, was later to serve as Treasury Secretary under President Richard Nixon. Ever more frequently, his practice was midwife to many of the dealings which were then transforming the face of Italian finance. Some of the established families which had hitherto dominated Italian industry were unable to put up the new capital required to keep pace with changing times, and were selling off their holdings. In their place, a new breed of entrepreneur was emerging. Technically its members represented State enterprise and the public sector; but in practice they moved like financial barracuda, acting sometimes on their own behalf, sometimes for their political patrons, but unfailingly with money from the public purse. Sindona, to his fingertips a political animal, fitted easily into this process.

The fiercest of the barracuda was Eugenio Cefis, chairman of ENI the state oil group. And his hand was behind the most dramatic example of this "politicization" of industry in 1968, when ENI secretly built up a controlling shareholding in Montedison, Italy's biggest, and hitherto privately owned, chemicals concern. But among those with goods for sale the most distinguished of all, by far, was the Vatican.

Pope Paul VI and his advisors had good reason for wanting to withdraw from Italian industry. Too visible an involvement with capitalism discomforted the Church, while the Rome Government's decision in 1968 to remove the Holy See's exemption from withholding tax on dividends made international investments look more attractive. Not least, its investments in Italy, even the huge international property group Società Generale Immobiliare of which the Vatican owned 33 per cent, was not faring well. Later SGI was to earn a tiny niche in history by putting up the Watergate building in Washington, the starting point of America's most notorious political scandal. But SGI had above all grown fat on the Roman postwar property boom, during which it had endowed the capital, to the dismay of the environmentalists, with a brand new Hilton Hotel on a wooded hill overlooking the old city centre. But those days were now gone.

The holding in SGI, and those in other Vatican companies, were in the portfolio of the APSA, the institution set up under the Lateran Pacts of 1929 to administer the compensation at last paid over by Italy for its annexation of the Papal territories. And if APSA wanted to dispose of SGI, whom more natural for it to approach for help than the keen-eyed Sindona, by now firmly in the Vatican's trust? Among those to have recommended him, moreover, was an energetic American bishop in the Curia called Paul Marcinkus, whose managerial talents had already caught the attention of the Pope. Indeed Paul VI would soon name him first secretary, and then chairman of the IOR.

Nor did Sindona let the Vatican down. Not only did he arrange to sell the interest in SGI, he actually bought it from the Vatican himself; and at double the going market price. Just why, only became clear long afterwards. Sindona had also secured the option to buy from the Vatican its choicest bank holding, the Banca Cattolica del Veneto. Later, in 1972, Sindona was to sell on this option at a usurer's price to Roberto Calvi.

Hardly had Sindona acquired the SGI holding in late 1968 than he embarked on a still more audacious project. He would attempt to capture the empire of Carlo Pesenti, a Catholic financier whose connections with the Vatican pre-dated even his own. On the face of it the venture seemed preposterous; for Pesenti's master company, Italcementi, could, after all, draw on the resources of three banks and two insurance companies.

In the event, however, Sindona's ambush came within an ace of success, and was thwarted only by the opposition of the Bank of Italy. As for Pesenti, he never entirely recovered from the experience. Obliged to borrow money from his own banks in order to buy Sindona out, Pesenti was in subsequent years to be forced to sell off those banks, one by one, to settle his debts. Truly, at the end of the 1960s, Sindona's pyrotechnics were the virtuosity of the master, from whom the pupil Calvi could only learn. And Calvi, ever the assiduous student, realized two things.

In the first place, Sindona appeared to have found the perfect means of getting round Italian legislation, framed to prevent a repetition of the financial disasters of the late 1930s, which forbade banks buying non-banking interests. The answer, Sindona was showing, lay in establishing foreign front companies—preferably in tax havens where local scrutiny was lax—to make those investments for him. Secondly, ownership of a bank offered the perfect means of doing this. For Sindona's basic ploy was to use the money of his banks to further his own ambitions. Through the technique of "fiduciary" or trustee accounts, he spirited huge sums out of Italy into foreign shell companies, owned either by himself or compliant associates. In turn, these might pass the money on to offshore "investment" companies, again either owned by himself or for which Sindona held the proxy of another. This money would then be used to carry out the purchase of the day back in Italy, or elsewhere. For the Italian authorities, the initial deposits from Italy to abroad were unexceptionable. If there were suspicions, who was to prove that, far from being employed for the declared purpose of, say, financing exports, the funds were being channelled back for speculation at home?

An asset, once bought, might then be shunted around Sindona's companies at ever higher prices, liberating still more "profits" for further speculation. If the price seemed excessive, then Sindona's banks would step in again, pushing up the value of the shares in question, by buying on the tiny Milan market. And this would in turn bring further advantage. The public would be convinced that Sindona did indeed have the Midas touch; and the financier would be more easily able to pass on shares to ingenuous third parties at yet more outrageous prices. He himself would always retain majority control, usually concealed in an offshore labyrinth. On such fragile foundations was Sindona's pyramid erected. By these methods, he, Calvi, and a few others would rule the Milan market of that time.

The Pesenti setback seemed barely to trouble Sindona. By now he was bent on even greater things. His goal was no less than to create the largest financial group, not just in Italy, but in all Europe. Sindona planned to secure first La Centrale, a dormant but cash-rich holding company; to La Centrale would then be added Bastogi, the so-called "drawing room" of Italian finance, another holding company with strategic interests throughout the country's industry and a point of encounter for the Agnellis, the Pirellis and the rest of Italy's traditional industrial élite. And, finally, from this springboard he intended to launch an assault on Banca Nazionale dell'Agricoltura, Italy's largest privately owned bank. It was, with hindsight, a hopeless venture. But Sindona thought he had the weapons to succeed. With the Vatican's assistance, he had already acquired a second bank in Milan, Banca Unione, to set alongside Banca Privata Finanziaria. Then there was Hambro's, a partner by now in Banca Privata Finanziaria and which had been involved in the SGI deal. There was the Continental Illinois, and, of course, the Banco Ambrosiano of Roberto Calvi.

Early in 1971, Hambro's made the offer for a controlling block of La Centrale shares, then in the hands of Pirelli and other leading industrial groups. The price was pitched temptingly, and it was a period when industry at large was finding the going hard. No longer could it easily afford the luxury of resources tied unprofitably up in ventures like La Centrale. The deal went through, and on August 5, 1971 the 51-year-old Calvi joined the board of the holding company, alongside such eminent names as Evelyn de Rothschild and Jocelyn Hambro. The first phase of Sindona's scheme had been carried out.

Bastogi, however, was a very different story. Once again, Hambro's and Ambrosiano were at Sindona's side. On September 10, after heavy prior buying of Bastogi shares on the Milan market, a consortium organized by Sindona launched Italy's first ever contested takeover bid; it offered 2,800 lire per share for a minimum of 33 per cent of Bastogi, 1,000 lire more than the going market price. Milanese finance was electrified, and the moment made history. But Sindona had grievously miscalculated. The authorities, already uneasy at his methods and motives, had been alarmed by the La Centrale affair. Now the "lay" financial establishment of Italy made common cause against him. In the vanguard of the opposition were the Bank of Italy, and a shadowy, elusive figure called Enrico Cuccia.

Ecclesiastical imagery runs strong in Italy, whether Catholic or "lay". Cuccia could not be more strongly identified with the latter camp. But as managing director of Mediobanca, the publicly-owned investment bank, Cuccia had earned the nickname of the "high priest" of Italian finance, dispensing blessing or disfavour on every major mooted project. In the case of Bastogi, his disfavour was icy, and the big "lay" banks like Banca Commerciale followed Cuccia's lead.

Hostile buying steadily forced Bastogi's share price up and above the level offered by Sindona's consortium, and the bid was doomed. Hambro's were called sternly to heel by the central bank. Within a year, and further alarmed by a central bank report on Sindona's Banca Privata Finanziaria, the London merchant bank had severed every link with the Sicilian.

The failure of the Bastogi bid was a turning point for Sindona. His interest in Italy dwindled, and increasingly he directed his charm and plausibility further afield, to the United States. Many of his interests passed to Roberto Calvi. Sindona will crop up again frequently in this tale. It is instead now time to examine another formative influence on the rising Roberto Calvi, that strange brand of freemasonry practised by Licio Gelli.

CHAPTER FOUR

Freemasonry

CALVI AND THE P-2 were made for each other. Exactly when his liaison began with Licio Gelli and Umberto Ortolani, those two master illusionists of a nation peerless in the art, is open to question. Some trace it to a supper at the end of either 1969 or 1970 held in Rome, at which a co-operation pact was sealed among the four guests said to have been present: Sindona and his protégé Calvi, Gelli and Ortolani. Sindona himself claims, however, that he did not introduce Calvi to Gelli until three or four years later. Another version maintains that Ambrosiano's chairman was initiated into the P-2 at a ceremony in Zurich in August 1975, and yet another that the deed was done in Italy, in the back seat of a Mercedes, for a fee of 500,000 lire. The membership lists made public later showed only that Calvi had paid his dues since the start of 1977.

Such obscurity is in any case entirely fitting. Throughout his life Calvi was convinced that unofficial, hidden centres of power were those which mattered. The devious was always preferable to the clear-cut, and later in his career he would strenuously recommend to friends the reading of Mario Puzo's novel, *The Godfather*, if they really wished to understand the ways of the world. Calvi's world was one where clandestine protection and promotion were desirable, if not essential. Sindona's own history proved the usefulness of such as Gelli and Ortolani, expert at picking their way along the treacherous paths of the *sottobosco*, or undergrowth of Italian political life, where determining alliances and decisions were often made and taken.

Gelli's vehicle was a freemasons' lodge called Propaganda-2, or P-2 for short, a perverse and malign variant of an already mysterious growth. For non-practitioners, freemasonry everywhere conveys a vaguely sinister odour, but Italian history has seen to it that there the movement has a peculiarly underground character. When free-masonry originated in Italy, some 250 years ago, the temporal power of the Church in Rome perceived it as a potential focal point for insurrection by nationalists and anti-clericals. As early as 1738 Pope Clement XII described freemasonry as "Satan's synagogue". The fears, moreover, were well-grounded; prominent masons like Gari-baldi and Carducci played an essential part in the unification of Italy and the overthrow of the Papal states. The movement attracted people determined to modernize and liberalize the State, and cut back the influence of the Church. In the wake of his settlement with the Vatican in 1929, Mussolini outlawed anti-Catholic lodges. But after the war Catholic and non-Catholic lodges alike were un-molested, subject of course to the constraints of the 1948 constitution of Italy, which forbade secret societies. However a secret society was exactly what Gelli was fostering.

The P-2 originated in the late nineteenth century, so named to distinguish it from the existing (and by masonic standards) open Propaganda lodge, based in Turin. From the outset it was an anomaly, conceived as a special lodge for masons in particularly delicate or important positions. Accordingly, it dispensed with elabo-rate initiation ceremonies, and handed exceptional discretionary powers to its Venerable Master. He could decide who would be enrolled, and he alone would know the full list of members. Not surprisingly, when the P-2 scandal washed over Italy in the spring of 1981, many of those whose names featured on the lists of 962 members claimed, with likely justification, that they had no idea of who else was in the lodge, and indeed that they were unaware of having joined it at all.

For those very reasons, it was the perfect instrument for Gelli; an organization nominally affiliated to Italy's Grand Orient rite with its 20,000 members, but in practice ripe to be diverted to any end. For many decades the P-2 had languished. But under Gelli, who seems to have become organizing secretary in 1971, and *Maestro Venerabile* in May 1975, it revived with a vengeance.

Italy, it must be recorded with honesty, albeit bemusement, has produced few more remarkable individuals this century than Licio

Gelli. He was not even twenty when he took part in Mussolini's "volunteer" expedition to help Franco win the Spanish Civil War. In the War, he saw action in the Albanian campaign before fighting the Allies as they advanced up Italy from 1943 onwards. But having fought with the Fascists he deftly changed sides to help the Communist partisans rid his native Pistoia province, just west of Florence, of the grip of Mussolini's short-lived Repubblica Sociale Italiana. In the process, of course, he saved his own skin.

Thereafter he was to spend much of his life abroad, notably in Latin America, where he became a personal friend of Juan Peron, the Argentine dictator. But all the while he was developing his business interests in Italy, accumulating a considerable fortune. For a while he was a senior executive of the Permaflex mattress company, before leaving to help set up a textile company, Gio-Le, which thrived, thanks in particular to a lucrative import contract from Rumania. Much more important, however, were the contacts and friends he was cultivating on both sides of the Atlantic, and his lifelong passion for the garnering of other people's secrets.

One friend in particular was to become important. He was a Roman lawyer called Umberto Ortolani, with extensive business interests in Latin America, including his own bank, Banco Financeiro, in the Uruguayan capital of Montevideo. Ortolani, who was to become Gelli's most trusted lieutenant in the P-2, was as wise as anyone in the ways of political Rome, and especially where those ways crossed those of the Vatican in its midst. His connections there were excellent, and included the Holy See's new financial adviser, Michele Sindona. They also extended to Uruguay, where Ortolani held the quaint, but not entirely empty, title of honorary ambassador of the Order of the Knights of Malta, not to be underestimated as an agent serving world-wide Catholicism.

What the ultimate goal of the P-2 was, perhaps only Gelli knew. He would describe himself as "part Garibaldi, part Cagliostro", the latter a reference to the Italian adventurer-cum-charlatan who charmed half Europe in the late eighteenth century, founding at every stop a Masonic lodge of his own "Egyptian order", said to possess undreamt of secret powers. Nor do we know whom Gelli was serving; the CIA, the KGB and the Italian secret services have been variously identified as his employers. Ultimately, perhaps, he was only working for himself, cajoling or intimidating others into accepting his nostrums. And many believed him.

At the end the P-2's membership lists read like a state within the state, full of top officials from Italy's discredited former secret services, senior army officers, naval admirals and commanders of the country's several police forces; as well as some leading public sector industrialists, bankers like Calvi, journalists, publishers and a handful of politicians. Gelli would hold court three days a week in rooms 127, 128 and 129 of the Excelsior Hotel on the Via Veneto. The hotel's staff were trained to see that visitors' paths did not cross; to make doubly sure the suite had two separate entrances, so that a caller arriving would not see a visitor departing.

Aspiring members of P-2 would be told to present themselves for initiation in a dark suit. Gelli would wear a blue apron trimmed in red; a masonic triangle would be around his neck, and he would wear a black cloak. For the ceremony itself, the initiate would take off his jacket, roll up his trousers to the knees. Then he would kneel for Gelli to lay the ritual sword on his shoulder.

The slant of the P-2 was broadly anti-Communist and right-wing. Attempted coups, more or less serious, were more than one between 1960 and 1975 in Italy, and several of those said to have been involved were to feature in Gelli's motley army. There are numerous pointers too that the P-2 may have had a hand in rightwing terrorist outrages dotting recent Italian history, from the so-called "strategy of tension" which emerged in the late 1960s to the Bologna station bombing of August 1980. The aim, presumably, to soften up public opinion for takeover by a more authoritarian regime. But it is not certain that Gelli himself seriously entertained such designs; the tenuous structure of the P-2 would have militated against them in any case. Equally possibly, the grandmaster's business was power, whose manipulation became an end in itself. Gelli and Ortolani gave the lodge Latin American dimensions, and entry to regimes there broadly sharing their own philosophies. Sindona was to contribute the wealth of his Italo–American contacts, and Calvi, quite simply, money.

By the end the lodge had been identified as a clearing house for almost every scandal to have shaken Italy in the last fifteen years. In that sense, at least, Gelli was the ideal destabilizer, beloved of secret services everywhere. But his greatest skill was the accumulation of information. As an excellent biographer has written: "It certainly hasn't been Gelli who invented intrigue and conspiracy (in Italian public life). His contribution to Italy's progressive degradation is different. Gelli increased the level of national corruption. He perfected and made widespread the use of the photocopy and the spool of tape. The exploitation of secret documents and tape recordings of private conversations have now become almost daily weapons in the political struggle."†

Possession of such material was the cement of his power over his acolytes, and his ability to blackmail them if necessary. In this skill Gelli was undeniably brilliant—even if the lingering mediocrity of the man has made many believe (not least for their self-respect) that the truly guiding hand behind the P-2 must have belonged to another. For Gelli was marketing illusions. The main appeal to the bulk of the members of his lodge was the apparent short cut it offered to powers, riches and the best jobs; and for such an advantage, surrender of secret information to the grandmaster must have seemed a reasonable price to pay.

In that sense, the P-2 was simply an extreme manifestation of the basic instinct of every Italian. In a land where the state is rarely powerful, neutral or efficient, the safest means of personal advancement are recommendation and knowing the right people. The other side of this coin is gullibility, a quality which Calvi also possessed. For so ardent a believer in the merits of the back door, the P-2 was a perfect means of discreet access to the inner circuits of power.

Then there was Ortolani, and his Vatican connections. For the blood of the Milanese Curia ran in the veins of Ambrosiano, and its backing was something he could not afford to lose. Later Ortolani and his family seem to have grown into some of the few personal friends that Calvi could claim; but in professional terms Ortolani was to constitute the perfect bridge between the two historically rival bodies with whom Calvi allied himself, the Church and freemasonry.

Thus the way ahead looked clear and Calvi the pupil was over the years between 1969 and 1974 to develop gradually into Sindona's peer and then his natural successor. At the beginning of 1971, Calvi earned

†Gianfranco Piazzesi: Gelli, Garzanti, 1983.

the key promotion to the rank of *direttore generale*, or general manager. His power in his bank would soon be complete. Carlo Canesi had already decided to step down as chairman at the end of 1971. For a while, disturbed at the involvement of Calvi with Sindona's increasingly controversial ventures, Canesi is said to have toyed with the idea of bringing in an outsider as Ambrosiano's new chairman. But Calvi had by now made himself indispensable.

In the end a compromise emerged. Ruggiero Mozzana, already 69, would succeed Canesi, while Calvi would take on the additional duties of *amministratore delegato*, or managing director. Although he was not to move into the chairman's office until 1975, the reins of power were in effect already his.

Upon his appointment as general manager, Calvi had wasted no time in putting his plans into effect. The Americas beckoned, and like Christopher Columbus in 1492, his first landfall in the new world was the Bahamas. The explorer had come ashore at the island of Salvador. Calvi's goal, however, was Nassau, by then one of the hottest offshore centres in international banking—and, equally important, governed by a code of banking secrecy to rival that of Switzerland. A subsidiary in the Bahamas, therefore, would not only fit in with Calvi's preferred image as an internationally-minded banker, determined to broaden Ambrosiano it would also later permit him to conduct his most sensitive business safe from the prying eyes of the Italian monetary authorities.

Calvi, at the head of a small group of foreign department executives from Ambrosiano, arrived for the first time in Nassau from the chilly Milanese winter in January 1971. Sindona later claimed the idea was his, but scores of international banks, most of them American, were already established there; if only, in many cases, with a shiny nameplate and a couple of secretaries minding the telex machine. The offshore, or Eurodollar, market was booming and Nassau, with its agreeable climate, tempting banking legislation and common time zone with New York, was an ideal centre for booking such transactions.

The face of the city's old colonial centre was changing. Queen Victoria's statue still guarded Parliament Square, but along Bay Street the vibrant calypso clubs were giving way to glossy, hushed new bank premises. The Caribbean evidently suited Calvi, but it made little impact on his polite but distant demeanour. "He was terrible formal and austere, just not what you imagine an Italian to be like," someone who met him personally on that first visit would remember. The judgement was apt; years before in Milan some who knew the rising young banker had dubbed Calvi the "Prussian" for his remote efficiency.

Within two months Ambrosiano's beachhead in the new world, the Cisalpine bank of Nassau, was duly registered, and opened for business the following May. As its manager, Calvi chose a Swiss-born expatriate newly arrived from New York called Pierre Siegenthaler. In his early 30s, Siegenthaler was an Olympic-class yachtsman with some banking experience in the US, and some accounts have it that he was recommended to Calvi by Sindona. Siegenthaler had a taste for Gucci shoes and gold watches (but a habit in the early days of bicycling to work in a pair of jeans). In fact, though, he was to be the discreet executor of many of Calvi's most private schemes in the decade ahead.

The new bank was capitalized at $2.5 million, and initially operated from Siegenthaler's home. But that did not prevent it attracting over $200 million of deposits, largely from elsewhere within the Ambrosiano group, in a very short time. Calvi in the meantime was making other arrangements for a long stay. Early on he rented a villa for his regular winter visits to the Bahamas, but before long he had secured a residence at the exclusive Lyford Cay complex on the western tip of New Providence island, from which unauthorized visitors were barred by a private police force.

A founding shareholder of the Cisalpine Overseas bank was the IOR, the Vatican bank. And one of the early visitors to the rented villa, joking with Calvi and his wife and discussing water-skiing with his two teenage children was the IOR's new chairman and, since August 5 1971, a director of Ambrosiano's subsidiary in Nassau—Archbishop Paul Marcinkus.

CHAPTER FIVE

Vatican

THE INITIAL AND enduring impact of Marcinkus is physical. To talk to, he can be expansive or peremptory, charming—but occasionally brutal. But what lingers in the mind is the sheer bulk of the man, six foot three in his socks and built like the natural athlete he is. The impression is curiously heightened by the slight stoop he has now acquired—to which the weight of the Banco Ambrosiano scandal has undoubtedly contributed. In the days when he guarded Popes on their foreign travels, he would seem affable, wisecracking but vaguely menacing; a streetwise, sharp-eyed American who by accident had found himself in the closeted, insulated world of the Vatican. His recreations today, tennis and above all golf, are those of the self-made American business executive. His swing—at least in the days before notoriety prevented him getting out on to the course for a round—had something of the style of the late Tony Lema, "Champagne Tony", who won the British Open in 1962, and whom Marcinkus would remember with affection.

Yet this incongruous man of the Church, in some ways the most important figure in this story after Calvi himself, won the confidence of two Popes, Paul VI and the Polish-born John Paul II.

His origins were far more modest than those of Calvi. Paul Casimir Marcinkus was born on January 15 1922 in the tough Chicago suburb of Cicero, one of five children of Mykolas Marcinkus, an emigrant from Lithuania who found work as a window-cleaner. His early years were those of prohibition and gang wars. Al Capone was one of the city's more noted products of that era.

But at the Roman Catholic grammar school of St Anthony's, Marcinkus was a brighter-than-average pupil, and, of course, sports-mad. It was a complete surprise to his classmates when he decided to study for the priesthood. In 1947 he was ordained, and three years later he left for Rome to study canon law at the city's Gregorian University. His intention was to return to Chicago, but in his own words, "I just got trapped."† A temporary summer stint at the Vatican's secretariat of State so impressed his superiors that he was taken on permanently.

His drive, and ability to get things done soon won him an important admirer, Monsignor Giovanni Battista Montini, a high Curia official who would be appointed Cardinal Archbishop of Milan in 1954. Nine years later Montini returned to Rome, as Pope Paul VI. Marcinkus, in the meantime, was to serve as a Vatican diplomat in Bolivia and Canada, but it was his managerial and administrative prowess which really attracted attention. He also had the talent of being the right man in the right place. Paul VI was the first Pope to travel the world, but his first trip, to Jerusalem in 1964, proved so badly organized that in future he enlisted the services of Marcinkus—first as St Peter's own American-style advance man, and then as unofficial bodyguard and aide. In 1965 Marcinkus acted as interpreter when Pope Paul met President Lyndon Johnson in New York. In the Philippines in 1970 he helped save the Pope from attack by a knife-wielding Bolivian artist.

Then again, in the late 1960s, when deposits from US Catholic institutions with the IOR began to fall off, what better choice could Paul VI make to head the bank than a dynamic American prelate and proven manager, who originated from the largest US archdiocese?

Inevitably the swift rise of this foreign intruder with his no-nonsense ways aroused some resentment and jealousy within the Italian-dominated Curia. But America loves a success story; and some who crossed the Atlantic on Church business are said to have regarded a round of golf with Marcinkus at the Acqua Santa golf club down on the Appian way as a status symbol to match an audience with the Pope himself.

Such different views, of course, sharpened later, first with the Sindona scandal, and then the Ambrosiano affair. Americans who knew Marcinkus well were generally prepared to forgive him. He might have been gullible, they maintained, but at heart he was a "nice

†*Chicago Tribune*, March 13 1983.

guy", basically honest, loyal and good company, always ready to put himself out for a friend. From the other side of the cultural divide, many Italians who had to deal with him could find Marcinkus rude and abrupt. Some found it quite plausible that he was the Vatican end of a conspiracy stretching from Calvi, Sindona and the P-2 to the CIA and the Mafia.

Sindona himself has claimed that he had a hand in Marcinkus' appointment to the IOR, nor would that be surprising. Both were friends of Continental Illinois' David Kennedy, head of the biggest bank in the archbishop's home town of Chicago. The Sicilian was already helping the APSA dispose of its embarrassing holdings in Italian industry; while Paul VI had had reason in his Milan days to be grateful to Sindona for helping the success of Church-backed charities. In any event, Marcinkus was first named manager and then, in 1971, chairman of the Vatican Bank.

The enterprising archbishop thus became the latest embodiment of a dilemma which in varying degrees has haunted the Church since it ceased to be a temporal power in Italy in the nineteenth century. How was it to reconcile its rejection of crude liberal capitalism (a hundred years ago at its height) with the practical need of working with that system, to raise money to finance its mission?

Back in 1860 devout Catholics attempted to resolve the difficulties by instigating the device of "St Peter's Pence", individual contributions from the faithful donated each year to the person of the Pope. Catholic financiers rallied round, too, providing loans and other ingenious fund-raising proposals. One of them was a certain André Langrand-Dumonceau, who first earned the nickname of "Europe's financial Napoleon", only to go spectacularly bankrupt in 1870. A recent study† has observed that he was "the extreme example of a strategy worked out by Catholic financiers, French and Belgian in particular. They aimed to involve the Holy See in their business deals, thus profiting from the moral and economic good name of the entire Catholic Church." Something of the same could be said for the relations of Sindona, and then Calvi, with the IOR. But Marcinkus seems to have been unmindful of the precedents.

†Carlo Crocella, *Augusta Miseria*, Nuovo Istituto Editoriale Italiano 1982.

When he took over the IOR he already inherited some links with Sindona, notably the holding in Banca Privata Finanziaria. But the two, who got on splendidly, rapidly extended their collaboration. Sindona is fond of claiming today that he saved the Vatican from financial disaster by relieving it not only of SGI, but two other companies as well. One was Condotte d'Acqua (later to pass to IRI, the giant Italian state industrial conglomerate); the other was Ceramica Pozzi, a badly run manufacturer of, among other things, lavatories. In return the IOR bought into various Sindona enterprises, both in Italy and outside. Marcinkus, with his lack of financial training, was no banker. Indeed, it has been maliciously observed that his troubles began when he started to regard himself as one. The real expertise belonged to Luigi Mennini, the IOR's managing director, a rarely-seen figure with a lifetime's experience in the Vatican bank—and of the ways of Catholic Italian finance.

Just how and when Paul Marcinkus and Roberto Calvi met is not clear. Marcinkus has declared that he was put on to Calvi by the Milanese Curia; Sindona has asserted that he was responsible. But the fateful meeting must have happened in 1971 at the latest. For by the August of that year, as we have seen, Marcinkus was seated on the board of Calvi's Cisalpine Bank in Nassau. The moment marks the start of IOR's hidden association with Ambrosiano. The Vatican bank took an early shareholding of Cisalpine of two and a half per cent, later to rise to eight per cent. Nobody noticed, or paid attention to, the fact that Marcinkus was one of its directors. But then nobody was paying much attention to Calvi in those days.

The archbishop has since stated that he saw Calvi only two or three times a year, "to discuss ideas and arrangements". He maintains that apart from that first stay in Nassau, he hardly met the banker socially, although Calvi's family dispute this. What is true is that Marcinkus was an ever busier man, and that day-to-day dealings between Ambrosiano and the IOR were left to Mennini and his equally retiring deputy, Pellegrino de Stroebel, chief accountant of the IOR.

The personal relationship between the gregarious, direct Marcinkus and the diffident and elusive Calvi is not easy to visualize. Professionally, however, Calvi had much to recommend him. His bank had three-quarters of a century of links with the Catholic Church in Milan, his discretion was absolute, and his financial skills considerable. However mixed the feelings in the Vatican over the rough and tumble of international finance, it needed to increase its income—and the IOR was an obvious means to this end.

Of all the mysteries of the Eternal Church, few are greater than that of its finances. The sheer geographical extent of the institution is part of the difficulty, but a bigger reason is the Vatican's obsessive secrecy. Clearly its possessions are huge, in terms of land, art and property. But Michelangelo's *Pietà* cannot be sold off to balance a budget. Like any other state, the Vatican must try to match income to expenditure. But as rising government deficits around the world were there to prove, that task became from the mid-1960s steadily harder. Inflation was rising, and salary increases, not just for the Curia's staff but also the 1,400 predominantly lay workers who enable the Vatican to be administered, had to keep pace. Extended international travel by the Pope, new departments set up after the Second Vatican Council in 1962, more forceful diplomacy and a new sense of international mission, all cost money. To meet these outgoings, and cover a declared budget deficit which by 1980 had reached $25 million, the Vatican must have been forced to rely increasingly on its two sources of *undeclared* income: St Peter's Pence and the earnings of the IOR. Under Paul VI, however, the former were unable to keep up with the growing demands. It is held that the proceeds of St Peter's Pence fluctuate with the popular appeal of individual Popes. In the reign of John XXIII, with his earthy warmth, they had soared.† But his more detached, introspective successor, especially in the later years of his Papacy, was a less compelling figure. Income, it is said, stagnated. So that left the IOR.

The Institute for Religious Works had been created by personal decree of Pius XII in June 1942, when the war was causing extra problems for the Vatican's financial workings. Its stated purpose was, and is, to manage assets entrusted to it—cash, shares and property— in the interests of the world-wide Church. Completely independent of the APSA and the Prefecture for Economic Affairs of the Holy See

†Only now, with the global appeal of John Paul II, has the trend been reversed. Figures unprecedentedly released in November 1982 showed that in 1981, offerings of $24 million to the Pope, including $15.4 million of "St Peter's Pence", had helped the Vatican to show a general budget surplus of over $4 million.

(in effect the Vatican's Finance Ministry), the IOR is theoretically supervised by a panel of five cardinals. In practice, however, Marcinkus had a free hand, reporting only to the Pope himself. Traditionally the IOR has never given the smallest detail of its business, still less published a balance sheet, although that might change after the Calvi débâcle. But as a bank it is medium-sized at best. Calvi would describe it as colossal to his few intimates; the more likely truth is that it administers funds of probably no more than $2 billion, half the size of Ambrosiano at its height. Its own assets may not exceed $150 million. The IOR's operations are now computerized. But its visible premises, including an ill-lit banking hall complete with clerical tellers, seem as dingy as the courtyard of Sixtus V, through which it is approached. Marcinkus' own office is more like a comfortable smoke-filled study.

The IOR is best seen as an "offshore" merchant bank in the heart of Italy, serving the universal Church—and, it has long been said, not a few favoured Italians as well. The anomaly of the Vatican, a sovereign state subject to neither exchange controls nor border checks with Italy, would turn it into an ideal conduit for spiriting money out of the country as the lira weakened and currency regulations tightened. Money deposited in an IOR account at an ordinary Italian bank, or simply brought to the IOR's counter in a suitcase, could then be sent anywhere in the world. Just how much money has left Italy by this route is unknown. The Vatican indignantly denies that any does now; in 1948, however, a Curia prelate called Monsignor Edoardo Cippico was arrested and imprisoned for having obliged Italians in this way. But that was more than twenty years before the paths of Calvi and Marcinkus crossed. The banker had far more ambitious and sophisticated designs. For the services that the IOR—wittingly or unwittingly—would render him, he was prepared to pay. And that suited the Vatican.

No-one has seriously suggested that for all his opaque dealings with Calvi and Ambrosiano, Marcinkus was bent on self-enrichment. He lives simply, and Sindona, undoubtedly experienced in such matters, has said he was not to be bought with personal bribes.

But the Church's growing financial needs were another matter. Marcinkus was a "team player", ready to serve its interests by every means. Now the IOR had to perform; and if its success was his own success, then so much the better. His prospects of advancement and of becoming a cardinal, would after all only be served if he could show the Pope he was as efficient a banker as he was organizer and advance man. Just how much profit the IOR earned from Calvi is unknown. What is known is that 85 per cent of its earnings are made available to the Pope, and fifteen per cent retained for administrative and other provisions. But Calvi, it must be assumed, helped them swell; and the payment of unusually high interest rates by Ambrosiano on deposits made by the IOR was just one possible way.

The lasting appeal of the IOR for unscrupulous Italian financiers is twofold—or, less charitably, threefold. In the first place, it was an ideal, much respected, candidate for the role of fiduciary or trustee. The technique used by both Calvi and Sindona over the years was roughly comparable to football's wall-pass or "one-two". Player One, Calvi or Sindona, would transfer funds, or the shares of a company, to Player Two, the IOR. According to the instructions received from Player One, Player Two then either holds the asset in his own name, or passes it on to a pre-specified recipient, not infrequently on the other side of the Italian frontier. The IOR with one foot inside the country, and the other outside, was perfect for the role. In football, the move is supposed to split an opponent's tight defence; for Calvi it was regularly to defeat Italy's steadily tightening exchange controls. The second advantage was the IOR's secrecy and offshore status, making discovery of what was taking place particularly difficult. The third, less charitable, advantage was that the Vatican bank never seemed to mind.

Indeed the IOR developed a speculator's mentality, where risk took second place to the tempting rewards on offer. It retained some holdings in Italy, such as its interests in Banco Ambrosiano and Pesenti's Italcementi, and smaller investments in bluechip industrial companies like Fiat. But scandal or near-scandal would dog its name. In the United States, the IOR was fined for an improperly documented acquisition of a stake in a company called Vetco Industries. That year too, by at least one account,† it narrowly avoided being caught up in a giant counterfeit stock deal sponsored by the Mafia. Then came Sindona, and then Calvi.

†*The Vatican Connection*, Richard Hammer, 1982.

"The IOR is not a speculative organization, and I'm not a speculator," Marcinkus declared in a rare interview† after Ambrosiano lay in ruins, in the autumn of 1982. "But can you live in this world without worrying about money? Even the Church has to see to the financial needs of its dependencies." God had to make an accommodation with Mammon; or in other words, and to repeat a celebrated Marcinkus dictum: "You can't run the Church on Hail Marys."

The argument over whether Marcinkus was quite as innocent a victim as he proclaimed in his dealings with Calvi would continue long after the demise of Ambrosiano. It is unlikely that Calvi had already conceived the perverted use to which that partnership was to be put, but its components were by 1971 in place. Apart from the IOR, Compendium in Luxembourg was well placed to exploit the lax banking laws of the Grand Duchy. Just over the Swiss border in Lugano, there was Banca del Gottardo, with emanations, through its Ultrafin associates, in Zurich and New York. In Nassau, Cisalpine was starting to feel its way. Then there were the shell companies, the indirect subsidiaries which compliant lawyers would set up, never to be mentioned on any balance sheet. One such, established in Luxembourg at this time or a little later, was called Manic S.A.—a singularly apt name in the light of what was to follow. Manic, under the titular control of the IOR, was to rise later from its obscurity with a vengeance.

But the time had now come to develop Ambrosiano within Italy, and events seemed to play remarkably into Calvi's hands. Following the failure of the Bastogi takeover that autumn of 1971, Sindona had resolved to pull out of Italy. The controlling interest in La Centrale held by Hambro's was of no strategic value, and the London bank was in any event anxious to break with the Sicilian. Calvi, on the other hand, signalled his willingness to buy.

In November 1971 Hambro's sold its La Centrale stake, with 37 per cent of the voting stock, to Compendium in Luxembourg. With La Centrale, Calvi had the company which would handle his subsequent investments in Italy.

†*Il Sabato*, November 1982.

CHAPTER SIX

Empire Building

AT THE START of the 1970s, the Milan stock market was tiny and unregulated, even more so than today. As a theatre for speculation and financial manipulation it was perfect. The fewness of the companies quoted—never more than 150—meant that it was the smallest of fry when set alongside Paris, Amsterdam or Frankfurt, to say nothing of the London stock exchange or Wall Street. Rules of disclosure were minimal, and consolidated accounts were but a gleam in the eye of idealistic EEC officials in Brussels.

With comparatively small outlay, an imaginative and unprincipled financier could do much as he pleased, puffing up a share price on which to build paper pyramids of wealth. Reputations were made, and in Italy, as everywhere, there were those gullible enough to be convinced by them. Greed and fear, the dominant emotions in financial markets anywhere, were allowed play without hindrance. Nor did it seem that serious. Credit was easy, and OPEC's awakening of 1973 was still in the future. If the stock market was not fulfilling its theoretical function of providing venture capital, that did not seem to matter either. For Italy in the previous decade had achieved the fastest growth of any industrial nation except Japan.

And it was with truly Japanese diligence and inscrutability that Calvi set about realizing his goal of turning Ambrosiano into an Italian merchant bank. Throughout his life he would remain a strangely one-dimensional figure. Socially, he might not have existed, his culture was small, his life by most standards grey. These gaps his wife would try to fill, in her self-imposed mission of making Calvi outwardly, as well as inwardly, the perfect and complete banker. She would try to persuade him, with small success, to read books and take an interest in the arts. With her fondness of bright colours and antique furniture, she would try, again without great success, to persuade visitors of the taste and animation of their flat in Milan and country villa at Drezzo, close to the Swiss border. But, then at least, these shortcomings did not matter; her husband's dimension was finance, where he excelled, and the moment could not have been better.

Now that Sindona was losing interest in Italy after the Bastogi setback, Calvi, as managing director and chief executive of Ambrosiano, was his natural heir as leader of Catholic finance in Milan. He had both the conveniences of the IOR and the resources of his bank to hand. The combination of these with Calvi's own stealthy and perverted financial genius was to be irresistible. Between 1972 and 1975 he endowed Ambrosiano with two banks and a large insurance company, which in turn controlled other smaller banking interests. It would emerge as the most powerful private financial group in Italy.

In so narrow a market as Milan, a handful of manipulators was enough. Calvi, of course, was one, while two of the others were his mentor Sindona and a formidable lady called Anna Bonomi who ran a group called Invest. They were to be the main partners in the dealings which secured Calvi's Italian kingdom. There was also a third, more passive, partner—the IOR. The illegal nature of the transactions by which he won control for La Centrale of the Toro insurance company and a thriving Lombardy bank, Credito Varesino, would eventually lead to Calvi's downfall. But the acquisition of his other bank, Banca Cattolica del Veneto, is perhaps even more deserving of examination, as an illustration of both the laws of the financial jungle which then obtained, and the complicity between Calvi, Sindona and the Vatican bank.

All stemmed from two apparently unrelated events: the decision of Paul VI to reduce the Church's more conspicuous holdings in Italy, and the purchase by Sindona in 1969 of an insignificant leather tanning company called Pacchetti.

Banca Cattolica del Veneto had been in the hands of the IOR since the War. It was deeply entrenched in the Veneto, that region of Northern Italy inland from Venice, where respect for the Church is greatest and the Christian Democrat vote remains largest. Then, as now, the bank was a marvellous investment. Its property assets, notably the beautiful old buildings which would house its branches, were enormous. It was moreover flush with the savings of the faithful, and spread over one of the parts of Italy where the famous *economia sommersa*, or submerged economy, was most dynamic. Indeed, in 1981 the Banca Cattolica del Veneto announced the highest net profits of any bank in the country.

The same could not be said of Pacchetti, but Sindona had his own plans. Out of this nondescript concern, he intended to conjure a financial creature then unknown in Italy, but all the rage in the United States: the conglomerate. Sindona's model was Gulf and Western. Pacchetti saw its shares pumped higher and higher, and found itself the owner of an odd lot of companies in anything from steel to household cleansers. But after Bastogi, Sindona was interested in it no longer. It was time to find a buyer for Pacchetti, and a bait that would tempt him.

At this point, the three-way deal between himself, Calvi and the IOR was concocted. In return for buying Pacchetti, Calvi would gain the option to acquire from the Vatican a controlling interest in Banca Cattolica del Veneto. Everyone was content, Sindona was to make a great deal of money, Calvi would gain a bank, and the IOR could contemplate the genesis of a huge Catholic grouping around Ambrosiano, which would be a natural ally. In March 1972, La Centrale duly announced that it had paid the equivalent of $45 million for 37 per cent of the Veneto bank. On the face of it, an excellent arrangement for La Centrale, whose lustre had been tarnished by the departure of such as Evelyn de Rothschild from its board after the Hambro's disengagement.

Rather less appealing, had shareholders known about it, was the underside of the deal. Pacchetti had been sold by a Luxembourg shell company of Sindona's called Steelinvest, to a concern with the weird name of Zitropo Holding, also of Luxembourg. As would also later emerge, fat commissions seem to have been paid as well. Calvi was to hint that, yes, Zitropo might have something to do with Ambrosiano. But he was acting on behalf of an "important client", and more he could not say. In the light of what happened later, that client might even have been the IOR. As for Pacchetti, it was a child's doll to be cast aside. In a few months Sindona had inflated its price from 200 to 1,200 lire per share. Now it would be used as a staging post for shares traded between Calvi and the Bonomis, before being left to decay. By

June 1982, as the deluge overtook Calvi, its shares were worth just 75 lire apiece.

Apparently, though, someone did object to the sale of Banca Cattolica del Veneto by the Vatican. He was Albino Luciani, Cardinal Patriarch of Venice, in whose archdiocese the bank mainly operated. The story goes that he protested to Marcinkus at the IOR about the transaction, but received little sympathy. Later Cardinal Luciani was to become Pope John Paul I. But he reigned for only a month, in 1978, far too short a time to bring the IOR to heel.

But Pacchetti was not just a prime example of how the Milan market could be abused by the unscrupulous. Its sale to Zitropo was the first of the financial skeletons which Calvi was to hide away abroad. In return for Pacchetti, Zitropo/Ambrosiano paid Sindona $40 million. The money in fact came from Cimafin, a Liechtenstein front company, which in turn was lent the money by Compendium (later Banco Ambrosiano Holding) in Luxembourg. In the end, Pacchetti would cost Calvi, if subsequent capital increases and commissions were included, over $80 million at the then exchange rate. Thus Ambrosiano's foreign liabilities began, and thus Calvi began his habit of accumulating treasures in Italy at the price of troubles abroad. Zitropo was to be a millstone to the end.

But in late 1972, Calvi was blandly asking Ambrosiano's shareholders to agree to a capital increase, to enable the bank's foreign business to be "expanded further". As usual he was finding it hard to tell the whole truth, or even a significant part of it; and on that occasion the deception did not stop there.

Ever since the previous February, Calvi had been travelling through a separate financial labyrinth, which would lead to control of another rich bank. This time his object was Credito Varesino, based at Varese, to the north-west of Milan. As so often the IOR was a staging post. Put simply, Calvi bought Credito Varesino from the Bonomis; but his means were typically contorted. By the end of 1972, Calvi controlled 35 per cent of the new bank, a decisive interest—but for six months the shares involved were oddly left with the IOR. Calvi had sold them in April to Giammei, notoriously the Vatican bank's stockbrokers in Rome, for 11 billion lire. In October La Centrale, in other words Ambrosiano, bought them back, but for 31 billion lire. This remarkable difference of 20 billion lire was not, however, a profit for the IOR. It had merely acted as a screen, behind which Calvi could shift such a sum around his group.

With Credito Varesino safely netted, Calvi turned his attention to Toro, and the interests in other smaller banks in its portfolio. This time, he found the Bonomis in opposition, after Toro for reasons similar to his own. By early 1974, after a covert stock market battle, Calvi was the contender to triumph. The Bonomis had to give best, but remained allies of Calvi in some other of his obscure dealings until withdrawal in 1975. But by then, his basic design had been realized. Not only was Banco Ambrosiano an orthodox commercial bank, with 1,800 billion lire of deposits, but in practice a merchant bank as well—whatever the Italian banking laws might say.

Not until 1978 was the Bank of Italy to expose, in an outstandingly perceptive report, the most questionable side to some of those dealings in Toro and Credito Varesino. But Calvi's methods were already attracting criticism. Cesare Merzagora, head of Assicurazioni Generali, Italy's biggest insurance company, and something of a patriarch himself of Italian finance, wrote to the Bank of Italy complaining of Calvi and the unsatisfactory nature of the Pacchetti affair. Ambrosiano, he pointedly observed, had the reputation *until recently* of being well-run. Guido Carli, the Governor of the central bank, also publicly criticized the inadequacies of the Milan Market. But Sindona's generosities to the politicians had helped ensure that they were in no hurry to strengthen its rules.

In fact, the Bank of Italy did carry out two earlier inspections of Ambrosiano, in 1971 and 1973, proof that it already had its misgivings about Calvi. But the smokescreen proved too thick to penetrate, and nothing came of them. Meanwhile events at home and abroad were making Calvi's dubious activities a less pressing concern. For a series of upheavals in the international monetary system coincided with the beginning of the end for Michele Sindona.

The Sicilian had wasted no time in using the $40 million received from Calvi for Pacchetti. That same 1972, he bought control of Franklin National, the twentieth largest American bank. Franklin was to be used as the platform for a speculative extravaganza, made all the easier by the then liquid state of international capital markets. The

Vietnam war was at its height, and thousands of millions of dollars were leaving America, as the Nixon administration, under its much-criticized policy of "benign neglect", countenanced a succession of payments deficits.

Sindona, and his top foreign exchange specialist Carlo Bordoni, thus could borrow money to speculate on everything: from lire, dollars and Deutschmarks to gold, silver and commodities of many kinds. As far as the lira was concerned, Sindona speculated on its decline. Alas, however, it was the dollar which weakened, devalued by ten per cent in February 1973, and undermined further by Middle East war and the sharp rise in the price of oil which followed. The mark, which Sindona was expecting to fall, instead rose almost without interruption. As his losses accumulated, he was forced to resort to ever riskier expedients to recover them. Payments to the politicians in Italy multiplied; the Christian Democrats admitted receiving $3 million from him, but the true figure probably was considerably higher. During this period too the shadow of the Mafia lengthened over his affairs.

But both Sindona and Calvi suffered another misfortune at about that time: the appointment as Treasury Minister of the redoubtable and uncompromising Ugo La Malfa.

La Malfa was one of the founders of the postwar Italian republic; by background and instinct he was a part of that "lay" establishment whose financial embodiments were the Banca Commerciale and bankers such as Enrico Cuccia, Sindona's great foe. Like both of them, La Malfa was Sicilian by birth; but despite, or perhaps because of that, his lifelong ambition was to haul Italy northwards to the modern mainstream of Western Europe, to let daylight into the confessional booth.

The story of Roberto Calvi would demonstrate how hard that task would be. But until his death in 1979, the name of La Malfa was synonymous with an intellectual honesty and determination unusual in Italy. In that summer of 1973 he lost no time in proving where his sympathies lay. Calvi, Sindona and the Bonomis he branded as *golpisti della Borsa*, or "coup-makers of the stock market". More important, he raised interest rates, and thus put an end to the policy of easy money, under which such coup-making flourished.

The plight of Sindona became desperate. To raise the dollars he urgently needed, he planned to transfer back to Italy control of SGI, the property company he had purchased from the Vatican in 1969, and subsequently run from abroad. But someone had to provide the money—and as often in the dealings of both Calvi and himself, that someone would be the small shareholder. Sindona intended that a Milanese financial company of his called Finambro would buy SGI. Finambro's capital would be raised for the purpose to 160 billion lire from a mere 1 million lire. The public would be able to subscribe only to non-voting shares, thus leaving Sindona with practical control. Unfortunately however, schemes of that dimension required Ministerial approval from Rome; and this La Malfa refused to grant.

Sindona was cornered. Despite ever more urgent solicitation of the politicians, his two Italian banks, Banca Privata Finanziaria and Banca Unione, saw their troubles steadily worsen. Hope flickered briefly in mid-1974, as the Nassau subsidiary of the Banco di Roma, the big state bank traditionally closest to the Vatican and the Christian Democrats provided him with a most timely loan of $100 million. But neither that, nor permission granted *in extremis* for a merger of the two banks sufficed. The newcomer, Banca Privata Italiana (BPI), was all but stillborn. On September 27, 1974, it was placed in compulsory liquidation after just eight weeks of life, and Milan magistrates issued warrants for Sindona's arrest, on charges of fraud and falsifying balance sheets. But with uncannily happy timing the bird had flown the day before to Taiwan, a country with which Italy had not signed an extradition treaty. Less than a fortnight later, the American part of his group collapsed, as the Franklin National Bank was declared insolvent in New York.

Shortly afterwards Sindona resurfaced in a permanent suite in the opulent Pierre Hotel, overlooking Central Park in New York. There he would mingle public complaining that he had been the innocent victim of a witch-hunt conducted by Cuccia, La Malfa and others of the "lay" establishment of Italy, with the private conviction that he would manage to avoid trouble on both sides of the Atlantic. In America, after all, he was not without friends in the Republican administration; while his old associates at home would be kept to heel by the threat of exposure of a tantalizing list of 500 prominent Italians, said to have exported currency illegally through his banks.

He was correct, but only in part, about Italy. The "list of 500", as it swiftly became known, did periodically cause a flutter in Italian political circles, and somehow he never was extradited back to face judgement in Milan. Indeed, notwithstanding his conviction and sentencing in 1976 to three and a half years in jail *in absentia* (for falsifying the accounts of Banca Unione), the Christian Democrats—or at least some of them—continued their efforts to persuade the Bank of Italy to consent to a painless solution of Sindona's difficulties right up until 1979.

But long before that, his banks around Europe had failed. In Switzerland, Finabank had accumulated losses of $50 million when it was closed by the Berne authorities in 1975.

To this day, no-one knows how much the Vatican lost with Sindona; Marcinkus has claimed that if earlier dealings are taken into account, the Holy See in fact shows a profit on the association. In any event, the archbishop kept his job and his influence, despite estimates elsewhere that involvement with Sindona cost the Vatican anything from $30 million to $300 million.

Back in Milan, Calvi also looked at first to have survived with reasonable comfort the tempest caused by Sindona's passing. Indeed, the latter's departure for the United States, the quiescence of the Bonomis, and the ebbing energies of Carlo Pesenti had left him seemingly alone on the winning side. But appearances were deceptive.

After a brief rally in 1973 (partly thanks to rumours that the little loved La Malfa might resign as Treasury Minister) the Milan market began to fall in earnest as Sindona's misdeeds unravelled. *Austerità*, moreover, was the watchword of the day, as Italy too faced up to the harsh economic realities imposed by more expensive oil. Shares in Calvi's companies were worse affected than most, because of his known close links with the bankrupt Sindona. But there was another ingredient to his misfortunes: an apparently deliberate effort to provoke his downfall. Not only was Ambrosiano stock being heavily sold on the over-the-counter market, but gossip was doing the rounds that both the Milan bank and Banca del Gottardo in Switzerland were experiencing difficulties.

Whether the whispering campaign existed—or whether it was an early product of Calvi's persecution complex—cannot be said with certainty. He was however sufficiently alarmed to notify the Bank of Italy of "false and tendentious" rumours, aimed at disrupting Ambrosiano. Much more important, Calvi took the episode as a signal that he should begin protecting himself and his bank by all means to hand.

A perspicacious book which took stock of Italian finance at about this time observed: "Calvi is condemned to expand. There is little prospect of an orderly retreat, for almost inevitably these enterprises end in disaster."† Eight years were to elapse before that prophecy was fulfilled. But for Roberto Calvi the long defensive battle was already under way.

---

†Scalfari and Turani: *Razza Padrona*, Feltrinelli, Milan, 1974.

CHAPTER SEVEN

Defence

DESPITE THE FADING pink paint on the cosy eighteenth-century façade overlooking Largo Bellotti, Banco Ambrosiano's headquarters just behind La Scala had many of the qualities of a fortress. Once inside, the visitor would find sombre windowless corridors stretching before him. The senior directors' offices on the fourth floor were only attainable after a special key on the third floor had activated the lift to go higher. To Roberto Calvi, now Ambrosiano's unchallenged but wary master, the fortress would have seemed under special threat when he gazed out over the rooftops of Milan in those closing months of 1974.

Not only were unknown assailants trying to undermine the bank, but the political climate in Italy at large was changing to his disadvantage. The country was moving leftwards, a process reinforced by the widespread indignation felt at the Sindona affair, and the evidence it had afforded for the dubious overlap between high finance and low Christian Democrat politics. The beneficiaries were the opposition Communists, who were promising a wholesale cleansing of Italian public life, and not least of the country's banking system, if they came to power. And for a while it seemed as if they really might.

In the summer of 1974, as Sindona's improbable financial edifice was coming apart, the Christian Democrats chose to ally themselves with the Church against the pressures for modernization of Italian society, in a referendum on divorce. The outcome was humiliating defeat. In regional elections the following year, the Communists won an unprecedented 36 per cent of the popular vote. If that trend continued, they might even overtake the Christian Democrats to become Italy's largest party at the general elections to be held by 1977 at the latest, but probably rather sooner. The fear must have been deep in Calvi that Ambrosiano might be threatened not only by financial takeover, but by political one as well. Accordingly, he started to take precautions in both directions.

In each case, the mechanisms were to hand, ready for employment: the network of foreign subsidiaries created by Ambrosiano between 1960 and 1973, and that adept of the black political arts, Licio Gelli. As we have seen, the exact date of Calvi's meeting with the Venerable Grandmaster of the P-2 is uncertain. What does seem certain is that partnership in earnest began around 1975.

Already, however, Calvi was setting about his financial purpose. He would buy control of his bank, and—with the assistance of the Vatican—transfer that control abroad. The mystery at the heart of the Banco Ambrosiano affair was beginning, in the shape of an obscure company called Suprafin.

Suprafin had been established in Milan in November 1971 by two of Calvi's most trusted associates: an accountant of Armenian extraction named Vahan Pasargiklian, later to become managing director of Banca Cattolica del Veneto, and Gennaro Zanfagna, a Milan lawyer. Capitalized first at two million lire, then 500 million lire, and finally one billion lire, Suprafin was controlled by a Luxembourg holding company called Anli. Early on it appeared to be primarily just another tool, along the lines of the inglorious Pacchetti, for the manipulation of the Milan market by Calvi and the Bonomis. In November 1972, the latter bought one third of its shares, to be relinquished only in 1975, when the Bonomis severed their ties with Calvi. From very early on Suprafin would deal in Ambrosiano shares, to smooth out violent price fluctuations. But after the disgrace of Sindona and the rumours about Calvi, the selling of Banco Ambrosiano turned in that summer of 1974 from a trickle into a flood.

Hardly a day went by without Suprafin buying where others were selling. And, of course, not only was the share price being supported, but Ambrosiano—or whoever truly owned Suprafin—was quite illegally strengthening control of the bank itself.

Initially most of the shares thus bought made the comparatively short journey to Liechtenstein. One of the first recipients, for example, was an *anstalt* in Vaduz called Ulricor, set up by an obliging lawyer there in March 1974, with a capital of just 20,000 Swiss francs.

Seven months later it was buying 170,000 shares in Ambrosiano or 1.7 per cent of the total—in keeping with its suitably innocuous declared purpose of "taking shareholdings on behalf of itself or others in industrial and commercial enterprises". Ulricor was to remain faithful right up to the end. In June 1982 it ranked as the eighth largest single shareholder, with 1.2 per cent, or 590,000 shares of the much enlarged capital of Ambrosiano. The original buying was carried out upon instructions from the Banca del Gottardo (in other words from Calvi); between 1974 and 1976 two of its administrators, with power of attorney, were Fernando Garzoni and Francesco Bolgiani, chairman and general manager respectively of Banca del Gottardo. And Ulricor, it was generally assumed, was technically owned by the IOR, the Vatican bank.

The Ulricor pattern was to become familiar. In 1974, three more strange-sounding names from Vaduz—Sapi, Rekofinanz and Sektorinvest—became prominent in the register of Banco Ambrosiano shareholders. Shortly afterwards two more, called Finkurs and Sansinvest, popped up. The next year Liechtenstein was supplemented by the more distant and even safer shelter of Panama, where registered companies did not even have to provide accounts. The first Panamanian shareholders were two insubstantial creatures called La Fidele and Finprogram. In October 1977 another four companies coalesced to join them in the steamy heat of Central America, bearing the fetching names of Orfeo, Lantana, Cascadilla and Marbella. The quartet was set up simultaneously to take delivery of 1,020,000 Ambrosiano shares, equal to 5.1 per cent of its capital. All were subsidiaries of Manic S.A. in Luxembourg.

In all, the diligent Suprafin had expedited abroad no less than 15.4 per cent of Banco Ambrosiano; a proportion which, given the fragmented structure of the capital of Calvi's bank, amounted to control. The recipients, as we have seen, were shell companies, consisting of little more than an entry in a lawyer's books; but all of them were in one way or another managed by Calvi and his bank, whatever the confusing changes of name they might sometimes later undergo. The buying orders placed with Suprafin had come first from Banca del Gottardo and then from Cisalpine Overseas, Ambrosiano's subsidiary in Nassau. The head of Lantana, which like its three Panamanian sisters had a token capital of $10,000, was Pierre

Siegenthaler, President of Cisalpine and also by now the honorary consul of Italy in the Bahamas.†

In 1978, as will shortly be explained, the Bank of Italy's inspectors guessed at, but unfortunately could not prove the gathering fraud. For Suprafin's purchase of Ambrosiano shares had cost 37 billion lire, or some $60 million at the then exchange rate. This outlay would follow the Pacchetti deal as the second—and easily the most important—cause of final calamity.

Obscuring everything was the collaboration, witting or unwitting, of the Vatican Bank, which extended well beyond the IOR's probable ownership of Ulricor. For as early as November 1974 the Banca del Gottardo had set up in the name of the IOR yet another Panamanian company. It was called the United Trading Corporation, and would, like Manic in Luxembourg, be no small cog in the machinery of financial deception Calvi was so skilfully constructing.

With little delay, United Trading Corporation was busy establishing various nominee subsidiaries, including two in Liechtenstein called Imparfin and Teclefin. When the Bonomis (and Anli) withdrew from Suprafin, these two little companies stepped in to replace them. So it was that the IOR came to possess the company which had purchased on the Milan stock market effective mastery of Banco Ambrosiano. Formal acknowledgement came in a letter, dated January 20 1975, which the Vatican bank sent to Calvi, stating in carefully chosen words that Suprafin "was of its pertinence"; in simpler terms, that the IOR owned it. The Vatican bank merely requested Ambrosiano to manage Suprafin on its behalf, and supply periodic reports of its activities. Whether those reports were sent is not known. Indeed, the letter itself subsequently became something of a puzzle. Some would take it at face value; but other students of the intrigue offered a different theory—that the letter, whatever the date it bore, was in fact written and provided early in *1978*, just before the inspectors of the Bank of Italy exposed the function of Suprafin, as Calvi surely knew they would.

In Italy it is not necessarily illegal for a company to acquire shares in itself; but the maximum permitted level of purchases must be published in its annual report and approved by shareholders. Hence

†L'Espresso, September 6, 1981.

71

the need for the IOR to be interposed, if Calvi was to preserve his scheme; and thence the possibility that the letter was made available long after its purported date.

The central bank in 1978 would not conceal its suspicion that in practice Suprafin to all intents and purposes belonged to Banco Ambrosiano itself. But of course its officials had no power to visit and question Marcinkus, Mennini and de Stroebel, safe in a foreign country in the heart of Rome. For the time being Calvi's financial fortress was impregnable. He was by then looking to his political defences too.

There are few more depressing aspects of the career of Roberto Calvi than his relations with Italy's politicians. From 1975 onwards, both directly and indirectly, his bank dispensed money across the political spectrum. The beneficiaries included the Christian Democrats, the Socialists and even the Communists. By the end, in June 1982, the Communists would owe Ambrosiano 11 billion lire—not to mention more than 20 billion lire borrowed by the Rome newspaper *Paese Sera*, strongly sympathetic to the party, and indirectly owned by it.

In all, it has been calculated,† Ambrosiano would lend the parties some 88 billion lire to purchase their good will. As Calvi's predicament worsened later, he would invest more and more time, as well as money, in his attempts to cultivate their support. But despite increasingly frequent visits to Rome, his understanding of the politicians was limited to a grasp of their financial appetites. Taciturn and never entirely sure of himself outside the ambit of the bank, Calvi was rarely at ease with them socially, unable entirely to master the subtle and shifting alliances, the gossip, the assurances lightly given but often unfulfilled.

But that still lay in the future. In the mid-1970s, Calvi seemed to have found the ideal bridge between his own diffidence and centres of power in Rome, in the person of Licio Gelli. Calvi, needless to say, never had a press officer as such. *I contatti con quelli là, me li tiene quello lì.* "This one here, he looks after dealings with that lot," he would confide. Thanks to Sindona, among other reasons, Gelli must have known many of Calvi's less reputable secrets; but the arrange-

†*Mondo Economico*, September 29, 1982.

ment was mutually beneficial from the outset. In return for his brokerage of political alliances and protection, helped by a steady flow of sensitive information from well-placed collaborators, Gelli gained first access to, and then partial dominion over, a powerful private banking group. Gelli and the P-2, moreover, constituted the initial bond between Ambrosiano and Rizzoli, the largest and most important publishing house in Italy.

In its heyday the P-2 was constructed around a tripod. Two of the legs were Gelli/Ortolani and Calvi/Banco Ambrosiano. The third was Rizzoli and its most coveted asset the *Corriere della Sera*, the Milanese newspaper with the richest tradition of any in Italy, and unrivalled sales of some 500,000 copies. At its height, Rizzoli was printing one in four of all the newspapers read daily up and down the country. Ultimately, association with Ambrosiano would lead it along a path to the brink of bankruptcy. But for a long while the combination of money, newspapers, and political leverage seemed irresistible.

CHAPTER EIGHT

Rizzoli

DESPITE THE WRETCHED likeness of their endings, the Rizzoli story has a romantic quality which that of Calvi lacks entirely. Angelo Rizzoli, the founder of a dynasty he boasted would be eternal, built up his publishing fortune from the humblest of origins. Brought up in an orphanage, at the age of nineteen he was running a tiny printing press, turning out labels for crates of fruit. By the 1960s he was the most powerful publisher in Italy, a legacy which passed first to his son Andrea, and then to his grandson Angelo junior. To the end of his life, the old man never forgot the lessons of his youth: "My children have had the misfortune to be born rich," he would tell friends. But even in his most sober musings Angelo Rizzoli cannot have imagined that a fortune worth over $100 million could be largely destroyed by his heirs in the space of just a decade.

The fatal step was one which was supposed to seal the Rizzolis' success—the acquisition of the venerable *Corriere* in 1974. Founded a century before, the paper was presently owned by the Crespi family, the oil magnate Angelo Moratti, and the Agnellis, masters of the Fiat car company, and the leading industrial family of Italy. "A dream held by three generations of my family has come true," proclaimed the young Angelo on July 17, 1974, the day Rizzoli took over after paying 44 billion lire for the privilege. The size of the mistake was soon plain.

The Rizzolis, of course, were neither the first nor the last industrialists in Italy or elsewhere to have been beguiled by the prospect of owning a newspaper. But the *Corriere* soon revealed itself as a particularly bad buy. That first year of 1974, it lost 12 billion lire, and the Rizzoli company did not possess the management expertise to push through the changes required. Within a year the deficit, and the cost of financing the borrowings for buying the *Corriere* in the first place had driven the young Angelo and his finance director of eighteen months, Bruno Tassan Din, to do the rounds of the banks asking for money.

The two made a curious pair: Angelo Rizzoli, corpulent and slow speaking, was the brooding heir; part playboy, part over-conscious of the responsibility his birth had thrust upon him. Tassan Din on the other hand, with his thick mane of grey hair and aquiline features, had arrived at Rizzoli with the reputation of a financial magician. His quick tongue was matched by a natural cunning. Later he was to be portrayed as the malign, scheming adventurer who brought Rizzoli to disaster; sometimes he would be described as being Rasputin to the uncertain, ingenuous Tsar Angelo.

In the summer of 1975 they both received an unpleasant surprise: the big State banks would not lend them money. Suspicion gradually turned into certainty as to the reason: that the *Corriere* of the day was showing rather too little respect for the Christian Democrats and the Socialists, the two dominant parties of the establishment, and political patrons of the public sector banks. Providence, however, was to place a saviour to hand, in the person of Umberto Ortolani.

If the unctuously intimidating Gelli was Calvi's bridge to the P-2, Umberto Ortolani was to perform that function for Rizzoli. Angelo's father, Andrea, had used Ortolani as a consultant for his business ventures in South America, where the latter already had interests of his own in the local right-wing press. Andrea Rizzoli put Ortolani in touch with his son and Tassan Din, and through him the two met Licio Gelli. Gelli's own banking contacts within the rapidly expanding P-2 did the rest.

Money, previously so hard to find, now miraculously arrived, both from Banco Ambrosiano, and from other banks of whom senior executives were later shown to be involved with the P-2. Thus began the three-way relationship between Calvi, Rizzoli and the P-2 which was to run through the rest of Calvi's life. "Ambrosiano was a tap for us," Tassan Din recalled, when it was all over, years later. But the partnership between bank and publisher rapidly surpassed that of ordinary lender and borrower. With the backing of Ambrosiano, Rizzoli launched itself into a headlong expansion, as if growth alone could burst the skin of financial difficulties.

Tassan Din was authorized to purchase an insurance company, Savoia, and then two small banks. One of them, Banca Mercantile of Florence, was later sold to Ambrosiano after a bewildering string of transactions in which the IOR again would figure as a passive partner.

In March 1976 Calvi, by then chairman of Ambrosiano, co-opted Andrea Rizzoli on to his bank's board. The appointment was recognition not so much of the close banking relationship between them, as of the fact that—unknown to the other board members—Rizzoli had temporarily become the largest shareholder of Ambrosiano. In return for his financial largesse, Calvi was using the Rizzoli name to conceal the true ownership of a block of Ambrosiano shares, held before by a Swiss front company called Locafid. Locafid, in turn, was run by his own Banca del Gottardo.† Rizzoli's involvement was short-lived, for the shares quickly disappeared into the fastness of Panama. But once again the "fiduciary" technique was at work; and Rizzoli, so heavily indebted to Ambrosiano, was an ideal candidate for the role.

But the real attraction of the publishers lay elsewhere. In Italy, perhaps more than anywhere, ownership of a newspaper was an essential part of the struggle between the competing interest groups and factions. From its columns, friends could be favoured and rivals denigrated; the owner himself would be presented in the best possible light. Subtle or less subtle hints might be dropped, incomprehensible for the general reader, but crystal clear for those to whom the message was addressed.

Visible ownership was, of course, hardly to Calvi's taste. Far better to exert influence from the wings of the stage, through provision of the funds which Rizzoli so badly needed. But that he relished such a role behind the publishing group and the *Corriere*, can hardly be doubted.

In the mid-1970s control of a newspaper was a subtle status symbol. It would place him on equivalent footing to the Agnellis who ran *La Stampa* of Turin, second only to the *Corriere* in terms of sales, or Montedison which had brought *Il Messaggero* in Rome. *La Nazione* in Florence, and *Il Resto del Carlino* in Bologna were owned by Attilio Monti, an oil magnate. Years before a far more potent oil industrial-

†See shareholding list of 1973, Appendix.

ist, Enrico Mattei of ENI, even launched his own paper, *Il Giorno*, in Milan.

Calvi was thus in excellent company, and in any case his fame was beginning to spread. In 1974 Giovanni Leone, the then President of the Republic, made him a *Cavaliere del Lavoro*, a distant equivalent of a British knighthood, for his services to the economy. Calvi, however, would rarely use the title.

Even Giovanni Agnelli, then President of Confindustria, the Italian employers association as well as chairman of Fiat, expressed a curiosity to meet this new leader of Milanese finance. A dinner was duly arranged; it was a quintessentially Italian occasion, discreet and non-committal, at which these two representatives of such different traditions, the cosmopolitan, patrician industrialist and the shy and devious Catholic banker, could size each other up. The evening would later be described as "hallucinating".

Aimless small talk was punctuated by frequent silences. Calvi only talked easily about his experiences in Russia. Oddly, he and Agnelli were near contemporaries who had served in the Soviet campaign at much the same time. But the two had little else in common. At last the dinner ended, after which Agnelli remarked of Calvi with effortless dismissal: "But how can anyone go through their life looking at the point of their shoes?"

As always, Calvi was not of the real establishment. He gave huge sums to the Bocconi university, to the prestigious Biblioteca Ambrosiana in Milan, and wanted to become a director of the Cini Foundation, the eminent cultural body in Venice. He would pay the membership fee for the club; but then would not cross its threshold. The encounter with Agnelli was an illustration of how in the presence of the truly well-born and well-connected, he could be dazzled and discomforted. Even within the orbit of Ambrosiano itself, he was not immune to such considerations. Years earlier he had asked Alessandro Cordero di Montezemolo, bearer of one of Italy's most aristocratic family names, to be chief executive of La Centrale. The experience was short-lived, as di Montezemolo rapidly disagreed with Calvi. "I'm not going to go around blindfolded," he is said to have emphasized, when Calvi predictably tried to circumscribe his freedom of action.

Di Montezemolo resigned, and today is chairman of a large firm of insurance brokers in New York. Had Calvi been prepared to tolerate a few such robust critics, he would probably not have met the end he did. But it was already too late to change his ways.

Throughout his life Calvi would rarely seek the counsel of an impartial outsider. "When two people know a secret, it's not a secret anymore," was one of his favourite aphorisms. Opposition would be seen as evidence of conspiracy to overthrow him. One of the few who did attempt resistance was Luigi Agostoni, deputy general manager of Ambrosiano and a director until he resigned in October 1975. His departure did cause some people to wonder. But for the rest, the board was subservience itself. In any case it did not seem to matter much then, as Calvi and the P-2 enfolded Rizzoli in their coils.

Most of the remaining independence of the publishing group disappeared in the summer of 1977, on the occasion of a capital increase from 5 billion lire to 25.5 billion lire. The provision of new funds was vital, both to keep pace with Rizzoli's expanding debts, and in some measure to offset the harm caused by the Government's delay in permitting an increase in the cover price of newspapers. Ostensibly the entire sum was put up by the family, to leave it in 91 per cent command of the group. The truth was somewhat different.

Rizzoli's true financial position, and the real identity of its owner were to remain mysteries until almost the end of this story, obscured respectively by a string of scarcely intelligible balance sheets and a screen of front companies and trustees. In effect, however, the family had lost control.

The money the Rizzolis used to subscribe to the capital increase was put up by Banco Ambrosiano; it went in good measure belatedly to complete payment for the 33 per cent of the *Corriere* they had acquired from the Agnellis back in 1974. In return, moreover, Calvi insisted that 80 per cent of Rizzoli's capital be lodged with Banco Ambrosiano as security for the loan. Later this majority interest in the publishers appeared to have been passed on by Calvi to the IOR, under one or other of the circuitous transactions they were then elaborating. As a result control of Italy's most important paper for a long spell may—theoretically at least—have been in the hands of the Vatican. The entire arrangement, Tassan Din has since stated, was orchestrated by Ortolani, who naturally would receive a handsome commission for his pains.

But there were other and more visible consequences of the new balance of power. Ortolani joined Rizzoli's board, as did Calvi's trusted Gennaro Zanfagna, who had been involved with the birth of Suprafin back in 1971. Piero Ottone, the independent-minded editor of the *Corriere*, who had so disturbed the Christian Democrats, would depart, to be replaced by his deputy, Franco Di Bella. Four years later, in 1981, Di Bella in his turn would be compelled to resign. The records maintained that he had been a paid-up member of the P-2 since October 10, 1978.

For Tassan Din, on the other hand, the successful conclusion of the capital increase was the signal to embark upon a hectic shopping expedition. Rizzoli, with the financial support of Ambrosiano, bought newspapers left and right, often with an eye on the political favours that might be purchased too. The group launched new publications of its own, notably *L'Occhio*, supposed to be Italy's mass selling equivalent of the Daily Mirror, but which lost money from the start. Rizzoli invested much in the burgeoning Italian private television of the day, and planned ventures in Malta and beyond. For with Calvi's money and Ortolani's guidance, Tassan Din enlarged Rizzoli's Latin American interests, notably in Argentina.

Everyone could count themselves satisfied. Tassan Din could theorize about turning Rizzoli into a global communications conglomerate; the inroads of the political parties into the Italian media were fostered, while in the end, Gelli and Calvi exerted unsuspected control. Expansion, however, brought above all an expansion of losses. By 1980 Rizzoli's financial disarray was such that end-of-month salary payments were occasionally in doubt up to the last day, while Tassan Din would in time become as tireless an advocate of retrenchment as he once had been of growth.

CHAPTER NINE

Revenge

BY EARLY 1976 the post-Sindona squall seemed to have blown itself out, and thanks to the surreptitious activities of Suprafin, Ambrosiano's share price had steadied. Within the bank, the new chairman was remote, vaguely feared, but seemingly infallible. Most of his interest would be devoted to La Centrale, of which he was by now also chairman; the everyday banking business of Ambrosiano scarcely bothered him. But the unfailing growth shown by its balance sheet would still most doubts.

True, some may have had misgivings, but proof did not exist. Ambrosiano that year was permitted by the Rome authorities to borrow $100 million abroad, on the loose justification that the funds would be used to help finance Italian exports (a pretext which would crop up regularly in the future). The subsidiary in Luxembourg, which had changed its name from Compendium into Banco Ambrosiano Holding, was granted permission to triple its capital; this meant that the Milan parent could "export" almost 300 million Swiss francs to subscribe its 70 per cent share of the increase.

There were even signs that the tangle of overlapping shareholdings was being sorted out. The Luxembourg holding company would take charge of the foreign subsidiaries, notably Banca del Gottardo and Cisalpine Overseas in Nassau. Control of La Centrale was transferred from Luxembourg to the parent bank in Italy, where La Centrale would hold Ambrosiano's domestic interests, in Banca Cattolica del Veneto, Credito Varesino and Toro. For a moment, a measure of clarity was seemingly returning to Calvi's affairs—but predictably, it was not so. For several of these transactions had the familiar dark underside, of which a currency crisis would indirectly force exposure.

Never, before or since, has the Italian lira been so roughly treated as in the year of 1976. Three times in the space of ten months it was the target of speculators. In that period, its value against the dollar fell by 50 per cent; at one point the usable foreign exchange reserves of the Bank of Italy dwindled to beneath $500 million. International markets were full of talk of the "Italian risk", a *portmanteau* expression which denoted huge deficits, inflation well into double figures, and the possibility of Communist victory at the general election held that summer. As the country's credit rating fell, the Rome Government introduced drastic measures to stem the flood of capital which both individual citizens and companies were despatching to the safety of Switzerland and beyond.

Law "159" of April 1976 has survived to this day. It turned the illegal export of currency from a simple "administrative" offence into a penal one, inviting arrest and imprisonment. The "159" was a blunderbuss, a desperate measure for desperate times, whose indiscriminating nature was to be bitterly criticized. Given the shortcomings of bureaucratic Italy, the argument ran, hardly a company did not have to breach it on occasion if foreign competition in export markets was to be overcome. The law, to make matters worse still, was also retroactive.

For Calvi, there were two consequences, one general and one particular. In broad terms, the "159" made it harder to operate those convenient offshore companies with impunity. Previously, if a foreign debt became too much of a concern, the possibility existed of settling it by sending lire out of Italy. After April 1976, that safety valve was largely removed. Foreign debts could now only be paid off by contracting new ones abroad; most often these would be denominated in the ever more expensive dollar. The tiny Liechtenstein and Panama companies were obliged to borrow, to subscribe their share of the capital increase carried out by Ambrosiano in 1976, from 10 billion lire to 20 billion lire.

But the new law had even more specific relevance to Calvi. On November 17, 1975 he conducted a transaction which—though he could not possibly have imagined it then—would lead to his ruin. That day La Centrale, now Ambrosiano's arm in Italy, bought 1.1 million shares in Toro, on the face of it enough to secure outright majority control of the insurance company. Curiously, however, the sellers, all companies based in Liechtenstein, were instructed to make the shares available by Banca del Gottardo, Calvi's arm in Switzerland. What was more, the sellers were all, directly or indirectly, within Ambrosiano's orbit already. One of them was even Sapi, one of those mysterious offshore shareholders of Ambrosiano itself. It would later transpire that the shares in question *had been bought by La Centrale itself*, in the days when La Centrale was controlled through Luxembourg, in 1973 and 1974. They were then tucked away in the foreign nominee companies like Sapi.

Yet when La Centrale "re-imported" the shares into Italy in November 1975, it would pay three times the going price for them on the Milan stock market. Calvi would later claim that the exceptional price was justified, because the extra shares gave him full control of Toro. But since they had in truth been at his disposal since 1973 and 1974, and since he did not report the transaction (as he was obliged to do by the retrospective provision of Law 159) the deal would be construed as an illegal export of the difference between their value on the Milan market, and the price actually paid—in the event 23 billion lire. In 1976 Calvi performed a similar trick with a block of shares in Credito Varesino.

All of this would be unearthed by the Bank of Italy's inspectors in 1978. But why did the central bank choose to have a close look at Banco Ambrosiano at all? The answer may be traced to Michele Sindona, Calvi's former mentor and comrade-in-arms, now down, but very far from out, in the Pierre Hotel in New York.

Despite the 4,500 miles which divided them, Sindona was never long out of touch with Italy and his old friend Licio Gelli. He had already convinced himself that the collapse of his Banca Privata Italiana was unfair, that he was the blameless victim of a vendetta carried out by his "lay" enemies like Cuccia. Now, he further reasoned, all could be put right with a little assistance from grateful associates from more fortunate times.

And who owed him more than Calvi, whom he had helped so much? The chairman of Ambrosiano had after all continued to thrive; while his bank had ample resources to settle the liabilities of Banca Privata Italiana, and thus enable its liquidation proceedings to be halted.

For that second consideration was by 1977 becoming steadily more important. A lawyer called Giorgio Ambrosoli, who had been appointed by the central bank in Rome to carry out the liquidation of

Sindona's Italian interests, was moving painstakingly towards the truth about some of the most questionable business channelled through his banks, including transactions involving the political far right in Europe and beyond, and the Mafia. In America, meanwhile, Watergate and the fall of Nixon and Sindona's Republican party friends, had brought a new moralistic president to power, in the person of Jimmy Carter. Less chance than ever existed of persuading United States investigators to look kindly on the demise of the Franklin National Bank.

That summer Sindona and his lawyers held what amounted to a council of war in New York, to examine how his erstwhile allies in Italy might be induced into working for a "technical" solution to his difficulties at home. The natural first choice was the Banco di Roma, still influenced by the Christian Democrats. Failing that, however, Calvi should be summoned to give assistance.

Evidently they made little progress with the Banco di Roma, for Sindona soon turned his attention to Calvi—but at first to small avail. Either (mindless of how Sicilian potentates can react when an earlier favour is not repaid) Calvi mistakenly calculated that Sindona was a spent force, who could be safely ignored; or he judged that the risk was too great in a venture of that kind, in reforging links with one whose downfall in 1974 had brought himself perilously close to the precipice. Perhaps both considerations played a part. But Sindona was outraged at such abandonment by an indebted friend, and he plotted spectacular revenge.

The chosen instrument was another of those strange *condottieri* who feature in the Calvi story. Once Luigi Cavallo had been a Communist, and a resistance fighter in the Second World War, but for many years now his prime employment had been as an *agent provocateur* at the service of the highest bidder. In the 1950s Fiat had employed him to set up docile in-house trade unions to counter the influence of the increasingly militant ones outside. Cavallo was said to collaborate with a variety of secret services. Above all, he was a practised executor of smear campaigns against pre-selected targets in the Italian financial world. The campaigns, one must presume, were paid for by former colleagues of the victims, who considered themselves betrayed. For Cavallo usually appeared to be well supplied with documents.

Probably for reasons of his own safety, he resides these days in Paris. But his mouthpiece was (and still is) the so-called *Agenzia A*, based in Turin. Periodically, *Agenzia A* would come to life, as a smartly printed pamphlet containing the detailed accusations of the moment. It would be distributed, free of charge, to potentially interested readers such as magistrates, financiers, politicians, as well as journalists. No matter that the contents were unreliable, and obviously far too delicate to publish. Suspicions would be kindled, often to be proved not entirely inaccurate, should the particular episode subsequently gain public notoriety.

For Calvi, however, Sindona and Cavallo devised something even more unnerving, given the secretive nature of their target. Purported details of all Calvi's most unmentionable dealings with the Sicilian would be provided for the general Milanese public to see.

November 13, 1977 had gone down in the city's financial legend as the "day of the tazebao". That morning central Milan, and in particular the crowded tiny streets around the headquarters of Calvi's bank, resembled Peking, as scores of posters, printed in white, blue and yellow appeared overnight from nowhere, plastered on available walls. No matter that Calvi, as usual in his office early, managed to have them down before mid-morning: the damage, above all psychological, had been done.

The banker can only have been horrified by his public denunciation. The posters claimed that he had arranged to have "tens of millions of dollars", stemming from ventures with Sindona, paid into Swiss bank accounts held by himself and his wife. After the unsuccessful Bastogi takeover bid, Calvi had, in the words of the poster, "appropriated for himself" $4.8 million. On November 11, 1972, he had received $3.3 million as a personal commission on the Pacchetti/Banca Cattolica del Veneto transaction. The money, the posters alleged, had been paid into accounts bearing the code names of Ehrenkranz and Ralkov G 21, at the Zurich branch of Credit Suisse, and into numbered accounts 618934 and 619112 at the Chiasso (Switzerland) branch of the Union Bank of Switzerland (UBS). Three questions had to be answered, the charge sheet continued: first, from where did Calvi obtain the $200 million he had used to buy control of his companies? Second, how big a profit did he make on selling their shares around the Ambrosiano group? And thirdly, why did the *Corriere della Sera* never mention the misdeeds (including illegal currency exports, tax evasion and falsified balance sheets) of "its effective owner"? Each of the demands would prove to be farsighted. And in case they had escaped notice, copies of *Agenzia A* containing further details were distributed a few days later.

Understandably, and with the good offices of Licio Gelli, Calvi hastened to make peace. According to Sindona's lawyers much later, Calvi consented to provide money for both him and his family. Shortly afterwards, $500,000 passed from Calvi to Sindona, camouflaged by a spurious transaction purporting to cover the sale of a luxurious villa in Northern Italy. As an additional precaution, the movement of Ambrosiano shares into Panama accelerated.

Unfortunately for Calvi, however, Cavallo had also delivered a separate attack, which no amount of money would be able to ward off.

On November 24, 1977, he wrote a lengthy letter to Paolo Baffi, who had replaced Carli as Governor of the Bank of Italy in the summer of 1975. He reminded Baffi of an earlier letter to the central bank, in which Cavallo had enclosed photocopies of documents containing apparent evidence of Calvi's secret accounts in Switzerland. The new letter listed all the accusations which had figured in the Milanese *tazebao*. Cavallo ended with the threat that if the Bank of Italy did not now move against Ambrosiano, he would sue it for failing to carry out its legal duties.

It was not Cavallo's letter alone which prompted Baffi to act, although it was another reason for further scrutiny of Ambrosiano after its rapid expansion of the last few years, and the accompanying rumours, few of them very complimentary. Senior officials at the central bank were at least equally disturbed by first a telex, and then a letter, from Cesare Merzagora—who had written to Carli as long ago as 1972 about Ambrosiano. This time the gist was the same, but the wording still more alarmed: how *could* the Bank of Italy tolerate any longer what Calvi was doing? Baffi gave the go-ahead for a full scale inspection of Banco Ambrosiano. On April 17, 1978 a team of twelve inspectors arrived in the pink-fronted building on Via Clerici, and although no-one could have said so then with certainty, the fate of Roberto Calvi was sealed.

CHAPTER TEN

Inspection

THE BANK OF Italy is a most remarkable institution. Visitors should not be misled by the row of tall palm trees outside, which lend an oriental flavour to the heavy nineteenth-century of its headquarters and muffle the din of the traffic on the Via Nazionale. The central bank is arguably the most professional and West-Europeanized part of the apparatus of the Italian State. To foreigners, indeed, it has often *seemed* the Italian State.

A central bank anywhere is a venerable and dignified organization, of great and, above all, discreet authority. In Italy, where Governments and Treasury Ministers come and go with disconcerting frequency, and where economic crisis—in recent years at least—has been a constant, this is doubly true. Since the end of the Second World War alone, the country had had 43 Governments by mid-1983, each with an average life of slightly over ten months. The Bank of Italy, on the contrary, has been headed by just seven Governors this century, fewer even than there have been Popes on the throne of St Peter. More often than not, they have reflected the older liberal, "lay" aspirations of the founders of the modern Italian state.

During the early 1970s, as deficit followed deficit and a new financial crisis tumbled upon the last, the central bank was regarded abroad as the guarantee of Italy's credit worthiness as a borrower. The high calibre of its officials, with their pronounced *esprit de corps* and familiarity with foreign languages, set it apart from the rest of Italy's decrepit institutions. How remarkable it was, Pushkin once observed of the Russian language, that so backward a people could produce so sophisticated a means of expression. The same was said of the Italian State and the Bank of Italy. In those years too, as the country moved politically leftwards, and the Ambrosiano/IOR scandal was undreamt of, the common witticism ran that only three institutions worked on Italian soil: the Communist party, the Vatican and the Bank of Italy.

Sometimes the Bank would straddle the paradoxes of modern Italy. At home it would be trying to block, with mixed success, the various routes an ingenious people had devised to export capital—whether by fiduciary account, suitcases of cash at the IOR, or motorboats plying across Lake Lugano. But in the monetary meetings abroad which then abounded, the Bank of Italy would be presenting elegant schemes to tackle more esoteric problems, dealing with the dollar "overhang", and currency "snakes", "crawling pegs", and "baskets".

If the Bank of Italy is so flatteringly perceived abroad, its prestige at home is no less. Its authority stems not merely from the breadth of its powers, but from its evident neutrality and independence, and aloofness from the political fray. And nowhere are the powers broader, yet more carefully to be exerted, than in the Bank's duty of superintending the domestic banking system.

In statistical terms alone the task is daunting. The central bank presides over a ragtag army of no less than 1,060 individual banks. They range in size from internationally known institutions like the Banca Commerciale or Credito Italiano, controlling funds of $25,000 million or more, to the tiniest *monte di pietà*, which centuries ago had started life as a pawnbroker's, and today might boast a single branch in a small town. All of them, though, have to comply with strict regulations imposed by the Bank of Italy. To ensure that they do so, the Bank's *vigilanza*, or supervisory department, will carry out up to 150 inspections annually, meaning that every bank, large or small, will have its books gone through every seven or eight years.

But from the mid-1960s on the job acquired an added political sensitivity. The banks were becoming sources of finance, above and below board, for the political parties; especially the Christian Democrats, but later, as Ambrosiano showed, for other parties as well. The public sector banks, controlling 70 per cent of total deposits and their chief executives political appointees, were the first obvious targets. But Michele Sindona was by no means the first private banker who showed how political support might be purchased. The banks moreover would help finance the rival empires built in those years by politically sponsored industrialists. It was the era of Italy's "chemical war", in which hundreds of billions of Lire were squandered on large and little-needed new plants, by flamboyant figures like Nino Rovelli of SIR, and Raffaele Ursini of Liquichimica. All was paid for by cheap loans from the State, channelled through a compliant banking system.

As the parties' appetite for funds increased, to finance their ever more unwieldy machinery of patronage, so did political interference in Italy's entire economic system. A master of the process was Eugenio Cefis from ENI, with his *coup d'état* at Montedison; but later others like Licio Gelli and Michele Sindona easily found accommodation within it. Inevitably, the Bank of Italy's inspectors were increasingly prone to uncover secret irregularities—and increasingly pressed to turn a blind eye to them.

During his long reign as Governor, from 1960 to 1975, Guido Carli did act to remove the worst abuses. His hostility played a large part in Sindona's downfall, as we have seen, but he has subsequently been blamed for not having done more. That is certainly unfair. If he was to move against a financier with the political connections of Sindona, Carli had to ensure that his own flanks were protected. Imperceptibly, he became as much a mediator as a judge; and unconsciously the Bank of Italy became an accomplice to the political warefare. Carli probably enjoyed this role. He is a suave, worldly figure, of the keenest intellect, and fond of dissertation. He had a natural taste for power, and feel for the political eddies. In Britain Carli could be easily imagined as a Secretary to the Cabinet, not infrequently disdainful of the politicians whom theoretically he served. The same could not be said of his successor Paolo Baffi.

The transition from Carli to Baffi at the time seemed completely unexceptional. The Bank of Italy's preference for the "internal solution" had been respected. Baffi moved up from the post of general manager to become Governor in the summer of 1975, during a brief lull in the almost permanent financial crisis of those years. His international standing matched that of Carli; but in many respects the two differed greatly.

If Carli adjusted comfortably to the politicians, Baffi did not. Born of humble family, he remains a most private man, of simple habit. He had spent his entire career at the Bank of Italy, which he joined in 1936. When he was Governor he preferred his unpretentious villa at the seaside resort of Fregene, 20 miles from Rome, to the grace-and-favour apartment in the capital which went with the job.

If a label is to be attached to Baffi, it is probably that of liberalism of the old school. Sound money, a limited role for the state and the free movement of capital and goods are among his cardinal beliefs. The best answer for Italy's economic problems, he has been heard to theorize, would be the abolition of exchange controls. Baffi has been called "a central banker's central banker", and few have won such widespread esteem. Under his guidance Italy staged an astonishing economic recovery between 1976 and 1979. His skilful handling of the lire's entry into the European Monetary System in 1979 was universally praised.

Baffi had also a lifetime of financial scholarship behind him. To be received by him made many visitors feel like inadequately prepared students before a kindly but slightly irascible professor—rendered still more intimidating by a machine-gun-like voice, and thick black spectacles perched owlishly across his nose. Baffi, in short, was everyone's idea of a central bank Governor. Except that is, for some of the politicians for whom he had little time.

Under him, and in charge of the supervisory department, was Mario Sarcinelli. His career, too, had been exceptional. Sarcinelli had joined the central bank in 1957 at the age of 23, with a special scholarship. He served in the research department, the traditional nursery for potential high-flyers. By the time he was 42, he had been promoted to the rank of *direttore centrale*, with responsibilities on the supervisory side. In this post, too, Sarcinelli performed outstandingly, and in 1976 was appointed one of the Bank's two deputy general managers, and a member of the four-man "directory" at its summit, along with the general manager and the Governor. Many felt that Sarcinelli would one day be Governor himself.

Italy by 1978 was on the way back to economic health, at least by its own standards. Foreign bankers spoke no more of the "Italian risk", and that year, aided by Baffi's judicious management of the exchange rate, the country recorded the largest balance of payments surplus of any major nation. But an important contributory factor was the tight credit policy enforced by the Bank, and Baffi's lack of sympathy for the industrialists who, with the aid of their political patrons, had prospered on the State's largesse.

Requests for funds, so readily available in the past, were coldly met. And chief among the victims of the stern *nouveau régime* was the chemical industry, bloated by the illusion of cheap, pre-Yom Kippur oil and the complaisance of the politicians. SIR and Liquichimica collapsed, and even the formidable Cefis was forced to leave Montedison. But this rigour earned the 67-year-old Baffi enemies; and he and Sarcinelli were to make more for the unforgiving way in which Bank of Italy inspectors were despatched into financial institutions most entangled with the politicians. No-one any longer was exempt. The inspectors went through the books of the banks of Pesenti, exposing the dubious means by which he had extricated himself from Sindona's grip. They examined the affairs of Italcasse, the central savings bank association which had long and notoriously operated a "black fund" on behalf of certain Christian Democrats and their friends in industry. In 1978 it was the turn of Banco Ambrosiano.

Sarcinelli knew full well that Calvi's bank, with its entrenched secrecy and cobweb of interests inside and outside Italy, would be an especially awkward assignment. No less than twelve inspectors (almost a quarter of the total) were sent to Milan, compared with just two who had drawn up the previous report on Ambrosiano in 1973.

At moments during the six months investigation, it seemed that even a twelve-man task force was not enough. As the group got to grips with Calvi's labyrinthine share dealings, Sarcinelli discussed with Giulio Padalino, the chief inspector up in Milan, the idea of sending reinforcements from other divisions of the central bank. In the event, much requested information on Calvi's foreign subsidiaries was simply not forthcoming. Calvi claimed that to have done so would have been to breach the banking regulations of other countries. The argument was hardly convincing. Calvi was after all chairman of both the Milan parent *and* of the two subsidiaries which aroused most suspicion, Banco Ambrosiano Holding in Luxembourg and Cisalpine Overseas in Nassau. But there was nothing at the time to be done. In the teeth of such obstacles it was not until November 17, 1978, seven months later, that the job was complete. The inspection of course was secret; but even if word had leaked out, it would have struggled for notice.

Those months of unglamorous drudgery in Milan were some of the most newsworthy in recent Italian history. Aldo Moro, a former Prime Minister and President of the Christian Democrats, was kidnapped and murdered that May by left-wing Red Brigades terrorists. The following month President Leone (who had made Calvi a *Cavaliere del Lavoro* back in 1974) was driven from office by scandal. In the space of three months, there were three different Popes. Paul VI died on August 6, to be succeeded by Albino Luciani, Cardinal Patriarch of Venice, who took the name of John Paul I. "The Smiling Pope" reigned for just 33 days, until his death on September 29. Then, on October 17, at their second conclave in less than eight weeks, the Cardinals of the Catholic Church chose Carol Wojtyla, Archbishop of Cracow, to be the first non-Italian Pope in 450 years.

All were exceptional events. But hardly less exceptional, in its own abstruse way, was the Bank of Italy's report on Banco Ambrosiano. Its language was dull and bureaucratic, and its length, including 26 appendices, ran to over 500 pages. What was exceptional was the quality of its financial detective work—and the conclusions it reached.

The report identified every basic ingredient of the future disaster, as well as providing the groundwork for the charges on which Calvi was to be convicted in July of 1981. Given Ambrosiano's refusal to come clean about its foreign subsidiaries, the inspector's findings could only be couched as heavily underlined suspicions. Suspicions, though, which proved uncannily exact. For that reason the document should be studied in detail.

The overall verdict on Ambrosiano was "Not at all satisfactory". The report then explained why. Ambrosiano had expanded with extraordinary speed in the last few years. True, results were there to show for it, but they had been achieved thanks to frequent infringement of the supervisory department's regulations. The bank had constructed a foreign network which allowed it to move large sums around, free of scrutiny by the Italian currency authorities. Any technical judgement on the soundness of Ambrosiano was impossible without greater detail of the operations in Luxembourg and Nassau, the nature of whose assets remained a mystery. These assets in turn

91

were so substantial that any discrepancy might make a large difference.

Given a central bank's taste for caution and understatement, it was a harsh assessment. Even more damning was the recommendation of the inspectors: "There is a clear need to cut back the network of subsidiaries which Ambrosiano has created abroad. They must also be forced to provide more information and figures about their real assets, *to avoid the risk that a possible liquidity crisis on their part might also affect the Italian banks, with all the unfavourable consequences that might entail.*" The circumstances of the collapse four years later could hardly have been set out more clearly.

The report then went on to point a heavy finger at the mechanism of the fraud Calvi was elaborating. It identified the crucial chain of command, from Milan, through the Banca del Gottardo in Lugano, to the key—Cisalpine Overseas in Nassau. Now Cisalpine had borrowed more than $200 million from Banco Ambrosiano in Milan. On the other side of its balance sheet were $183 million of assets, described only as unspecified "financings". But where had they gone? The inspectors recorded other clues. On the board of the Nassau bank sat not only Calvi, but Archbishop Paul Marcinkus, chairman of the IOR, which Carlo Olgiati, Ambrosiano's general manager, had told them was the owner of Suprafin. Now Suprafin had been the mysterious buyer of fifteen per cent of Banco Ambrosiano's shares between 1974 and 1977. These shares had in turn been despatched, on buying orders placed by Cisalpine through Banca del Gottardo, to that clutch of Liechtenstein and Panamanian companies, with names like Cascadilla and Orfeo.

What the inspectors could not *prove* was that these fanciful creatures were the property of either Ambrosiano, or of the IOR. But they certainly had their suspicions. The growth of the mysterious assets in Nassau "might not be unconnected with the massive purchases of Ambrosiano shares"—in other words, that Banco Ambrosiano had lent the money to Cisalpine to buy, in effect, control of itself. At another point, the report remarks that "it cannot be excluded" that the Liechtenstein and Panamanian companies were part of the Ambrosiano group. As for the IOR, the Vatican bank said it had only 1.37 per cent of Banco Ambrosiano. But again, it "could not be excluded" that it owned more, in the person of the Panamannian companies which had bought such large blocks of Banco Ambrosiano, with the express blessing of Cisalpine. And on Cisalpine's board, of course, sat Archbishop Marcinkus of the IOR.

Nor, the report illustrates, was Ambrosiano a bank whose shares were innocently spread among tens of thousands of small shareholders. In fact 32 per cent of its capital was in the hands of 22 large shareholders—all of them in one way or another "friendly" to Ambrosiano.† If Calvi and the IOR were behind the offshore companies, then he had succeeded in making Ambrosiano takeover-proof.

But there was more. The inspectors judged Ambrosiano to be undercapitalized. They found breaches of the banking law, and severe organizational shortcoming—principally that Calvi was running Ambrosiano as he pleased. Board meetings did take place once a month, as prescribed by Ambrosiano's statute; but mainly to endorse decisions which Calvi had taken, and often implemented beforehand.

They must have been remarkable occasions, rather like a priest celebrating mass. Calvi would deliver a brief sermon, to which the other directors would reply with a respectful Amen. A twenty-minute monologue by the chairman would typically be followed by a rapid runthrough of the major credits extended by the bank in the previous month. Calvi routinely would enquire if there were any questions. Invariably there were none, and proceedings were over. The report condemned the board for its "supine acquiescence", while Ambrosiano's official auditors were described as "superficial and unquestioning".

As both chairman and managing director, Calvi enjoyed unfettered control. On his own he could authorize major loans, allowing the relationship with important borrowers like Rizzoli to be conducted as he wanted. The system was also ideal for Licio Gelli, in that financial operations within the orbit of the P-2 could be carried out without query. Already one of Ambrosiano's biggest borrowers, the inspectors had found out, was the Genghini construction group in Rome, later to collapse in a 450 billion lire scandal. Its founder, Mario Genghini, had made a spectacular career as a property magnate, with links to the politicians. He was also a member of the P-2.

†See Appendix A.

The central bank's conclusion was that Ambrosiano's internal organization was in some respects "patently inadequate" for a bank of its size and ambition. The inspectors suggested that "a first step" might be to withdraw authorizations so far granted, and thus force a restructuring of Calvi's bank, "so that the real destination of every single financial transaction abroad can be followed". The restructuring, of course, never took place.

In October 1978 Padalino discussed the report's findings with Calvi. And although he did not show it, the banker was more than a little alarmed. Yet again he pleaded his good faith in his foreign operations. The trouble was, he maintained, that the accounts of both the Luxembourg and Bahamas affiliates had been drawn up in accordance with local rules, which prevented him from providing more details to the Italian authorities. But the crocodile tears were still wet as Calvi was strengthening his defences.

There were a number of reasons why he decided to reduce the role of Cisalpine Overseas in Nassau. Siegenthaler was probably getting pangs of unease, especially after the creation of four Panamanian shell companies (with himself as chairman of one of them) to hold Ambrosiano shares. Coopers and Lybrand, the Nassau bank's accountants, were worried about the size of its lending to the IOR, and probably to those mysterious little companies sheltering behind the legal ownership of the Vatican bank, including Manic S.A. in Luxembourg, and the United Trading Corporation, set up on its behalf in Panama four years earlier. Graham Garner, of Cooper and Lybrand's office in Nassau, asked Siegenthaler to ensure that the lending did not grow further. He also intimated that changes in accounting standards might force his firm to disclose the relationship between Cisalpine and the IOR.

Above all, however, Calvi realized that Padalino and his inspectors had grasped the function of Cisalpine in his elaborate device for despatching control of his bank abroad. But contingency plans were ready. For on September 29, 1977 Ambrosiano Luxembourg had set up in the even remoter haven of Managua, the capital of Nicaragua, a new bank called Ambrosiano Group Banco Comercial. It was capitalized at $20 million, and had the bland-sounding purpose of "conducting international commercial transactions".

During 1978 and 1979, a good part of the unspecified "financings" by Cisalpine was transferred to the books of the new bank in Managua. The arrangement seemed if anything better. Ambrosiano was exempt from tax, apart from a nominal contribution to the Nicaraguan treasury. The new bank was in effect run from Nassau by Cisalpine. Calvi (probably with Gelli's intercession) was on good terms not only with the then dictator Anastasio Somoza, but also with the ever more menacing Sandinista opposition. To the end of his life he retained a Nicaraguan diplomatic passport, and in 1979 Calvi attempted to lobby the Rome Government for an increase in coffee imports from Nicaragua. To the Sandinistas, he would later confide, he had given large sums to buy seed grain on international markets.

Curiously, of the foreign banks in Managua at the time of the left-wing takeover in early 1979, Ambrosiano's subsidiary was the only one not to be nationalized by the new revolutionary regime. By the end of that year, Calvi was to transfer his most delicate business again, from Managua to Lima, Peru. But in those anxious months, while the Bank of Italy's inspectors were swarming over his bank in Milan, Nicaragua looked an ideally safe hideaway. However, even these considerations were quickly to become secondary. The Bank of Italy report expressed the reservations we have seen. But it also identified what appeared to be two clear breaches of currency regulations. Since 1976, these had been criminal offences.

Sarcinelli and Padalino must have suspected they would make some interesting discoveries at Ambrosiano. But the cupboard was even fuller of skeletons than they could have expected. For failure to report those secret share dealings involving La Centrale, Credito Varesino and Toro between 1973 and 1976 looked to be a *prima facie* violation of currency regulations by Calvi, in his capacity as chairman of La Centrale.

The special internal procedures of the Bank of Italy then took over. Although the supervisory department was in the business of banking, not of police work, it was bound from time to time to come across breaches of the law, particularly after the 1976 currency legislation, and its retroactive penal provisions. But the central bank had equally to avoid provoking public panic among savers and depositors. For that reason, cases which looked as if they might lead to criminal charges were first examined by an internal committee of experts and lawyers, whose conclusions would be automatically endorsed by the Governor.

This committee met in late 1978. It decided that there was indeed a *prima facie* case against Calvi. It was also agreed that, given the location of Ambrosiano's headquarters, the case should be entrusted to Milan, rather than Rome, where the risk of political interference was in any case greater. The task of submitting the report to the Milan judiciary fell to Padalino, as the senior inspector directly involved.

By coincidence, the day Padalino did so, Calvi came down from Milan to talk over the report with Sarcinelli. The Ambrosiano chairman was as evasive as ever—as with so many others at different times who dealt with Calvi, Sarcinelli could not understand what he was getting at. But Sarcinelli made *himself* perfectly clear: Ambrosiano should provide the missing information on its foreign subsidiaries, and the Bank of Italy would press him until he did. Calvi astonishingly protested that he already *was* supplying the facts, adding rather mysteriously that he travelled a great deal, but was always reachable through his secretary in Milan.

The two were not to meet again. Sarcinelli showed Calvi out of his office with the hardening suspicion that something was very badly wrong at Ambrosiano; and Calvi must have been more alarmed than ever at the central bank's determination to establish the truth. A day or so later, those apprehensions grew greater. Sarcinelli had not mentioned that the Milan magistrates were now about to look into those murky share dealings. But the following issue of *L'Espresso* weekly magazine reported that the matter had indeed been passed over to the judiciary. Although the leak almost certainly originated in Milan, Calvi sent a telex to Baffi to protest bitterly at this apparent breach of confidence.

In fact Calvi need not have worried unduly. For within a few months Sarcinelli, not he, would be in prison, while the magistrate to whom the case first fell, would be dead.

Emilio Alessandrini was one of the most promising and esteemed of the younger generation of Milan magistrates. He was a specialist not only in financial investigations, but also in the left- and right-wing terrorism plaguing the country in those years. On the morning of January 29, 1979, Alessandrini had just dropped his son off at school when his orange Renault 5 was ambushed by a commando of gunmen from the left-wing *Prima Linea* ("Front Line") terrorist group, a sister organization of the Red Brigades. He was killed instantly. Luca Mucci, the magistrate who took over the Calvi case, had to start again from scratch. Both a precious life, and time, had been lost. Calvi and the P-2, it must be presumed, had nothing to do with the Alessandrini murder. The same could not be said with such certainty about the events about to unfold at the Bank of Italy.

CHAPTER ELEVEN

The Bank of Italy Affair

ITALY'S WONDROUS CAPACITY to absorb the most grievous of set-backs, self-inflicted or otherwise, is well known. But it was tested as rarely as before on Saturday March 24, 1979. At dawn that day Ugo La Malfa, the old foe of Calvi and Sindona, was struck down by a massive cerebral haemorrhage from which he was to die two days later. With La Malfa vanished what small hopes remained that a new-born government, one of whose few distinctions was his presence within it, could survive and elections be avoided.

But while La Malfa's political friends and enemies alike were arriving to pay their last respects, calamity of a different kind was overtaking the Bank of Italy. In the middle of the morning officers of the *Carabinieri*, the country's paramilitary police force, entered the central bank to arrest Sarcinelli. The deputy general manager of the Bank of Italy was taken to the *Regina Coeli* (Queen of Heaven) prison on the bank of the Tiber in central Rome, charged with deliberately concealing evidence from Rome magistrates investigating the collapse of the now bankrupt SIR of Nino Rovelli. A similar charge was brought against the Governor himself, and Antonio Alibrandi, the magistrate conducting the inquiry, let it be known that only Baffi's advanced age had spared him too the indignity of prison. In the most astonishing manner, the "Bank of Italy Affair" had begun.

No episode before or since has illustrated more clearly the sinister side of public life in Italy, the contrast between the platitudes dispensed by the politicians in public, and the private, historical reality of fiercely competing interest groups and factions.

*   *   *

Just who was behind the attack on the Bank of Italy, no-one to this day can say with certainty. The "smoking gun" in Italy is rarely found: despite Gelli's mania for files, photocopies and tape recordings, pressures and connivances are often undocumented, even unspoken. But the circumstantial evidence is overwhelming, that an attack it was—or rather a counter-attack, carefully framed to teach the central bank a lesson it would not forget.

Probably the investigation of Ambrosiano was not the only reason. Rather, the inspection of Calvi's bank in 1978 was but the latest of a series of challenges to the complicities and financial conveniences of the system, which could not go unanswered. Objectively the campaign of Baffi and Sarcinelli to throw light on the dark corners of Italian banking could not be faulted. Realistically, however, to have tried to do so without adequate political "cover" beforehand was perhaps naïve and inviting reprisal. The Italian system implied a paradox: that even the central bank's power could only remain intact if wielded moderately.

On successive occasions the Bank of Italy had trodden on the toes of the politicians. Carlo Pesenti, that most Catholic of financiers, had been ordered to straighten out irregularities in his banks—with the result that in December 1978 he was forced to sell off one of them to pay his debts. Then it had exposed the existence of Italcasse's "black" funds (to have most eyecatching consequences in 1980). Even more serious, the central bank had blocked efforts by the Christian Democrats to secure the "technical" solution to the problems of Michele Sindona, which would have allowed that notable benefactor of the party to return to Italy unmolested. All this, and now the assault on Calvi's Ambrosiano, linked to the P-2 and also another prime source of largesse for the parties—not only the Christian Democrats.

It is too much to believe that the issue of warrants against Sarcinelli and Baffi by the magistrate Alibrandi so soon afterwards was a coincidence. Not just its timing, but the sheer disproportion between the imprisonment order and the dubious, highly technical nature of the supposed offence suggested that Sarcinelli was being deliberately punished.

Italy's postwar constitution had given the judiciary both independence and great discretionary powers. But that absence of control presupposed that magistrates would use their authority to investigate and arrest with responsibility, and remain free from political conditioning. Instead, and inevitably, the magistrature, too, was dragged into the thickening fray. So-called *magistrati d'assalto*, literally "assault judges", emerged, not averse to publicity, and liable on occasion to put political convictions, left-wing or right-wing, ahead of judicial neutrality. And it was Sarcinelli's misfortune that the Rome public prosecutor's office, which handled the Bank of Italy affair, was notoriously the most politically conditioned of any. If the Bank of Italy had entrusted Milan with the penal investigation against Ambrosiano, it was fitting that the banker or his protectors should fight back through Rome.

The opportunity was an investigation already under way into presumed irregular Government subsidies to SIR. Nino Rovelli, who combined Clark Gable's looks with keen political antennae, had swiftly understood the chance of aggrandisement offered by the Government's well-intentioned, but misguided, strategy of the 1960s of developing new primary industries in the backward Italian South. He chose to expand in Sardinia, remote and poor even by the standards of the South. Rovelli borrowed very large sums from the *Credito Industriale Sardo* (CIS), a state-owned bank set up specially to help Sardinia. He bankrolled Cagliari's football team, local newspapers and national politicians. But the chemical plants Rovelli promised took a long while to materialize. Between 1973 and 1974 oil prices quadrupled. SIR began to sink in an ocean of debt and Rovelli disappeared to Switzerland as magistrates began to examine just where the money had gone.

The Bank of Italy inspected CIS in 1977/78, but its internal committee decided that the report, whatever the injudicious lending to Rovelli, warranted no legal action. It was, therefore, put on file. Meanwhile, in 1978 the magistrates had questioned Baffi about CIS and SIR, but showed little interest in the report.

Their attitude changed abruptly in early 1979. Alibrandi and another magistrate on the SIR case, Luciano Infelisi, suddenly descended on the central bank, and seized documents on the affair, including its report on CIS. No matter that the offence in question was disputed (for whereas the penal code obliges a public official to disclose knowledge of a crime, Italy's banking law permits the governor and its vigilance department not to pass on findings to the judiciary if *they* deem that no offence has been committed). On March 24 Sarcinelli was arrested, on the charge that by failing to hand on the CIS report, he had served "a private interest" in the course of his official duties. But well before that, he had begun to suspect that something was afoot.

The first straws in the wind were vicious articles in a few right-wing papers, attacking Sarcinelli over Italcasse, and intimating that he and Baffi were Communist sympathizers. OP, a scandal sheet run by a journalist called Mino Pecorelli who on occasion worked closely with Gelli, described Sarcinelli as "the Red functionary". Pecorelli was to be shot dead in Rome a few days before the Bank of Italy affair began, in circumstances still a mystery today. Then in February, Sarcinelli was phoned by his lawyer during a skiing holiday, to be warned that some sort of attack was being prepared. Alibrandi and Infelisi, the two magistrates involved, were both of the political right. Afterwards one was even quoted as saying that he had wanted to teach Sarcinelli a lesson.

But if arrest was only a partial surprise to its victim, it astounded and outraged everyone else. Most Italian politicians, as well as bankers, economists and public figures were bewildered and indignant.

Were the circumstances not so serious, it would have been laughable to suppose that Baffi and Sarcinelli, of uncontested integrity, could have been party to a corrupt cover-up. But while the Bank of Italy's horrified staff proclaimed the first strike in their history, the Government was mindful of the possible damage to Italy's standing in the outside world, which held the central bank in such regard.

That Saturday evening Filippo Maria Pandolfi, the Treasury Minister, went on television to declare his confidence in the Bank, and its honesty and impartiality. As nearly as he could, Pandolfi stated that the magistrates had behaved recklessly and that the Bank of Italy was blameless. Central bank Governors from several European countries made exceptional public statements to the Italian press, expressing their own solidarity with Baffi and Sarcinelli, and their conviction that the charges were groundless.

There was one contrasting voice, however. The *Corriere della Sera*, funded by Ambrosiano's support for Rizzoli and conditioned by Gelli, was notably cool to Sarcinelli's plight.

Sarcinelli was to leave prison a fortnight later, hurt and confused, but already suspicious of the origin of the attack. In Milan the word was going around that Calvi in some way was connected with the attack on the central bank; while Sindona from New York was soon boasting that he had secured his revenge on the institution responsible for his persecution and downfall. Even after his release, the magistrates remained opposed to Sarcinelli's reinstatement. Giulio Andreotti, the caretaker Prime Minister until elections were held in June, stayed largely aloof from the controversy, an attitude which aroused some speculation over his own motives. Not for the first time Andreotti was being oddly ambiguous.

With Sarcinelli's removal, the *vigilanza* lost many of its teeth and some of its nerve. In June he was allowed to resume his post at the Bank of Italy, but had been moved by then to the harmless—as far as the politicians were concerned—international monetary side. Only many months later was the slate rubbed clean, when the charges against both Baffi and himself were dismissed for the trumped-up nonsense they were. But by then the desired effect had long been achieved—and a new Governor had taken over from Baffi.

The annual meeting of the Bank of Italy, held every May 31, is by tradition the foremost financial occasion of the year, akin to Budget Day in Britain. But in 1979 it acquired an unusually emotional overtone. As was his custom, Baffi read aloud the bank report's key "final considerations," of his report in his clipped, staccato fashion. Normally that would have been all, but not in 1979. The audience of bankers, industrialists and economists interrupted the speech twice with loud applause, first when Baffi defended the Bank's right to discretion in discharging its task, and then when he emphasized his and Sarcinelli's respect for the law. And then, quite exceptionally, Baffi read out to a hushed audience a statement of his own.

He spoke for the first time in public of the trials of the bank. With Biblical dignity he declared his hope that its detractors "would find pardon in remorse for the ill they have done, fuelling a campaign based on a tissue of false and tendentious arguments, and motivated by who-knows-what obscure design". Baffi then announced that he would resign before the end of the year, as soon as a stable Government had been formed after the election.

Baffi insisted that at 67, and after 43 years at the Bank of Italy, he had never intended to stay in office beyond 1979. In fact, pain and disillusion at the concocted scandal by which he had been smeared were decisive factors. An attack in its way as destabilizing of Italy's financial structure as the Red Brigades' murder of Moro had been of the country's politics, had been carried through successfully.

Over the next three months soundings took place on the choice of Baffi's successor. Distinguished names were mooted, as the best guarantee of preserving the bank's independence; so were some less distinguished ones, a clear sign of a desire to bring the Bank of Italy politically to heel, once and for all. In the end the internal solution, as usual, prevailed. Baffi resigned in mid-September, to be replaced by his deputy, the general manager Carlo Ciampi. If his name was less familiar, Ciampi was highly respected. But the Bank's unknown assailants had succeeded in relegating Sarcinelli to the sidelines. The new general manager to replace Ciampi was to be Lamberto Dini, brought back to Rome after twenty years' service at the International Monetary Fund in Washington, the last three as Italy's executive director on the IMF's board. The Bank of Italy was to be sadder, perhaps wiser—and certainly badly shaken.

But in that ill-starred year of 1979, the Bank's tribulations were not finished. Slowly the vicissitudes of Baffi and Sarcinelli were pushed into the background by the election, and the increasingly desperate attempts in the weeks that followed to form a Government. First Andreotti tried, then the Socialist leader Bettino Craxi; and then Pandolfi himself. It was not until early August, two months after voting, that Francesco Cossiga, a Christian Democrat and Interior Minister during the harrowing period of the Moro kidnapping, succeeded in forming a Government, albeit dependent on Socialist abstention for survival. In the meantime the shadow of Sindona was lying more darkly than ever over Italy—and particularly over the city of Milan.

Ever since his exile began, the Sicilian had been trying to secure painless settlement of his Italian problems by whatever means to hand: blandishment, bribery or threat. The most spectacular pressure, as we have seen, was exerted on Calvi. But another target was Sindona's particular *bête noire*, Enrico Cuccia of Mediobanca, in Sindona's eyes both at the origin of his problems, and possessor of the key to their solution.

Cuccia refused to treat with Sindona, only to find himself subjected to a crescendo of Mafia-style intimidation. He would receive periodic threatening phone calls, in what Cuccia described to magistrates as a "typical Italo–American Brooklyn accent"; his daughter would sometimes be followed by sinister individuals. Exasperated, Cuccia even went to New York in 1979 to meet Sindona, but found only the familiar impossible demands. Cuccia had to arrange for the Italian arrest warrant against Sindona to be withdrawn (despite Sindona's sentencing to a three-year jail term *in absentia* in 1976!); he had to find the money to bail out Banca Privata Italiana; even, as a fellow Sicilian, to provide money for Sindona's family. In October 1979, a bomb was exploded under the front door of Cuccia's flat in Milan.

It is easy to understand Sindona's increasing desperation between 1976 and 1979. The likelihood that he would have to face trial, and almost certain imprisonment, in New York for the Franklin Bank collapse was growing by the month. In Italy meanwhile Giorgio Ambrosoli, the Banca Privata liquidator, was discovering more and more. It was essential that Sindona was able both to leave the US, and return, a free man, to Italy. But that in turn meant squaring Ambrosoli.

Ever since his appointment as BPI's liquidator in September 1974, Ambrosoli had nursed no illusions about the nature, and the dangers, of his task. Early in 1975, in a moving and prophetic letter to his wife, he wrote: "Whatever happens, I'll certainly pay a high price for taking on this job. But I knew that before taking it on and I'm not complaining, because it has been a unique chance for me to do something for the country . . . The job gives me an enormous power, but I've worked only in the country's interest, obviously making only enemies for myself." The principal enemy, plainly, was Sindona and the interests he represented. But even Ambrosoli cannot have imagined how high the price would be.

With the months and years of patient sifting, so the numbers on the coded accounts, the random telex messages, the transfers of funds between the various obscure corners of Sindona's empire began to make sense. And the threats increased. Sometimes callers would use Sarcinelli's or other names to get past his secretary to deliver unambiguous warnings. But Ambrosoli persevered. And as he dug steadily deeper into Sindona's affairs, new light was thrown on some of Calvi's contorted dealings with the Sicilian, in those halcyon years between 1971 and 1974.

At the beginning of July 1979, Ambrosoli reported that he had discovered a 6.5 million-dollar commission paid by Sindona in connection with the Zitropo/Pacchetti deal, which gave Calvi the key to acquiring the rich Banca Cattolica del Veneto from the IOR. The money, he stated, had been divided between "an American bishop and a Milanese banker"—an evident reference to Calvi and Marcinkus. The Cavallo wall posters in Milan appeared to have given fairly thorough documentation of Calvi's share—the $3.3 million paid into coded accounts in Zurich and Chiasso, but Marcinkus always denied taking such a commission. In any case, Ambrosoli was to have no time to elaborate upon his finding.

At around midnight on the night of July 11/12, he was dropped off by friends with whom he had shared a late supper, outside the building where he lived in Milan. "Are you Avvocato Ambrosoli?", asked a group of men who stepped out of the shadows. "Yes, what do you want?" The strangers shot Ambrosoli dead at point-blank range and vanished into the night. Sindona was later named as a prime suspect of having enlisted the American gangsters believed to have killed Ambrosoli "on contract", although in early 1983 formal charges had not yet been brought against him.

The state paid small tribute to the courageous lawyer who had given his life in its service, in the process probing its most embarrassing secrets. The funeral of Ambrosoli took place a few days later in the stifling mid-summer heat of Milan. It was a simple affair with just four wreaths and a handful of mourners, of little public note. Only Baffi was there, bespectacled and bowed, in silent acknowledgement of the loss.

The country, too, paid little attention. The attention of the media was fixed upon the almost simultaneous murder in Rome of a colonel of the para-military *carabinieri* together with his driver, at the hands of a commando of Red Brigades terrorists. For 1979 was a year in which terrorism seemed to be spinning out of control, when hardly a day went by when the early morning news bulletins were not punctuated by the first report of a new ambush, new deaths. Of what importance was the mysterious assassination of a little-known lawyer in Milan? For the central bank, however, it was another heavy blow after the "punishment" inflicted on Baffi and Sarcinelli. Its discomfort was made worse by a vague sense of guilt. Should not Ambrosoli have been better protected, and should he have been left alone to carry out so difficult and dangerous a task?

Milan's general atmosphere of menace stretched even further. Padalino, the chief inspector of Ambrosiano who was there frequently as the magistrates assessed the apparent currency offences committed by Calvi, fell victim himself. An initial evaluation by the *Guardia di Finanza* tax police had concluded that Calvi's explanation for the high prices paid on the suspect share deals, that they were necessary to ensure majority control of Varesino and Toro, was acceptable. Padalino that summer found himself being threatened and warned about his report, that it could even be construed as a libel of Ambrosiano. Calvi or his protectors seemed to be getting to the judiciary even in Milan, despite its reputation for independence and freedom from political control. The inspector even became physically afraid. At his hotel he would insist on having colleagues in the next room, with a connecting door.

In fact Ambrosoli had not died in vain. Had he lived, he would have been a key prosecution witness at Sindona's forthcoming trial. But in the months before he was murdered, he had transmitted vital evidence to the US authorities investigating the Franklin National Bank insolvency. As Sindona well knew, his days of liberty were numbered.

On August 2 he staged a final gambit by arranging to have himself "kidnapped" on leaving his apartment at the Pierre for an evening stroll. In keeping with Sindona's persecution mania, word was put about that left-wing terrorists were responsible. Few took that theory very seriously. In fact, armed with a false passport in the name of Joseph Bonamico, and disguised with moustache and beard, Sindona went on a tour of Europe, from Austria to Greece, and to Palermo in Sicily. His known aim was to drum up support for the trial which was now inevitable, and—in ransom demands purporting to come from his "kidnappers"—blackmail his former political accomplices into making a last effort to clear his name. Certainly there were other purposes too. On October 16 the charade ended when Sindona was discovered wounded in a New York telephone booth. His strategy had failed. The enigmatic "list of 500" capital exporters has still not been revealed, while the politicians he once knew still prosper.

At last, six years after his bankruptcy, Sindona was tried before the Manhattan Federal District court. He was convicted and sentenced to 25 years in jail for crimes including perjury and misappropriation of funds, plus a 30-month term for simulated kidnapping. The model prisoner Michele Sindona is unlikely to be leaving Otisville Penitentiary on parole before 1988 at the earliest. To while away the time he reads the works of Nietzsche, to find philosophical justification for his view of himself as a financial superman brought low by the jealousies of lesser men.

CHAPTER TWELVE

New Ploys

JUST AS HE had survived the crisis of 1974, so Calvi seemed to have beaten off both the vengeance of Sindona and the attentions of the Bank of Italy. But the spiteful "tazebao" campaign mounted by Luigi Cavallo had profoundly unnerved him. The wall posters had been followed by pamphlets, purporting to come from left-wing extremist groups calling themselves "Proletarian Autonomy" or "Banking autonomy" and threatening him physically. No matter that they were the likely work of Cavallo and Sindona. They were all too plausible in a period when terrorist violence was an everyday occurrence.

Calvi became obsessed with his own safety. In the bank he was secure, inside his vast triangular office with its black vinyl walls and bright turquoise carpet, sealed off by the double-locking lift and bullet-proof windows. The office was as impersonal as its occupant. There was hardly a book to be seen, just his bare antique desk with a few papers upon it, and maybe a bottle of mineral water. At his left elbow was an enormous telephone console. In front of the door leading to a waiting room lay a valuable antique Persian carpet. Calvi would tell some visitors it was worth 250 million lire; even if they doubted that figure they would respectfully step around it. In the corner to his right was a wall safe, whose keys Calvi alone carried, attached by a chain to his belt. Inside the safe were his secrets.

But equivalent protection was now required outside. Back in October 1975 Calvi had taken on as his personal bodyguard one Federico Gualdani, a burly expert in the martial arts. By 1978 Gualdani was in charge of eight "gorillas"—a retinue of an unusual size even in Italy, where terrorism and kidnapping had turned personal security into a thriving industry.

This private army looked after Calvi 24 hours a day. They guarded

108

his family, his Milan and Rome flats, his villa at Drezzo. They travelled with him everywhere, in a fleet of armour-plated Alfa Romeos with bullet-proof tyres. At the end, Calvi's personal safety was costing Ambrosiano over $1 million a year, three times his gross salary as chairman of the bank. In a curious footnote to the story of the bank, Gualdani in late 1982 was to enter a claim for over $400,000, as compensation for premature termination of his contract. Calvi's protection eclipsed that of Government ministers and fellow bankers, matching even those of the threatened Latin American dictators under whose regimes he sheltered.

But in Latin America, he was taking new financial precautions as well. Nicaragua might offer perfect secrecy, but its political stability was another matter. Central America was turning into one of the world's most volatile areas. Calvi's carefully cultivated relations with the left-wing *sandinista* guerrillas, who had come to power in Nicaragua in early 1979, offered some guarantee, but it was as wise to look elsewhere. Quickly Calvi's eyes, guided by the Latin American connections of Gelli and Ortolani, lighted on Peru. And as the Bank of Italy affair was gestating at home, he moved with much alacrity.

Silva Rueta, the Peruvian Finance Minister of the day, was in Paris in January 1979 to attend a meeting to discuss rescheduling of his country's foreign debt. Calvi went to see him in the French capital to propose that Ambrosiano be allowed to open a full-scale subsidiary for offshore business in Lima. Rueta seems to have been much impressed. Calvi's bank was already the biggest in private hands in Italy, it had helped Peru finance the purchase of Italian warships a few years before; and had extensive connections with Latin America. Later in 1979, Ambrosiano was to open a lavish banking subsidiary in Buenos Aires, called Banco Ambrosiano de America del Sud.

Permission was granted, and in the course of the year Calvi went to Lima twice to supervise arrangements. On October 11, 1979, Banco Ambrosiano Andino was formally inaugurated, on the upper floors of a shiny new office block called Edificio Alide, in Paseo de la Republica. Under Peruvian legislation of 1976, it was authorized to carry out foreign currency business only, with either local or foreign-based banks. And so, halfway across the world, was born the bank that would be Calvi's innermost sanctuary, where his most unmentionable business was conducted. To run it, Calvi chose his two most trusted, and trusting, lieutenants from Ambrosiano's foreign side.

Filippo Leoni, joint general manager in Milan in charge of foreign business, became Andino's first chairman. His deputy, in Lima as in Milan, was Giacomo Botta, cadaverously thin with a fondness for expensive English-looking suits. The careers of these two, who in the end probably knew more about the far-away mysteries of Ambrosiano than anyone except Calvi himself, had grown in the shadow of their chairman. Both came from comparatively modest origins, and both had risen rapidly through the bank (more rapidly than strictly justified by ability, those who were suspicious of Ambrosiano would maintain), thanks to their loyalty to Calvi and their obedient execution of his wishes.

A small irony was that Leoni had a morbid fear of flying. If he went to Luxembourg he would insist on going by train; and it is said that on the one occasion he went to the United States, he took a boat from Gibraltar. But despite his Latin American duties, Leoni never had to travel very far. For if Banco Andino's nameplate was in Paseo de la Republica, Lima, its heart and mind remained firmly in Milan, or at best in nearby Switzerland or Luxembourg where board meetings were mostly held. There was no need to go to Lima, since nothing much ever happened there. Decisions were taken in Milan, and conveyed through Banca del Gottardo, or Cisalpine in Nassau.

From late 1979 on most of the loans extended to Panama and Liechtenstein were transferred to Lima. With this ready-made business, and some dealings with local banks (notably Banco de la Nación which held two per cent of Andino's capital) Calvi's new creature could boast "assets" of $890 million by the end of 1980, after barely a year of activity. From nothing, it had become twice the size of Cisalpine.

To the extent that it was known about, such breathtaking growth should have aroused suspicion. Even so, it was odd that Ambrosiano was so interested in Latin America, whose economy even then was wobbling. But to anyone who asked why the bank was not more concerned with major international centres like London or Paris, Calvi would either murmur something about excess taxes, or proclaim that South America was world banking's next Eldorado. The correctness of that claim would of course be demonstrated by the debt crises which swept across Mexico, Argentina, Brazil and Venezuela—and through the international banking system—not long afterwards. Less surprising was that despite the strictures of its report in 1978, the Bank of Italy permitted it, or at least allowed Botta and Leoni to hold senior posts at Andino. The attack on Baffi and Sarcinelli had had its effect.

But the insertion of first Managua and then Lima into the mechanism of fraud was not the only new screen Calvi introduced between the inquisitive and the truth. Where his own safety, financial or physical, was concerned, he was not one for half measures.

Between 1977 and 1980 a new litter of tiny companies, usually with a nominal capital of $10,000, was born in Panama and Liechtenstein. They were registered through resident agents there, but owned by Manic S.A. of Luxembourg and thus indirectly by the IOR. By the end they numbered seventeen; but the Panamanian offspring which most need to be remembered were called Belrosa, Bellatrix, Erin, Laramie and World Wide Trading. An obscure Liechtenstein *anstalt*, called Nordeurop Trading Company Establishment, was another newcomer. In time it would be replaced by Astolfine, to emerge as the most voracious Panamanian company of all. Alongside operated the opaque United Trading Corporation, set up in 1974 on the Vatican Bank's behalf by the Banca del Gottardo, and Zitropo, that veteran from the days of Sindona. All of them would achieve debts, and notoriety after Ambrosiano folded, quite out of proportion to their unnoticed and motley origins.

Their purposes were no less motley. The main one, of course, was to finance those other Panamanian and Liechtenstein companies owned by Manic with the strange sounding names, and which owned so much of Banco Ambrosiano itself: Cascadilla, Lantana, Orfeo, La Fidele, Finprogram and so on. Those financings, and the debts they implied, soon began to grow, as interest fell due and fresh money had to be found, to subscribe to the capital increases which Ambrosiano was forced to carry out, first in 1979 and above all in 1981. Physically, as might be guessed, the shares never strayed from Milan, safely on deposit with Ambrosiano. When his bank's annual shareholders' meeting came round each April, Calvi would strangely but conveniently emerge as proxy-holder on their behalf.

But the little companies of the second generation also served as repositories for others of Calvi's secrets. Among these the more innocent were concealed holdings of shares in companies and banks already controlled by Ambrosiano. There was, for example, six per cent of Banca del Gottardo, meaning that Ambrosiano owned not 45 per cent of the Swiss bank, as it always declared, but an outright majority of 51 per cent. Another of their "assets" was that block of Pacchetti shares, for which Calvi had paid so much in 1972. At the end ten years later, their book value in Zitropo's portfolio was $82 million; their real worth, when they were sold in autumn 1982, was just $4 million. Then there were funds which Calvi seems by then to have been channelling to Gelli and Ortolani. The tiny Erin was, for example, the recipient from Banco Andino of a $37 million loan destined for Bafisud Corporation of Panama, an emanation of Ortolani's Banco Financeiro in Uruguay. There were transactions involving Rizzoli, and others where the IOR was a direct destination of funds. These, it was later claimed by the IOR, were passed straight on to the United Trading Corporation, which it technically owned, but which it never administered.

As the months and years went by, the dealings between these tiny companies and Ambrosiano's various banks became steadily more entangled. But the process of deception was established—basically that of Sindona before Calvi. As their indebtedness increased, so the value of their own assets, pledged to Managua and then Andino as collateral for the credits advanced, was increased. As the difference between Pacchetti's theoretical and real valuations above shows, the process was to culminate in absurdity, when the moment of reckoning came in 1982. But that was still some way off. Calvi had just one more immediate problem to tackle.

The Bank of Italy inspectors who prepared the excellent report of 1978 had identified the weakest spot in his defences, which even the transfer from Nassau to Managua and Lima had not removed. It was, in effect, the first link in the chain—that $200 million lent initially from the Milan parent, with the help of which Cisalpine had extended the unspecified "financings", at whose nature the report had guessed so accurately. These were now being extended by the banks in Nicaragua and Peru. Therefore, to ensure complete concealment, Calvi had to find the funds abroad, so that no trace of the foreign *imbroglio* would feature on the books of Banco Ambrosiano itself. The task, given the rumour which surrounded Calvi in Italy, might not have been easy. But at this juncture a crucial benefactor emerged from an unlikely quarter: the huge state-owned oil concern ENI.

From 1978, the year of the inspection, until the end ENI was to be another bridge linking Ambrosiano with the politicians. Since its inception just after the Second World War, it had been far too important to be ignored by the parties. Under its legendary first chairman, Enrico Mattei, the inroads had been kept to a minimum. By force of his extraordinary personality, and the skill with which he exploited the growing appetite of the party organizations for money, it was Mattei who dominated the politicians—to the extent that he was considered the most powerful single figure in all Italy. But after his death in a mysterious air crash in 1962 near Milan, the roles gradually reversed.

Mattei's successors were weaker, and the group's own financing needs grew. These could be met from two obvious sources: the banking system, or its only shareholder, the State. Both, however, were increasingly in the grip of the parties, whose own rivalries were increasing. Gone was the cosy command of the Christian Democrats, who had run the country unchallenged since 1945, as Italian politics adjusted to the postwar social transformation. The changes led to the birth of the formula of the "centre-left", drawing the Socialists first from Opposition in the late 1950s, and then from 1963 directly into Government. Some of the consequences were beneficial—on paper at least—like the long-overdue nationalization of the electricity supply industry, and a re-organization of the chemical sector.

But the trend had a less wholesome effect, of intensifying the battle for control of the appendages of the State, citadels of patronage and finance. The main struggle was between the Christian Democrats and the Socialists and their factions, with smaller bones being tossed to the smaller parties of Government, the Social Democrats, Liberals and Republicans. No citadel was more highly prized than ENI.

Mattei's bold and controversial forays into the international oil business had endowed it with a huge foreign substructure, while the rise in oil prices, especially after 1973, meant that ever larger sums of money flowed through its accounts. Today ENI ranks as the fourth largest industrial corporation in the world outside the US. Unfortunately, so furious did the contest become for its control between

113

Christian Democrats and Socialists that between 1978 and 1983 its chief executive changed no less than six times. Sometimes he would be called chairman, on other occasions "commissioner", when a truce could be delayed no longer. It has been a typically Italian miracle that despite this self-inflicted injury, ENI has succeeded in functioning at all, thanks to a dedicated middle management. But there are two fairly constant threads through these embattled years, Leonardo Di Donna and Florio Fiorini, who between them ran ENI's important financial department.

At the risk of crude oversimplification, Di Donna was the representative within the group's top management of Bettino Craxi, the Socialist leader, and Craxi's dominant faction within his party. Di Donna's presence was a rock on which at least four of ENI's chairmen and commissioners foundered. However fierce the public criticism of him, the Socialists insisted that Di Donna should stay, even after revelation in 1981 of his name among the members of Gelli's P-2.

And Craxi, perhaps, owed him not a little. For, the story ran, Di Donna alerted Craxi to the ENI–Petromin affair. That most extravagant example of the seemingly unbreakable bond between the Italian oil industry and scandal, concerned the payment of a seven per cent commission on a direct oil supply deal between the Italian group and Petromin, the State-owned Saudi Arabian oil company. Just where this huge sum (no less than $115 million had the contract been completed) was destined—to Italian politicians, Saudi princes or both—it is still impossible to say. Saudi Arabia, in any case, broke off the arrangement when the affair became public in late 1979. Most important, however, the revelations discredited Giorgio Mazzanti, ENI's then chairman and identified with the Socialist faction hostile to Craxi. Mazzanti was forced to resign, while Craxi was empowered to beat off a real threat to his position from his party opponents. Gelli's own genius at playing on both sides at once is shown by the fact that not only Di Donna but also Mazzanti were listed as members of the lodge, although the former denied involvement.

Well before that, however, Di Donna was doing business with Gelli's financial arm, the Banco Ambrosiano of Roberto Calvi. How their association began has never been made clear. The common link of the P-2 is a possibility, but political connections in any case existed already. Since 1975 Calvi's bank had been helping to finance the

Socialist party, and in the normal run of things would have had dealings with ENI in Italy. But from 1978 on, that relationship blossomed far beyond Italy's borders, and at an ideal moment for Calvi.

The Bank of Italy inspectors completed their fieldwork at Ambrosiano in Milan on July 19, 1978. Hardly had they done so than 5,000 miles away, in Nassau, the ENI connection was operational. Cisalpine Overseas was then headquartered in the IBM building, a stylish modern office block on East Bay Street owned by the American computer company. But it had close, indeed personal, links with another tenant of the same building—Tradinvest Bank and Trust of Nassau, ENI's financial affiliate specially tailored for the Bahamas offshore centre. On its board sat Pierre Siegenthaler, President of Calvi's Nassau bank, as well as two more junior managers of Cisalpine, Calvin Knowles and Sue-Anne Dunkley.

On July 21, Tradinvest agreed to lend Ambrosiano Holding of Luxembourg $45 million for five years. Inside a fortnight another $15 million followed, then another $20 million, this time from another ENI financial company in the Caribbean, Hydrocarbons International of Curaçao. Before the end of the year yet more money had flowed into Ambrosiano Holding, this time 100 million Swiss francs. The lender was ENI's embodiment in the Grand Cayman Islands, one of Nassau's most pressing rivals in the Caribbean offshore business.

Thus, within the space of four months, Italy's biggest oil group had come to Calvi's aid with no less than $130 million. And where ENI trod, others followed. In 1979, Banca del Gottardo, Ambrosiano's Swiss arm, had arranged two syndicated credits for over $60 million, in which some of the world's biggest banks took part. In 1980, Midland Bank of France was arranging a loan of $40 million, and in 1981 International Westminster led a group of banks who provided $75 million for Ambrosiano's Luxembourg Holding company. ENI's accommodating finance department had started a process which would lead to one of the angriest postscripts of the Ambrosiano collapse—the legal conflict over who should make good some $450 million of loans contracted by the Luxembourg affiliate between 1978 and 1981.

But the generosity of Di Donna and Fiorini did not stop at $130 million. No matter that ENI's experts made the alarming discovery that it was alone providing 60 per cent of the medium term funds secured by Ambrosiano Luxembourg, a dangerously high exposure by a single lender, and that the balance sheet valuation of the latter's assets looked unrealistically high. By mid-1979, Di Donna was writing to Calvi to assure him that if Ambrosiano would lend more to the oil group in Italy, then ENI would be quite happy to provide more help to his bank's foreign subsidiaries. He was as good as his word. Tradinvest provided $31 million to its next door neighbour Cisalpine in Nassau, and in 1980 capped all with a peculiar financing agreement with Banco Andino in Lima. Tradinvest would lend $50 million to Andino, in return for a credit of 100 million Swiss francs from Ambrosiano. This latter sum materialized only in part, and then after some delay. But why did Ambrosiano have to be involved at all? Could not ENI simply have used some of its own dollar balances to buy Swiss francs on the foreign exchange market?

But what, some wondered within ENI, was it doing acting as a bank? Some did protest that ENI should use its money for investments in industry, or at best short term deposits. What was it doing tying up money for five years, and with a bank of dubious reputation? For a few at ENI were aware of the Bank of Italy's findings. But their counsel went unheeded, to be remembered only when Ambrosiano collapsed, leaving ENI as its largest single creditor, for $160 million. Of that sum, much may be lost for good.

Without the providential support of Di Donna and Fiorini, Calvi might have been cut short in his enterprise. With their assistance, Banco Ambrosiano in Milan reduced its direct lending to foreign subsidiaries from $200 million in 1978 to a much less suspicious $40 million within two years, and Calvi was permitted to claim that he was following the Bank of Italy's instructions. In broader terms, ENI served as a good reference to Ambrosiano abroad, a little like the notorious letters of comfort the IOR was to provide *in extremis* in 1981. Others, particularly foreigners less wise in the ways of Italy, might be deceived into thinking that all was well.

And ENI's motives for the helping hand to Calvi? There have been various theories, but a conceivable explanation lay in politics. Some felt that the transactions could conceal financial aid for the parties at home. But no-one could be sure, and the truth—as so often in the Ambrosiano story—would remain elusive. What is certain is that

ENI's concern for Calvi continued until the very end. In June 1982, as Ambrosiano disintegrated, Fiorini came up with an ingenious plan that would have led in effect to ENI taking over Banco Ambrosiano! As a means of preserving $160 million of bad loans, the scheme probably had something to commend it, but as a use of public money it did not. In any case, Fiorini forgot to tell Enrico Gandolfi, ENI's stern commissioner of the day, and paid for the oversight with his job.

CHAPTER THIRTEEN

Messages from Licia

As THE 1970s closed, Calvi was to outward appearances at the height of his powers. With that disconcerting blend of shyness and arrogance which marked him in those years, he went about his business. He travelled ceaselessly, to Rome to see Gelli and his political contacts, and abroad to visit the scattered outposts of his realm.

Apart from the handful in the know, his staff at head office took the expansion at face value, unaware of the debilitating underside and unconcerned that the chairman was so often away. Ambrosiano's board, made up of members of a docile Milan establishment and cronies of Calvi from Rome, asked no questions. At a lower level in the bank, the growth seemed merely proof that a skilful Catholic banker could with determination mount a challenge to the "lay" establishment of Italy. If the central bank had probed Ambrosiano, if gossip abounded that Calvi was so secretive because he had much to hide—might that not be just a sign of the jealousy of less able rivals? Within Ambrosiano, Calvi was the master, his potency only enhanced by mystery. The foreign department in particular was happy in the belief that the growth abroad showed how it was running rings around lumbering competitors like Banca Commerciale.

On the few occasions that someone would express anxiety, Calvi might hint at the identity of his ally-cum-shareholder in foreign parts. Don't worry, he would say with the flicker of a smile, "It's all priests' business." *Dietro ci sono le tonache*, "the cassocks are backing us." And as further proof, there was the presence of Alessandro Mennini, one of the many sons of the IOR's Luigi, as a rising young executive on the foreign side. Rarely was additional elucidation demanded, and none was ever forthcoming.

And perhaps, during the weekends spent with his family at Drezzo, or on his foreign travels where the Italian press and its insinuations did not arrive every morning on his desk, Calvi would feel that his worst forebodings were unjustified. The Bank of Italy's teeth had been drawn, while Mucci seemed to be making little headway in his investigation into the apparent criminal offences unearthed by its 1978 report. In October 1979 he again questioned Calvi about the inflated price of the Toro and Credito Varesino transactions between 1973 and 1976, but there was no way to break through the stonewalling answers. Gelli's protection, if increasingly irksome, was also paying dividends: Calvi and Sindona settled their differences, thanks to the grandmaster's good offices.

Drezzo became particularly important at this stage. There Calvi would play out his role as a family man, busying himself with the modest pleasures of the countryman which perhaps he was at heart: cutting wood, looking after the hens and cows on the dozen-or-so-acre estate, and above all the two handsome white *maremmani* sheep dogs to which he was attached. No matter that later visitors would find even Drezzo cold and gloomy; for Calvi it was a refuge.

Life there was simple, and meals, even when important guests were present, unelaborate. His wife or daughter would usually serve at table. Calvi would show his guests the converted barn where he kept a modern sculpture of a church portal of which he was most proud. In the evenings, he could perhaps read about criminology. Those who knew Calvi well were surprised at his knowledge of financial frauds of the past. He was fascinated in particular by those which involved electronic gadgetry and computers. Of course, it is not difficult to see why.

For the rest, he remained a creature of the shadows. If duty compelled him to attend some meetings of the Italian banking association he would sit through proceedings, impassive and unmixing. His contribution would be brief at best. On the Milanese cocktail and reception circuit, he was virtually unknown. The ideal was for someone to appear on his behalf. In finance, too, the principle was the same, as a revealing episode at about this time displays.

An old-established private banker in Milan had heard that a small American bank was for sale, and was asked if he was interested in buying it. He wasn't, but was informed that Calvi might be. The banker went to tell Calvi about the idea. Calvi listened intently, but then indicated that he couldn't become involved himself because of possible problems with US regulations. There was a silence. Then Calvi came up with his suggestion: why didn't the banker buy it himself? But no, came the answer, he wasn't interested, and in any case didn't have the money. "Ah," said Calvi, "but you've missed the point. The money will be no problem." The other banker, realizing what Calvi was offering, politely declined, and left. In a sense it was the old "fiduciary" approach at work, but it also revealed Calvi's perennial tendency to try and entrap new people in his web, for money in return. Ambrosiano, moreover, always had the reputation of being a bank which paid its staff well.

Only with foreign bankers, and in foreign places, would he unbend a little. Sometimes he would invite executives from the biggest international banks to one of those suave lunches bankers like to offer each other, in the private dining room on the top floor, from where the view is best. Flanked by Leoni or Botta, Calvi might expound on the international monetary system, as he believed bank chairmen should. The meal would be simple but excellent, with immaculate service. At the end, over coffee and liqueurs, the pitch might come: how advantageous it would be if the guests' bank did more business with Ambrosiano. But Calvi would imply there was no urgency, that it didn't really matter. The wiser guests might leave wondering why Ambrosiano was so busy in Latin America of all places. The wisest of all never did lend Ambrosiano money.

Similar encounters might take place in New York in the autumn, with Calvi the guest. It was part of an annual itinerary taking him to Washington for the annual IMF meeting, and then to Nassau, Managua and Lima. He might converse amiably at the IMF with other Italian bankers, people with whom in Milan he hadn't exchanged a word in the other 360 days of the year. But talking with him, people would often have the impression that he wasn't really listening, that his mind was elsewhere. And so it probably was; for Ambrosiano's need to borrow, despite the *deus ex machina* of ENI, was remorselessly increasing.

In 1979, Calvi did settle the least serious of the objections of the Bank of Italy, by announcing that Banco Ambrosiano's capital would go up from 20 billion to 30 billion lire. But its perverse shareholding structure meant that this measure, which ought to have strengthened the bank, in fact undermined it further. For if Calvi was to retain control, and the risk of an embarrassing slide in Ambrosiano's share price was to be avoided, then the tiny companies in Panama and Liechtenstein would have to put up their due. And that would be paid for by more borrowing.

By the end of 1979, the exposure of the front companies, channelled by now through Banco Andino in Lima, stood probably at between $400 million and $500 million. Worse still, the dollar was about to rise rapidly against the lira, and international interest rates were moving higher. To borrow would cost more, while the assets against which the loans were secured, mainly lira-denominated shares in Milan, would be worth ever less in dollar terms. At home, other Italian banks, scenting trouble and by no means well-disposed to Calvi, were unwilling to lend to the foreign subsidiaries of Ambrosiano, of which so little was known. They would normally insist on dealing only with the Milan parent, more measurable and of better name.

Indeed, the exception in Italy to this rule was essentially only one, apart from the ever-obliging ENI which wasn't a bank at all. It was Banca Nazionale del Lavoro (BNL), Italy's largest bank, and whose general manager Alberto Ferrari was also in the P-2. Indeed, he and Calvi by some accounts had been initiated together, in Zurich in August 1975. Over the years BNL was to provide $50 million to Ambrosiano's Luxembourg holding company. Perhaps it and ENI should have had their suspicions. The same could not be said for the foreign banks, less wise in the ways of Italy, which were induced to lend Ambrosiano money.

The initial approach would be normality itself. Representatives of Ambrosiano's foreign department, often Alessandro Mennini and Carlo Costa, its two best English speakers, would visit a potential victim, quite possibly for one of those bankers' lunches. The question would be raised: would the bank consider making a loan to the Ambrosiano group? The money, it was sometimes assured, would help finance Italian exports, in conjunction with SACE, Italy's export credit guarantee organization. Then might follow a presentation of Calvi's bank, complete with impressive but, of course, doctored figures and charts. If these first contacts showed promise, then negotiations would continue—primarily with Ambrosiano's head office in Milan—and agreement would be reached.

Less normal was what happened thereafter. The lenders, encouraged by the implicit guarantee of the Milan parent, and happy to commit their surplus funds for profitable and apparently respectable purpose, would sign the contract with one of Ambrosiano's foreign subsidiaries. Little did they imagine that the proceeds would go to finance a clutch of nameplate companies in Panama and Liechtenstein; and that the main thing being exported from Italy was the control of Banco Ambrosiano. Still less did they conceive of the bizarre methods by which this would be done.

Calvi was meeting the insistence of the Bank of Italy that the parent bank no longer finance its subsidiaries abroad by breathtaking sleight-of-hand. The top foreign officials in Milan like Leoni and Botta simply became directors of the foreign subsidiaries. Thus the name of the borrower would be changed from Banco Ambrosiano (Milan) to Banco Ambrosiano Holding of Luxembourg or Banco Ambrosiano Andino, but everything else would be the same. The Luxembourg holding company, in theory in charge of Calvi's foreign dominions, in 1978 consisted of just two secretaries. At its height, its employees numbered only ten. Its board, headed by Calvi himself, comprised just senior executives of his group. The one Luxembourg citizen who was a director never attended meetings, which invariably took place in Lugano or Zurich. Much the same, as we have seen, went for the bank in Lima. Such structures were not in themselves an unusual international banking practice. But they meant that the entire mechanism, outwardly so different from its predecessor, could be directed by the same three or four people in Milan.

The Luxembourg holding company was just a funding office to satisfy the voracious appetites of Managua and Lima for money, to be devoured in turn by the companies in Panama and Liechtenstein. Ambrosiano in Managua was run by Cisalpine in Nassau. The instructions went from Milan to Nassau via a "representative office" of Cisalpine in Avenue des Citronniers in Monte Carlo, where a direct telex line was installed. Almost weekly, secretaries from Ambrosiano's foreign department in Milan would travel the 180 miles to Monte Carlo with a batch of messages. So frequent were the exchanges that a touching familiarity would creep into them. Addressed to Pierre (Siegenthaler), they would be signed Giacomo, Licia or Angelica. Giacomo, of course, was Giacomo Botta. Licia was Licia Ghiggi, Botta's secretary, and Angelica was Angelica Nidasio, an employee of Ambrosiano's foreign department. Later on, the Christian names would give way to a more mysterious "XY".

A later system for sending money to Banco Andino was not very different. Instead of the direct telex line from Monte Carlo, another Luxembourg subsidiary, called Ambrosiano Services was established. Its main "service" was to pass on similar instructions for loans by Banco Andino. The instructions were given by telephone from Milan to Luxembourg by senior officials like Botta.

The money spun from one front company to another with bewildering speed. One memorable message from Botta to Siegenthaler on June 26, 1979 sent the same nine million dollars on a book-keeping world tour: from Nicaragua to Liechtenstein to Panama to Luxembourg, to Nassau and then back to Nicaragua where it started. The purpose, investigators presume, was to "generate an income" in Luxembourg. The example is extreme, but it conveys the conjuring to which Calvi had to resort for survival. The pace of the lending accelerated in 1980. Between February and October that year, Banco Andino approved sixteen separate loans for $348 million to the hungriest front company of all, Nordeurop in Liechtenstein, later to become Astolfine SA in Panama. The Andino board (in other words Leoni, Botta and Costa) assembled to give its formal blessing not in Lima, of course, but in nearby Zurich—and only after most of the money had been paid out. In this unorthodox fashion, 88 creditor banks of Ambrosiano Luxembourg were to be parted from $450 million.

The process continued, at ever more desperate speed, right up to the end. Money was shifted here and there, to plug a hole, to enable one company to show an accounting profit, to whisk a suspicious loan temporarily from under the nose of an auditor. The ploy was fiendishly complex, but brilliantly simple in its results. For although everything was directed from Milan, nothing showed up on the books of the parent bank itself. And if anyone were to find out, then the ultimate owner of the companies would emerge as the IOR in the Vatican, thanks to its ownership of the two companies Manic and United Trading Corporation, set up all those years before. The proof of this vital secret was stored in Switzerland, at the Banca del Gottardo.

But if Calvi's financial defence cost money, so did his political defence. One expensive favour was the purchase by La Centrale of a controlling interest in the Venice newspaper *Il Gazzettino*, traditionally the voice of the potent Christian Democrat establishment in the deeply Catholic Veneto region. The paper was losing money heavily—until Calvi's appearance on the scene in 1979. Thereafter, when La Centrale had taken over, money suddenly became available. *Il Gazzettino* was safe for the Christian Democrats, at a cost for the Ambrosiano group of some 30 billion lire over the years. But Calvi did not forget the Communists, on the opposite end of the spectrum. As we have seen, *Paese Sera*, the Communist-backed daily in Rome, was lent 20 billion lire by Banco Ambrosiano between 1978 and 1982.

Calvi sought added protection from Catholic quarters. Carlo Pesenti, after himself and Sindona the third of the Vatican's allies in Italian finance, joined La Centrale's board, as did Luigi Lucchini, standard bearer of the dynamic small steelmakers in Brescia, whose fame was already reaching beyond Italy. The press wrote of a new "Lombard League".

In fact, however, the day-to-day administration of La Centrale was in the hands of Michel Leemans, a Belgian brought to Milan by Calvi long before. Leemans was never to hold any formal post at Banco Ambrosiano itself. But by a strange quirk, just as Calvi was always to conduct the most sensitive transactions of La Centrale himself, so Leemans was to be the last representative of Ambrosiano in 1982, when all was about to be lost.

And as 1979 gave way to 1980, the portents of disaster were becoming more visible. Most ominous, the judiciary seemed at last to have decided that the Bank of Italy was a less worthy object of their attentions than the financiers whose murky affairs the central bank had investigated.

The first victim was Italcasse, where the central bank's inspectors had in 1977 unearthed irregularities severe enough to warrant a judicial follow-up. That investigation had, of course, contributed to the political assault on the Bank of Italy two years later. But at dawn on March 4, 1980 the findings brought even more spectacular consequence, as no less than 38 senior bankers from the savings institutes under Italcasse's umbrella were arrested. They were charged with making irregular loans to various favoured borrowers, including the Caltagirone construction group from Rome, a big benefactor of certain local Christian Democrat politicians.

It mattered little that such imprisonment before any trial was quite commonplace in Italy, and that the theatrically-tinged affair would blow over, like so many others, leaving scarcely a ripple behind it. For Calvi, the message was clear. For whatever reason, the balance had shifted, and not to his advantage. The fact that the magistrate who ordered the arrests was Antonio Alibrandi, who only twelve months before had made the accusations against Baffi and Sarcinelli at the Bank of Italy, must have made him uneasier still. For what guarantee was there that the Milan judiciary's investigation of his own alleged offences would not now land him in a similar predicament?

Gelli, too, was increasing his pressures on Calvi, mixing promises of help with half-spoken threats to let spill other of the banker's embarrassing secrets. Relations between them worsened to the extent that in April 1980, when Calvi was in Zurich for Easter, he abruptly changed his hotel to avoid encountering Gelli, who, he discovered, had booked into the same one. Only Ambrosiano's small shareholders remained faithful, dismissing at the annual meeting all adverse gossip as "libel". Once again, a higher dividend would make them forget Calvi's reluctance to inform them of what his bank was really about. But the respite was short.

Within weeks, the overstretched construction group of Mario Genghini finally crumbled. On June 25, 1980 he was declared bankrupt by a Rome court, leaving behind him total debts of 450 billion lire, a third of them to Ambrosiano itself. The magistrates did issue an arrest warrant for fraud, but by that time Genghini was safely in Latin America. For Calvi the episode must have been proof that not even the P-2, of which Genghini was a member, could ward off financial reality for ever. Any doubts on this score were removed by the events of a few days later in Milan.

At last the specialized *Guardia di Finanza* financial police were reaching the same conclusions as the Bank of Italy eighteen months before. The *Guardia di Finanza* were now sure that the shares in the Toro insurance company despatched abroad by La Centrale in 1973 were *exactly the same ones* as it bought back at such an inflated price in

1975. In other words, in one guise or another, Ambrosiano had controlled the shares all along, and the excessive sum paid for their return in large part constituted an illegal export of capital. Calvi should have reported this under the 1976 law, but he had not. Thus armed, Luca Mucci, the magistrate still handling the case, ordered him to surrender his passport and warned that criminal charges might be on their way. Calvi's long, losing battle with the Italian courts had begun.

The loss of his passport was unnerving, humiliating and hugely inconvenient. Without it he would be prevented from his annual visit to the IMF meeting, a place where the chairman of Italy's largest private banking group ought above all to be seen. In many respects worse, he would be prevented from those important personal inspections of the foreign subsidiaries of Ambrosiano.

News of the sanction inevitably appeared quickly in the Italian press, and shares in Ambrosiano and its affiliates came under severe pressure on the Milan stock market. Under distinctly suspicious circumstances, Calvi did recover his passport, just in time to attend the Fund meeting that autumn. But other reminders followed, of just how thin was the ice upon which Catholic finance trod. The next eminent figure to be arrested that summer was Massimo Spada, once of the IOR and now chairman of Ambrosiano's own Banca Cattolica del Veneto, charged with involvement in Sindona's fraudulent bankruptcy in 1974. Worse still, the same fate would befall Luigi Mennini, the successor of Spada at the Vatican bank, on similar accusation.

For the Holy See, which had been trying with limited success to forget its imprudences in the Sindona affair, Mennini's arrest was a particular embarrassment. Despite his 71 years, his were the financial skills indispensable to the IOR. Calvi's discomfort was even greater. For he now began to doubt in earnest whether the Vatican's concealment of his own dubious dealings could continue.

The moment had come to seek a new source of support, if not of escape from the predicament into which he had built himself. The support had to be substantial, and beyond the control of the Italian authorities. And who met these two conditions better than the Arabs?

*   *   *

126

Calvi had long been fascinated by the thought of linking Ambrosiano with the oil wealth of the Middle East. In the mid-1970s he had vainly tried to set up an "Arab Mediterranean Bank", only to be deceived by a spurious Saudi Arabian intermediary who left Milan without even paying his hotel bill. But Calvi, with his love of the complicated and contorted, was not dismayed, nor his faith in Arab promise much damaged. As Leemans put it long afterwards: "If you offered him something straightforward, he'd dismiss it. But he'd be fascinated by something really far-fetched; like a child believing in a fairy story." Exactly what fairy stories he was told by the brash British financier Peter de Savary, we do not know. But by late 1980 Calvi was deep in plans for Banco Ambrosiano Overseas (as Cisalpine was now called) to buy twenty per cent of de Savary's Artoc Bank and Trust, also based in Nassau.

That winter Calvi went to Lyford Cay for what was to be the last time in his life. There was much to attend to in the Bahamas: not least progress in the construction of a new headquarters for Ambrosiano Overseas, a garish four-storey edifice far on East Bay Street, beyond the bridge to Paradise Island and the Nassau Casino. It was grandiosely called Ambrosiano House, and at a cost of $8 million was the biggest ever fixed investment by a bank in the Bahamas. On the top there would be a penthouse apartment, where the Calvis would stay on future visits. But most important was Artoc.

Coopers and Lybrand, the accountants which audited both Artoc and Ambrosiano Overseas, were the first to moot the idea of a link. De Savary had set up Artoc to cap his success as an oil trader in the Middle East. At the time it was equally owned by Arab and European interests. There were incentives for both sides. A deal with Ambrosiano might redress the previous financial dominance of the Arabs in Artoc; at the same time it could help open banking doors for Calvi in the Middle East, where Ambrosiano was still weak.

But the main attraction for Calvi was the prospect of rich new contacts in the Arab financial world. For an outlay of just $4 million, he gained not only twenty per cent of Artoc but also two seats on the board, alongside such figures as Abdullah Saudi, formerly Libya's representative on the board of Fiat (in which Colonel Gaddafi had bought ten per cent in 1976) and later to run the Bahrain-based Arab Banking Corporation. And there were others, Kuwaitis and Saudi

Arabians, who could conceivably organize the sum—maybe $700 million by then—required to get Calvi off his foreign hook.

The agreement with Artoc was signed in February. Calvi was in London for the occasion with his wife and a retinue of officials from Ambrosiano's foreign side. They stayed at the private St James' Club which de Savary owned, in relaxed good humour. There was a dinner one night at an Artoc director's home in a Chelsea square. It was a friendly occasion; the deal had been concluded, and in his own way Calvi opened up a little. Small talk, of course, was never for him. But Calvi expounded with conviction on the need for freedom, and to contain the Communists. It all sounded rather like Gelli and Sindona. As usual his subordinates around the table listened respectfully, acknowledging the rightness of the chairman's views.

The visit to London coincided with other reassurance that whatever his difficulties in Italy, the suspicions had not spread too far abroad, among potential lenders. Licia's and Angelica's furtive missions were still a secret of Avenue des Citronniers.

In what was to prove the last big loan arranged by Ambrosiano Holding of Luxembourg, National Westminster, the second biggest bank in Britain, raised $75 million on its behalf. The five year credit's original amount was $50 million, but the enthusiasm of the market was such that the figure was increased to $75 million. Nor was the interest rate on the loan so high as to indicate an undue degree of risk. Quite clearly in February 1981 Ambrosiano did not appear a dangerous proposition. Ambrosiano accepted the terms of the proposal on February 6, and on April 8 formal agreement was signed. The storm was then a month away.

CHAPTER FOURTEEN

Corriere

CALVI MUST HAVE had his forbodings as he returned to Italy in early 1981. The reason was not just replacement of the sub-tropical Bahamas by Milan's foggy winter chill. In his heart he surely knew that even the Artoc venture then taking shape was unlikely to be a match for the difficulties which were piling up at home. From every side old foes and new were pressing in.

After a two-year interval the Bank of Italy was again concentrating on Ambrosiano, albeit more circumspectly than in 1979, when the direct challenge of the inspection brought such rapid chastisement. But in late January 1981 the central bank finally won approval from the Government for new regulations governing foreign interests held by Italian banks. The regulations frowned upon foreign holding companies which were not themselves banks, and warned that such interests would only be permitted if a) they could be properly scrutinized by the Bank of Italy, and b) operated in countries with a proper system of supervision.

No names were mentioned, but the reference to Ambrosiano could not have been clearer. The Government's directive was to be the basis for the central bank's relentless bombardment of Calvi from the summer onwards, for details of what went on in Luxembourg, the Bahamas, Nicaragua and Peru.

Hardly less ominous, though it did not appear so at the time, was the appointment the previous October of a new Treasury Minister in Beniamino Andreatta. A Bolognese university professor of impulsive and independent spirit, Andreatta was a devout Catholic and a Christian Democrat, but by temperament he was less caring than his colleagues for the political niceties. The impetuosity of his judgement could be questioned; but in his way Andreatta shared the "lay" desire for a greater openness in Italian society. "A most Protestant Catholic", he was once described: another explanation of why he was to be peculiarly upset by the behaviour of both the Vatican and a bank supposedly the guardian of old-fashioned Catholic virtues. When the end came, Andreatta was to be implacable.

One of his early acts as Minister was to choose a new head for the decrepit Milan stock market supervisory commission, the Consob. When it was created in 1974, the Consob was portrayed as Italy's answer to the omnipotent Securities and Exchange Commission, which ruled over Wall Street. But these improbable expectations were never met, and in 1978 indignity was added to impotence when Giulio Andreotti, the Prime Minister, named a Rome theatrical impresario to its board. But the arrival of Guido Rossi in February 1981 was to jolt the Consob out of its lethargy.

Like Baffi and Sarcinelli, Rossi came from modest origins. But he had become Milan's leading corporate lawyer, and holder of that chair at the university of nearby Pavia. Harvard-trained and widely travelled, Rossi was everything that Calvi was not: rationalist, technocratic and above all a believer in clarity.

At the Consob he saw his task as one of throwing open the windows of the fetid and ingrown Milan market to the daylight of consolidated balance sheets, disclosure of true shareholdings in quoted companies, and modern trading rules on a par with those elsewhere in Europe. Like Baffi and Sarcinelli, he was to be criticized for being unrealistically rigid in his approach. Indeed, from the outset Rossi found himself beset by subtle bureaucratic obstacles, such as funds allocated to Consob by Parliament but which never seemed to materialise. "You're a brave man to try and reform the stock market," a wise Milanese broker told him once. "It's like trying to bring morals to a whore-house."

Inevitably such an approach brought him into confrontation with Calvi, the emblem of financial obscurantism, head of a bank whose ownership was a mystery, and long involved in share trafficking of the type that Rossi wanted to stamp out. Rossi moved in when the market was at last recovering from the disgrace and neglect which followed the ruin of Sindona. During 1980, share prices had on average doubled, and trading volume had multiplied tenfold. Rossi's ambition of widening the market was welcomed by those who wanted to use the new public interest in stocks and shares to restore its proper role, as a source of capital in a modern market economy. Otherwise the improvement might prove yet another speculative bubble, causing only disillusion when it burst. As far as Rossi was concerned, no more suitable candidate existed for admission to the market than Banco Ambrosiano.

Calvi's bank had long been heavily traded, but only on the informal *mercato ristretto*, or over-the-counter market. The anomaly stemmed from Ambrosiano's origins, and the right of choice that Ambrosiano's board still technically exercised over its shareholders. For Calvi, the arrangement was ideal. The *mercato ristretto* was subject to even fewer controls than its larger brother. Consolidated accounts were not obligatory, and trading took place only one day a week. This, in turn, allowed Ambrosiano to control its own share price easily and cheaply. The consideration was vital. The last thing Calvi could afford, after borrowing so much to buy effective control of his bank, was to see the price of its shares, the main collateral for those debts, plunge.

Hardly had Rossi taken over at Consob, than he informed Calvi of his wish. Ambrosiano was after all, he argued, the most important private banking group in the country, with over 30,000 shareholders. But Calvi was appalled. Such a step would oblige Ambrosiano to publish detailed accounts, consolidated to include the secret foreign operations. More important, it would become far harder, and more expensive, to prop up the bank's share price. Worst of all, Calvi suspected that Rossi would simply order the full market quotation, whether he liked it or not.

At their first meetings, in that early spring of 1981, Calvi attempted to dissuade Rossi. Ambrosiano's image would suffer, he implied, giving no reasons. Rossi was distinctly bemused and pointed out that, surely, to be traded on the major Milan market ought to *enhance* the bank's prestige. But Calvi still opposed the idea. He would alternate the same arguments with long moments of silence, always his defence when under pressure. Rossi, who previously had never met Calvi, was no less astonished by his mechanical capacity to tell one lie after another, by his very ordinariness. How could so unimpressive a figure be where he was, Rossi wondered. His curiosity was further aroused by the capital increase Calvi had just announced at Ambrosiano's annual meeting, to the ever-admiring shareholders. Their apparently unshakeable faith in Calvi was as well. For they were being asked to provide in all 240 billion lire of fresh funds, a large sum by any standards. What the shareholders did not know, of course, was that those Panamanian and Liechtenstein companies, whose existence only a few were aware of, would be borrowing still more money to subscribe to their quota of shares. Calvi was to present the capital increase as a seal on Ambrosiano's expansion and success under his guidance.

In fact the new money was urgently required to offset losses the bank had incurred after Genghini's collapse, and might incur over the struggling Rizzoli. There was a smaller loss around then in Spain also, when Banco Occidental, in which Ambrosiano held a ten per cent interest, collapsed with $100 million of debts. For Rossi however, the sheer size of the sum that Calvi was seeking was just another excellent reason to force him on to the main market.

But for Calvi, fencing with the chairman of Consob rapidly became a secondary consideration. For April and May of 1981 brought a sequence of overlapping disasters, dispelling the almost mystical aura upon which his reputation rested. The mysteries were crudely revealed for what they were: membership of a sinister freemasons' lodge, improper entanglement with Italy's biggest newspaper and publishing group, and total disregard of Italian currency regulations. Those New Year forebodings in Nassau were to prove only too well grounded.

The weakest link in the chain was Rizzoli. By the autumn of 1980, the publishing group was in a wretched state. Tassan Din's reckless expansion of the previous three years, encouraged by Gelli and Ortolani with Calvi's acquiescence, had proved a calamity. Tassan Din, never short of ideas, had drawn up a new three-year plan; but this time the emphasis was on cutbacks and closures. Equally necessary, however, was a substantial injection of new capital, to reduce debts now costing Rizzoli 60 billion lire a year in interest payments alone.

The obvious options were two: either the sale of the group, with its tempting bait of the *Corriere della Sera*, to a third party; or a capital increase; which would have to be paid for by Ambrosiano. Tassan Din presented Calvi with the unpleasant choice, for both solutions had drawbacks. The advent of a major outside shareholder could lead to effective surrender of the *Corriere*, among the most potent weapons of the P-2. On the other hand, a direct shareholding by Ambrosiano would expose Calvi's involvement with the paper, and run foul of a regulation which banned such investments. In any case he already surreptitiously controlled 80 per cent of Rizzoli, following its previous capital increase in 1977. But with Gelli's and Ortolani's help, Tassan Din came up with an ingenious answer.

Angelo Rizzoli, who in theory still owned 90 per cent of the company his family had founded, would retain 40 per cent. The remaining 50 per cent would be held through an unspecified "institution", whose identity Calvi and Gelli refused to disclose. Was it the P-2 they were referring to, or could they have meant the Vatican bank? After all, 80 per cent of the publishing group's capital had been lodged with first Calvi and then the IOR in 1977; and if the IOR had acted as a front for Calvi so often before, why should it not do so in the case of Rizzoli? To preserve the illusion that the Rizzolis still ruled the group which bore their name, a controlling syndicate would be created, containing the 40 per cent of Angelo Rizzoli, plus 10.2 per cent supplied by the "institution". The money for the capital increase—150 billion lire—would, of course, come from Banco Ambrosiano, and Calvi would be the real owner of Rizzoli.

The scheme was elegant, but never materialized. For in mid-March 1981 Gelli, the self-proclaimed puppet-master, suddenly became a fugitive, his occult realm of the P-2 a matter for the magistrates and the police. Fittingly enough, the indirect cause of this disaster, which would have fatal repercussions later for both Rizzoli and Ambrosiano, was none other than Michele Sindona.

The decisive breakthrough was made neither in Milan nor Rome, but in Palermo, where Joseph Miceli Crimi, an Italo-American surgeon suspected of involvement in the huge drugs trade between Sicily and the US, was being questioned. Among his interrogators were Giuliano Turone and Gherardo Colombo, two magistrates from Milan who had long been probing the Sindona bankruptcy and its implications.

Turone and Colombo were less concerned with uncovering the

"Sicilian Connection" than establishing Crimi's exact role in Sindona's erratic voyage around Europe during his "kidnapping" in the summer of 1979. Crimi, an admitted freemason, had helped organize Sindona's hideaway in Palermo. But the magistrates also knew he had made a strange trip to Arezzo, and wanted to know why. At first Crimi stonewalled, claiming he was visiting his Italian dentist there for a check-up. Then on March 14, 1981, he unexpectedly gave way. He had been to Arezzo, he said, to see a fellow mason, Licio Gelli, about arrangements for Sindona.

The magistrates quickly followed up this new lead. Three days later a *Guardia di Finanza* detachment went to Gelli's villa in Arezzo, but Gelli was away and they found nothing of particular interest. The next stop was Gelli's office at the Gio-Le textile factory. And there, in an ordinary wall safe and a brown leather suitcase alongside it, were the secrets of the P-2. In the safe the *Guardia di Finanza* discovered the list of the 962 names of members of the lodge, together with bundles of payments slips and receipts. In the suitcase they found 32 dossiers, and the headings of another 400-odd. The magistrates could hardly believe it.

The membership lists amounted to little short of a parallel state. The names included those of two current cabinet ministers, large segments of Italy's military and secret service hierarchy ranging from the chief of the general staff to the past and present heads of the *Guardia di Finanza* itself. No less than 50 generals and admirals, serving or retired, featured on the lists. There were industrialists, financiers, diplomats, top civil servants, police officers. The journalists numbered 24, the parliamentarians (including two ministers) were 38—drawn from every major party except the left-wing Radicals and the Communists. Calvi was there, of course, as were Sindona, Angelo Rizzoli, Tassan Din, the *Corriere*'s editor Franco Di Bella, and Mario Genghini, that other notable beneficiary of Ambrosiano's generosity.

If the importance of the members was not enough, any doubts as to Gelli's penetration of the machinery of the Italian state were banished by the documents in the various dossiers, not a few of them highly confidential Government papers. Quite evidently Gelli had constructed a breathtaking mechanism for advancement, manipulation, and if he wanted, blackmail and extortion. He himself had vanished to the safety of South America, along, presumably, with many of the dossiers, whose contents would tantalize for many months afterwards. But enough was left behind to compromise Calvi further.

File heading No 351 read "Calvi—statement to magistrates by the Bank of Italy". It contained copious notes by Gelli himself, indicating intimate knowledge of the progress of the investigations into the alleged currency offences. There were documents too, some manifestly forged but enough to suggest that Gelli had his informers everywhere. Among them was a separate slip apparently indicating that $800,000 had been credited to a secret numbered account at a Geneva bank for the benefit of Ugo Zilletti, then the deputy chairman of the Upper Council of Italian magistrates, the apex of the judiciary, and whose head is the President of the Republic himself. The note was easily to be construed as payment for services rendered in securing the return of Calvi's passport. Zilletti adamantly denied the suggestion. But in April 1981 he was obliged to resign from his post.

Calvi curtly dismissed Gelli's file on his legal misadventures as a "contrived folly". But the consequences could not have been graver. As suspicions grew over the two years of meandering taken by the affair since Alessandrini had been murdered in 1979, Mucci was taken off the case, to be replaced by Gerardo d'Ambrosio, among the sternest of the young Milan magistrates. Day after day, fresh details of the scandal emerged in the press. At the same time, with Gelli on the other side of the Atlantic and his organization in ruins, the entire Rizzoli rescue plan had to be recast.

Whatever the "institution" destined to receive 50 per cent of the publishing group, it was no longer prepared to do so. Instead, the 10.2 per cent that would constitute the nominally controlling syndicate with Angelo Rizzoli was placed in the hands of Tassan Din. As for the remaining 40 per cent, Calvi had no option but to take that on himself, if the scheme, and with it prospects of Rizzoli's survival, were to be preserved.

On Easter Sunday, April 19, Tassan Din took the agreement first to Naples for signature by Angelo Rizzoli, who was spending the holiday at Capri; and then to Calvi at his villa at Drezzo. The momentous accord occupied just a single sheet of paper.

La Centrale, Ambrosiano's merchant banking arm, would acquire

40 per cent of Rizzoli for 116 billion lire. With this money, Angelo Rizzoli would repay Calvi the debt he had incurred to carry out Rizzoli's previous capital increase in 1977 (and thus retrieve the 80 per cent of the group's shares mortgaged through the IOR), and subscribe his share of the new one. In all, 150 billion lire of fresh capital would go to Rizzoli. Meanwhile La Centrale's foray into the publishing world would cost it the colossal sum of 176 billion lire: the price agreed with Angelo Rizzoli, plus 60 billion lire to cover its own portion of the forthcoming capital increase.

The stealth with which the deal had been executed was vintage Calvi. The first Leemans, who was after all La Centrale's managing director, heard about it was on April 22: "Do you know we're buying Rizzoli," exclaimed an executive at La Centrale, bursting into his office brandishing a news agency flash conveying announcement of the agreement by Angelo Rizzoli that day. Leemans rang Calvi in amazement: "Oh yes," came the reply, "I forgot to tell you. I was going to." It was only the following Sunday that Calvi gave Leemans and Roberto Rosone, Ambrosiano's general manager for Italy, a fuller version of events.

Calvi was relaxed and unperturbed, notwithstanding the unflattering comments aroused by the announcement. He was after all a banker of doubtful repute, under investigation for currency offences and apparently linked to the P-2 (although the membership lists had not been made public, the Zilletti affair made it more than likely that Calvi and Gelli were no strangers). What, it was asked, was he doing buying virtual control of Italy's most important paper? And was not such a transaction forbidden, after the Bank of Italy directive preventing banks moving into areas unrelated to finance? Rosone and Leemans were most worried about the cost. La Centrale would have to borrow the money to finance the deal, at a cost to itself of almost 40 billion lire a year in interest payments alone, they observed.

Not to worry, Calvi reassured them. Half a dozen potential buyers for the 40 per cent stake were already waiting: and in two or three months La Centrale would have sold out with a tidy profit. In any event, he had already secured the prior agreement of the Bank of Italy, the Treasury Minister and the party leaders in Rome. Maybe, Calvi was merely relaying assurances he had been given by Gelli (or Tassan Din), that the *Corriere* transaction would cause no problems.

Maybe he was telling a plain lie. Possibly, however, Calvi did have a prepared solution. For at about the time the Rizzoli purchase was going through, he arranged for $143 million to be transferred from Banco Andino in Lima to Bellatrix, one of the little Panamanian companies. From there the money—by coincidence or otherwise exactly equal to the price paid by La Centrale—was directed into two Zurich accounts, bearing the names of Zirka and Recioto. Was this to enable control of Rizzoli to be swiftly transferred outside Italy, just like control of Banco Ambrosiano itself?

But the question was rapidly to become academic, for, far from abating, public debate intensified about Ambrosiano, about its mysterious appendages abroad, and its impenetrable ownership. Political objections also mounted, a sign of unease among the parties that the mouthpiece represented by the *Corriere* might be passing into hostile hands, at a moment, moreover, when early general elections seemed possible. Nor were the Treasury Minister or the central bank giving any sign they had accepted the arrangement—indeed rather the opposite.

Calvi himself must have secretly foreseen the worst. For as he signed the agreement he asked Tassan Din quietly: "If I do sign, do you think I'll avoid going to prison?"

†Bruno Tassan Din, in an interview to *La Stampa*, February 16, 1983.

CHAPTER FIFTEEN

Prison and Trial

THE KNELL FOR Calvi was not long in sounding. The magistrate d'Ambrosio had swiftly concluded that the evidence against him, strengthened now by the contents of Gelli's files at Arezzo, warranted formal charges. Shortly after 7.30 a.m. on the morning of May 20, a detachment of *Guardia di Finanza* officials arrived at Calvi's flat in Via Frua in central Milan to place him under arrest. Four hours later he was in a prison cell in Lodi, twenty miles south of the city. There he was to spend the next two months, the most crushing of his life.

But the sombre early-morning round-up extended beyond Calvi. A clutch of other leading financiers, also held to be involved in the suspect transactions in Toro and Credito Varesino followed him behind bars. Calvi was arrested in his capacity as chairman of La Centrale; into Lodi and three other prisons in the Lombardy region disappeared four other Centrale directors past and present, including Antonio Tonello, chairman of both Toro and Credito Varesino. Two more were only allowed to remain at liberty because of their advanced age. They were Massimo Spada (who the previous October had been arrested on charges connected with Sindona) and Carlo Canesi, Calvi's first mentor at Ambrosiano. Canesi, indeed, was to die during Calvi's trial, at the age of 87.

Two other figures at the pinnacle of Milanese finance were also imprisoned. They were Carlo Bonomi (the son of the redoubtable Anna Bonomi) and Giorgio Cigliana, respectively chairman and general manager of Invest, the Bonomi group company, which was alleged to have abetted Calvi in some of the share dealings. Even though Calvi's own arrest had been half-expected, and the spectacle of financiers in handcuffs was nothing new, the implications of the magistrate's initiative left not just Milan, but Italy, aghast. It was as if a scimitar had decapitated two of the most powerful financial groups in the country, and had sliced deeply into its largest publishing empire. Nor were the day's excitements over.

Later that evening those other two Milan magistrates, Turone and Colombo, gave clearance for the Government to publish the P-2 membership lists, whose contents had in any case been abundantly ventilated by the newspapers. As the litany of names rolled on, from Calvi to Rizzoli to Di Bella to Tassan Din, the agreement between La Centrale and Rizzoli—and much else besides—began to make clearer, and most disturbing, sense.

Some at the *Corriere* were still able to joke acidly about their plight ("We've got 40 per cent of our owners in prison, and the other 60 per cent in the P-2"), but the paper was devastated. Several of its best-known journalists departed, and Di Bella the editor, after an initial attempt to brazen things out, was forced to resign shortly afterwards. So too was Arnaldo Forlani the Prime Minister, in whose Government, it had been revealed, were two alleged members of the lodge of Licio Gelli. He was to be replaced by Giovanni Spadolini, leader of the tiny Republican party, and Italy's first Prime Minister in 36 years who was not a Christian Democrat. Catholic politics, as well as Catholic finance, were on the retreat.

But the consequences for Calvi were gravest of all. On that May 20, he was destroyed.

Ironically the charges themselves were almost the least serious part of his predicament. "Of all the things I'm supposed to have done, why did they bother with those share deals?", he remarked sadly to his family later. And indeed, compared to the involvement with Gelli and Ortolani, and to his difficulties abroad, the currency offences were of little import—if offences they really were.

For some still maintain that Calvi had not created a surplus abroad, but had been forced to settle a loss, brought about by a fall on the Milan stock market, and the very great rise in the value of the Swiss franc against the lira. He himself believed the real blame lay with the IOR, in Calvi's eyes the true recipient of the surplus.

Indisputably, however, imprisonment dislodged the cornerstones of the elaborate edifice he had constructed. The tenuous props to his reputation were pulled away. The Vatican was at last to realize the enormity of the mess it had helped create. From that time on it backing for Calvi was tepid and grudging. The political support he thought he had secured proved insufficient; while both foreign bank and those within the Ambrosiano group who knew the truth (o suspected it) lost faith. Most immediately destructive was the psycho logical impact of jail.

For anyone to find themselves suddenly under lock and key and a the orders of others is, at the least, a jarring experience. For the aloo and private Calvi, accustomed to the unquestioning obedience o others, the shield of bodyguards and armour-plated cars, the shock was terrible. Prison crushed his spirit, making him even more morbid and suspicious than before. At Ambrosiano people would try to make light of it, talking of the chairman *in pensione*, but for the rest of hi days Calvi could never talk easily of the experience.

By Italian standards Lodi is a fairly comfortable prison. Even so Calvi for the first week there found himself sharing a cell with three petty delinquents who would play cards and have the radio or constantly, preventing him from resting. A visitor early on found him "completely submissive", meekly obeying the commands of guard half or a third of his age, red-eyed from lack of sleep.

Calvi's ordeal was hardly less upsetting for his wife and family whose faith in his powers until then had been undented. Clara Calv cast desperately around for ways to help her husband. At Ambro siano itself she found surprisingly little sympathy. But at this point a strange benefactor appeared—the first of the unappealing figure who crowd the final year of Calvi's life.

Francesco Pazienza was a financial soldier of fortune, working either on his own account or on hire for others. Trained as a doctor he gave up medicine for the greater rewards of the "internationa consultant". He was what the French aptly called a *brasseur d'af faires*. Pazienza was young, only in his mid-thirties, but he spoke fou languages, and vaunted contacts with the Italian secret services, the CIA and Italian politicians. Disconcertingly, he could mix charm with a brutal aggressiveness. Above all Pazienza seems to have had a sharp eye for human weakness, and a remarkable ability to win people': confidence on only slight acquaintance. Calvi, with his doubts, his fascination with the secret world and his conviction that concealed rather than open, power was what counted, was a perfect target.

140

The two appear to have met at an IMF meeting in Washington, where Pazienza was with a group of American bankers. By March 1981 they were in regular contact. Calvi gave him the title of "international adviser" to Ambrosiano. He also entrusted Pazienza with a supremely important task—the one which could solve all his difficulties. Pazienza was to find a buyer for the assets held by the IOR-backed Panama and Liechtenstein companies, above all the controlling interest in Banco Ambrosiano itself. The proceeds would enable the debts to be repaid, and the whole sorry tangle resolved.

Obviously, Calvi's arrest had abruptly halted these plans. But Pazienza then approached Clara Calvi in her hour of desperation. The day after her husband had been sent to Lodi, Pazienza telephoned to assure her that he was mobilizing his political contacts to help Calvi. But she would have to go to Rome. Clara Calvi has told how she accompanied Pazienza on a private jet down to the capital to put her case in person to the three politicians whom Calvi always claimed were his sponsors: Giulio Andreotti, the Christian Democrat party president Flaminio Piccoli, and Bettino Craxi, the leader of the Socialists.

Her argument was simple: her husband had provided much financial assistance to both parties: could not they now do something to help remove his troubles with the judiciary? The politicians made no promises, but said they would do what they could. In the weeks ahead Craxi and Piccoli did speak out in Parliament and elsewhere in favour of Calvi, to some effect. But they must have suspected already that the banker was *bruciato*, as the Italians graphically put it, "burnt out". With the P-2 intrigue laid bare, how far could they risk exposing themselves in favour of a man who for years had represented the financial arm of Gelli's lodge? The Vatican appears to have been reaching the same conclusion.

From 400 miles' distance in Rome, Banco Ambrosiano had until recently looked a more reliable proposition than it did from close at hand in Milan. But the P-2 affair, the clamour created by Calvi's open involvement with Rizzoli, and the unending rumours had begun to prise open even the Vatican's well-sealed eyes. Later the Holy See claimed that it was utterly deceived over the nature of its business dealings with Calvi; but the IOR knew full well at the least that these were close and substantial. There had been an additional warning that spring as well. Andreatta, the Treasury Minister, who had read the Bank of Italy report, went to the Vatican to urge it to cut loose from Calvi before it was too late.

What became of this episode is not clear. Although there is little doubt the visit took place, Marcinkus would claim that no-one told him about it. But debate over the complexities of the IOR's relations with Ambrosiano was about to be eclipsed by an infinitely more serious matter: the attempt on the life of the Pope on the warm Wednesday afternoon of May 13, 1981, which came within an ace of succeeding.

Those to whom Andreatta had conveyed his apprehensions were suddenly faced with the prospect of a Church without rudder, as its ruler, in whose hands all power was concentrated, fought with death. Financial decisions, which in any event would have gestated slowly, must simply have been pigeonholed.

Seven days after John Paul II was so nearly assassinated, Calvi was arrested. In the weeks that followed, Marcinkus was pressed by his family, on the grounds that much of the sum held to have been illegally exported had gone to a company owned by the IOR. Calvi's son Carlo telephoned Marcinkus several times to plead for the IOR to admit involvement, on the grounds that this would have considerably reduced the gravity of the case against his father. The problem was that the Banca del Gottardo in Lugano, through which the deals had been channelled, was bound by Swiss banking secrecy regulations. The IOR would have to volunteer the information itself.

Marcinkus however refused to help. "If we do, it's not only the IOR and the Vatican's image which will suffer," he told Carlo. "You'll lose as well, for our problems are your problems too." The reply was enigmatic. Did it mean that the worldly archbishop already knew all about the massive fraud, to be publicly displayed only a year later? Or was it simply to observe that for the IOR to intervene would merely show to what extent Ambrosiano had sheltered behind it?

Another episode indicates just how fervid was the Vatican's desire to keep its name out of the trial. One day his wife Clara and daughter Anna went to visit Calvi in prison at Lodi. They were driven there by Alessandro Mennini, the physical symbol of Ambrosiano's entwinement with the IOR, and a family friend of the children. Calvi was tired and fearful. He begged his family to see Marcinkus and Luigi

Mennini and insist that they help him out. Anna took notes of what her father told them, under the heading: "This trial is called IOR." Since February he had been pressing the Vatican bank, he said, but to no avail. It was now up to the family to try.

As they left the prison, Anna showed one of the sheets to Alessandro Mennini. Horrified, Mennini tried to wrench the paper from her hands: "You must never say this name (IOR), not even in the confessional box." Clara Calvi then snatched the papers herself and sat on them in the car to prevent anyone taking them. But, she has recounted, she never did go to see Marcinkus and Mennini's father.

Gradually the first impact of imprisonment lessened, especially after intercession by Pazienza and the prison chaplain saw him moved to a single cell. And from there, almost incredibly, Calvi began to take in hand again the reins of Ambrosiano. He alone knew all the secrets of the bank; and without his guidance Olgiati, the general manager, Rosone and Leoni in Milan were hard-pressed to cope. But the fears of these three were growing as foreign banks started to sever the lifeline of funds for Ambrosiano's foreign subsidiaries. After Calvi's arrest Midland Bank, for example, dropped a planned $25 million loan it was organizing for Banco Andino in Lima. Others just declined to renew credits as they fell due for repayment.

Most ominous of all, Banca del Gottardo in Lugano, through which much of the original web had been spun, indicated that it was no longer willing to continue its role in the clandestine foreign operations about which it knew so much. This was now taken over gradually by Ambrosiano Services in Luxembourg.

After a preliminary hearing on May 29, Milan's financial trial of the century began in earnest on June 10. Public interest was so great that the proceedings, originally intended for the Italian equivalent of a magistrates court, were shifted to the main courtroom of Milan's Central Assizes, complete with the special iron barred cage along one side where defendants in major terrorist and Mafia trials of recent years had been housed. Financiers, however, were deemed less of a public menace. Calvi and his fellow defendants were permitted to sit without handcuffs, on ordinary benches.

On the second day Calvi gave evidence for the first time. Sitting sober-suited in front of the interrogating judges, he spoke quietly, often consulting a pile of documents on his lap. Drawing heavily on the material seized from Gelli's archives in Arezzo, the prosecution brought some astonishing episodes to light. One suggested that Calvi had attempted to shift responsibility for the suspect share dealings on to the frail shoulders of Canesi. Another showed how Anna Bonomi was perhaps a less redoubtable financier than she seemed. In 1976, she had even been forced to pawn jewels to Calvi, in return for an urgently needed loan of 2 billion lire. These, however, proved sidelights. For the judges were making plain their scepticism over Calvi's version of the Credito Varesino and Toro transactions. The politicians, on the other hand, were more sympathetic.

First the Socialist's newspaper *Avanti* claimed that the arrest of Calvi was just a facet of the "battle raging on the stock market": in other words that the charges were a mere contrivance, to unsettle further a market, which was by then already falling steeply. In mid-July, indeed, panic selling forced trading to be suspended for three days, the first such interruption since 1917.

Then in the midst of the trial, a legal expert of the party claimed that the judges had been deliberately picked for their bias against Calvi. The magistrates were using arrest warrants "like bludgeons", and their power should be reduced. Finally, even Craxi himself, the party leader, was to complain at the judiciary's "rash and intimidatory" use of its authority.

In a sense events would bear him out. For even the outwardly imperturbable Calvi, now shorn of the P-2, spurned by the Vatican, and harassed by the judges, was about to give way.

On the night of July 2, he summoned three of the most implacable magistrates investigating his dealings with Gelli, Sindona and the lodge, to tell them a strange tale; of how he had been persuaded to provide $21 million to the Banco Financeiro in Montevideo, owned by Ortolani of the P-2. The money, he had been led to understand, would be channelled back to the Socialists in Italy, to enable the party to reduce its embarrassingly high borrowings from Ambrosiano.

The episode remains obscure. Maybe it was a ploy of Ortolani to extort money from Calvi. The Socialists dismissed the incident, maintaining it only showed how magistrates who sympathized with the Communist party in Milan were using a vulnerable Calvi to discredit them—just when the Socialists had taken votes off the

Communists in disturbing quantities at that summer's local elections.

A week later Calvi gave further evidence of how his legendary composure was no more. On the morning of July 9, his lawyer Valerio Mazzola, made a dramatic announcement to the court. His client had attempted to commit suicide the previous night, by swallowing barbiturates and trying to open his wrists. It was, said Mazzola, the desperate gesture of a man "unjustly and unnecessarily" imprisoned, who could no longer reason normally.

Was the suicide attempt genuine? Some maintained that Calvi indeed had tried to take his own life, convinced that a much longer spell in prison awaited him, and that his position was now without hope. But, others asked, was it not rather a despairing ploy? Might not Calvi have staged both "confession" and suicide attempt, to win sympathy and make the most theatrical appeal possible to his political backers for more help? Calvi himself later described his action as one of "lucid desperation".

Whatever the explanation, the trial was close to its end. On July 20, after nine hours of deliberation, Roda Bogetti, the presiding judge, returned with her colleagues to deliver their verdict. It was more severe than even the prosecutors had demanded.

Calvi was deemed "capable of conduct without scruples", and sentenced to four years in jail and a fine of 16 billion lire. Tonello received a three-year term and an 8 million lire fine. Lesser punishment was meted out to Giorgio Cappugi, La Centrale's former general manager, and Giuseppe Zanon di Valgiurata, its deputy chairman. Everyone else was acquitted, including Carlo Bonomi and Giorgio Cigliana of Invest, both of whom had been allowed bail more than a month before. Bonomi himself maintained later that they had been arrested and tried only to strengthen the case against Calvi, the real target of the prosecutors.

But Calvi's own prison ordeal was ended. His lawyers lodged immediate appeal against the conviction, and he was set free on bail. Although he was obliged to surrender his passport, Calvi was able, astonishingly, to resume his financial career as if nothing had happened. A week after his release, the board of Banco Ambrosiano unanimously reconfirmed him, amid applause, as chairman of the bank. Fleetingly, divine providence did indeed appear to be protecting *Il banchiere di Dio*. The truth, however, was very different.

CHAPTER SIXTEEN

Letters of Patronage

FOR WHILE CALVI was enduring his private agony at Lodi, and sitting grimly through the court hearings in Milan, more than one scheme was elaborated to remove him either temporarily or permanently from his post at Ambrosiano. But for a variety of reasons they all failed.

In Rome, the authorities still lacked conclusive proof against him—and without it they dared not move. The political voices raised in Calvi's favour were an unpleasant reminder for the Bank of Italy of the vicious attack on itself only two years earlier. Meanwhile the web that Calvi had spun in his time of unchallenged command of his bank, as subtle and as strong as spider's silk, made him effectively indispensable. And of course the Vatican, the only outside shareholder which might have unseated him, found itself trapped in the very same web. These two considerations combined, with the inevitability of real tragedy, to ensure Calvi's survival as chairman of Banco Ambrosiano. The result was that a crisis which in 1981 might just have been containable had, within a year, turned into a banking collapse without equal since the Second World War.

The first move came from the Vatican, dismayed by Calvi's judicial tribulations, and by his links with the most disreputable face of freemasonry. The soundings seem to have begun that spring. The whispered candidate of the Holy See for Calvi's succession was Orazio Bagnasco, a driving Catholic financier aligned with the Christian Democrats. Bagnasco, a collector of paintings of the seventeenth-century school from his native Genoa, had built his fortune on a network of property-based mutual funds, headquartered in Lugano in Switzerland. Lately, moreover, he had bought the CIGA chain of luxury hotels, among them the Gritti Palace and the Danieli in Venice.

If Ambrosiano's Catholic and private traditions were to be maintained, Bagnasco was one of the very few obvious choices. Indeed, several months later he did become vice chairman and heir apparent at the bank. But the initial attempt was to no avail. First came the attempt on the Pope's life; and then a few weeks later the IOR learnt the full implications of what it had done in connivance with Calvi.

In July 1981, as foreign creditors started to pressure Ambrosiano, it was plain that the IOR connection was its only immediate lifeline. On instructions given by Calvi from prison, Leoni, as head of Ambrosiano's foreign department and chairman of Banco Andino, accompanied Pellegrino de Stroebel on one of his rare sorties from the offices of the Vatican bank. Their destination was Lugano, and the head office of the Banca del Gottardo.

There, from the files of the bank so intimately concerned with the early framing of Calvi's foreign design, the chief accountant of the IOR had confirmation of what he may or may not have suspected. Manic SA and United Trading Corporation, those two front companies set up under the Vatican bank so long before, had spawned their tiny offspring. Between them, these owed Ambrosiano's Latin American affiliates over $900 million. The main asset which secured these huge borrowings was a large block of shares in Banco Ambrosiano itself. Thus the IOR was the technical owner not just of its declared 1.6 per cent, but of at least a further 10.2 per cent of Calvi's bank as well. On paper, *it controlled Ambrosiano*; and to reverse Marcinkus' remark to Calvi's son Carlo, Ambrosiano's problems were the IOR's problems too.

But the Vatican was not alone in its alarm. Inevitably, with Calvi away *in pensione*, those left behind in Milan began to discover more of the rottenness behind the seemingly respectable façade.

Just who knew how much and when, about the bank's real plight, would be for the Italian courts to decide. But some within the bank were worried enough to cast around for an alternative to Calvi. One of these was Roberto Rosone. Like his chairman, Rosone had spent his entire career at Ambrosiano, but previously mostly on the more tranquil domestic banking side. Rosone was blunt, rough-spoken, of modest culture. For that reason many would laugh at him for his thick provincially-accented Italian, and for his lack of social polish. Others would describe him as someone deliberately promoted by Calvi beyond his natural station as manager of a small-town branch of Ambrosiano, in the belief that he would always be loyal and cause no problem. The fact remains, however, that Rosone mounted the most serious effort from within the bank to have Calvi step aside.

Rosone had been worried by the Rizzoli deal, and disconcerted by the arrogant behaviour of Pazienza, Calvi's self-styled "international consultant", during a visit to Ambrosiano while Calvi himself was in prison. He had also been taken aback by Marcinkus' brusqueness when he went to the Vatican at that time to warn the IOR that if there was a crisis of confidence, Ambrosiano would have to call in some loans it had made to the Vatican bank.

His idea was to replace Calvi at least temporarily, until the annual shareholders' meeting the following April. The best candidate, Rosone felt, would be the previous chairman Ruggiero Mozzana. Mozzana was 78 years old and in poor health, but eventually agreed to the suggestion. With his direct superior, Carlo Olgiati, Rosone took the plan to Rome and the Bank of Italy. But it was turned down, for reasons not entirely clear. One drawback, obviously was Mozzana's age. But the central bank would afterwards emphasize that it suggested to Calvi to step down in 1981—indeed that it had already studied the idea of placing Ambrosiano in the hands of a Government appointed commissioner. But, it concluded, it had no choice in the matter once Calvi, proclaiming his indispensability at his bank, and arguing that to go would be tantamount to an admission of guilt, had insisted on staying. Andreatta, the Treasury Minister was of a similar mind to the Bank of Italy; but was fearful that had drastic action been taken, Calvi would have gone to a local tribunal and secured his reinstatement.

Thus it was, to the considerable bewilderment of many, that a convicted illegal exporter of currency who faced a four-year jail sentence, was allowed back to the helm of the largest private banking group in the country. On strictly legal grounds, the Bank of Italy could justify its attitude. Perhaps the magistrates could have ordered Calvi's suspension (as they had done with Sarcinelli at the Bank of Italy itself in 1979!). The central bank could only send in a commissioner to take charge of Ambrosiano for one of three reasons; a) if "very serious irregularities" had been committed, b) if it had suffered very serious asset losses, or c) if the Ambrosiano board itself requested such a step. Conditions b) and c) did not then obtain, while the Bank of Italy did not *know* enough to justify the first grounds. The question remained: after the report on Ambrosiano in 1978, and now Calvi's conviction, did it not *suspect* enough to move against Ambrosiano?

In the acrimony of aftermath, the main criticism of the Bank of Italy was that it lacked the courage to back its judgement. As someone remarked later: "If you want the ermine and sceptre of high office, you've got to be prepared to use its authority too." But then again, the expressions of sympathy over Calvi's "victimization" from the Socialists and some Christian Democrats could have contained the seeds of a second political attack on the central bank.

As it was, the Bank of Italy had to deny publicly the boast of Calvi to his directors on July 28 that he had its specific blessing to resume as chairman. But the board meeting did sanction some significant changes. Olgiati, the co-author of the attempt from within the bank to replace Calvi, resigned as general manager. He was substituted by Rosone, who was named deputy chairman as well. Leoni became joint general manager, but Botta (nominally at least) took over his responsibilities on the foreign side. And although no word was given, both had resigned earlier from the board of Banco Andino in Lima, the obscure hub of everything. Clearly, those who knew were scared stiff.

August is Italy's traditional holiday month, when the country comes to a halt. It should have been a badly needed break for Calvi after his spell behind bars, and to an extent it was. With his wife, he departed for a few theoretically restful weeks in Sardinia. Pazienza, an appreciated friend after his services to the family while Calvi was in prison, was much in evidence. He visited the Calvis in their villa, and took them out on his launch. He also promoted a fateful encounter between Calvi and an associate from Pazienza's Roman dealings, a Sardinian businessman named Flavio Carboni.

That summer Carboni was the gay, self-indulgent host with a pronounced taste for the obvious trappings of success, like pretty girls and Lamborghini cars. The Calvis met him on his enormous yacht, teeming with well-connected guests—a junior Government Minister, an ambassador, and other assorted dignitaries. As Calvi would learn, Carboni's acquaintances ranged across the entire spectrum of Roman society, from eminent politicians to underworld gangsters. But that day in Sardinia, the two just chatted a little and then parted. The banker had to return to Milan and to Rome—for even in August his problems had not lain still.

That month saw the start of the endless nagging by the Bank of Italy which ultimately provoked his ruin. If the Bank could not mount a frontal assault, it would kill him with a thousand bureaucratic cuts. First it demanded full figures about Ambrosiano's overseas affiliates, and a list of all shareholders owning 10,000 shares or more. In August also it threw a huge spoke in his wheel by removing the voting rights of the shares in Rizzoli and the *Corriere*, which Calvi had bought the previous spring. He was forced at once to promise that he would sell the holding quickly, to comply with the new regulations.

Even more pressing was incipient rebellion in Peru. If most people at Ambrosiano's headquarters still retained their faith in Calvi, those who manned the telex machines across the Atlantic and in Latin America were under far fewer illusions by now. No-one was more anxious than the successor of Leoni at Banco Andino, Giorgio Nassano. His job consisted primarily of following coded instructions by telex to credit the resources of his bank to the likes of Astolfine, Belrosa and Bellatrix in Panama. That August Nassano flew to Italy to demand guarantees from Calvi that these companies were credit-worthy, for the $900 million they were borrowing to no obvious purpose.

The meeting was heated, but Calvi was hardly in a position to bargain. He was forced not only to lift the veil on the Vatican's secret ownership of the front companies in Panama who were consuming Banco Andino's substance, but to promise that the affair would be straightened out by mid-1982. At the end of August he went to the IOR. The time had come for the favours extended by Ambrosiano in the past to be returned.

As a half-empty city basked in the summer heat, and John Paul II convalesced at his summer residence of Castelgandolfo in the nearby Alban hills, Calvi worked out his arrangement with the IOR. And after what de Stroebel had discovered a few weeks earlier in Lugano, the Vatican bank had little choice in the matter, if it were to preserve what chance remained of averting another disaster, worse even than Sindona.

By the end of August an understanding was reached. The IOR would issue "letters of comfort" admitting ownership of the nominee companies in Panama and Luxembourg to which the money had been lent, but on two conditions. First, the admission would entail no liabilities for itself, and that the whole tangle would be resolved by June 1982. On August 27 Calvi wrote the formal letter to the IOR, requesting the letters of comfort. Its text then set out the wording of the letters of comfort, ending with a paragraph confirming that whatever happened, the Vatican bank would suffer "no future damage or loss". His letter was on notepaper of Ambrosiano Overseas in Nassau.

In return, the IOR provided two "letters of comfort". One was addressed to Banco Andino, the other to Ambrosiano Group Banco Commercial in Nicaragua, which had retained a small portion of the loans on its own books. The texts were identical. The IOR stated that it "directly or indirectly controls the following entries". Then came a list of the debtor companies. "We also confirm our awareness," the letters ended, "of their indebtedness towards yourselves as of June 10, 1981, as per the attached statements of accounts."

These accounts were simply bald lists of the assets and liabilities, but they were comprehensive proof of the straits in which Calvi now found himself. The accounts of the borrowers from Banco Andino, for instance, showed debts of $907 million, of which $852 million had been provided by the Peru bank, and $55 million directly from Milan. To secure those debts, there was the ten per cent shareholding in Banco Ambrosiano itself, plus smaller interests in other companies controlled by Ambrosiano and the IOR. All were said to be worth no less than $1,200 million, compared with a real value of perhaps $350 million at best. The difference was the measure of Calvi's fraud, and the extent to which the value of the shares used as collateral had been pumped up to keep the demented system going.

The deed was done. It mattered little that letters of comfort notoriously have no legal value throughout the banking world, least of all ones which speak merely of "awareness" of debts. The directors in Nicaragua and Peru, and at the Luxembourg Services company where the letters were stored, could breathe more easily, half comforted at least that the Universal Church, in the fullness of its wisdom and authority, was the guarantor of their loans; in any case, they also had Calvi's assurance that within a few months the debts would be much reduced, if not repaid.

But Calvi gained little peace of mind, only time. On sober review his position must have appeared increasingly hopeless. His mood would oscillate erratically between brief moments of euphoria when he could convince himself that salvation was possible, and longer periods of disillusion and gloom.

For some while yet, the foreboding would only very rarely show through. Mostly he succeeded, as always in the past, in masking his feelings behind the distant, impassive façade. The inability to make a point clearly, the capacity to erect pyramids of lies in the face of hostile questioning, were unchanged. Some did claim that the tic on the left side of his mouth, beneath the thin moustache, would become more pronounced under pressure. But until the end, his self-control was remarkable.

The safety valve became his family, especially his wife and daughter in Milan to whom he would confide his darkest fears and suspicions. To them, Calvi would remain a victim of the jealousy and spite of others, blackmailed and exploited as no other in Italy. And they were largely correct. For if Calvi's troubles were self-inflicted, they were now so numerous that he could no longer hope to control events.

In that autumn of 1981 the aura of power and mystery which so long had protected him was dissolving. He had been sentenced to four years in prison, he had no passport. The discovery of the P-2 had contributed to a plethora of judicial investigations, frequently involving himself. The Bank of Italy was on his heels, so was a newly aggressive stock market authority. Now that Gelli was a fugitive in Latin America, Calvi was having to handle directly the politicians. And for all his faith in the powers they offered, Calvi never learnt to deal easily with them. New intermediaries stepped in like Pazienza and Carboni, whom Calvi believed was a substitute to Gelli as a duct to the hidden powers of freemasonry. There was also Giuseppe Ciarrapico, a publisher connected with Andreotti of the Christian

Democrats. Even the once sacred weekends in the country at Drezzo were made over to meetings and consultations.

Everyone wanted money, in return for an advantageous word here, an intercession with a threatening magistrate there. Calvi would pay scandal sheets thousands of pounds monthly to keep silent. Gelli, whose enforced absence from Italy had made him no less importuning, was a particularly unwelcome caller. He would ring the villa at Drezzo, on a private line whose number was known only to himself, Ortolani and a few others, identifying himself as "Luciani".

Now the Vatican could no longer be regarded as an ally. The letters of comfort were almost the last indulgence dispensed. On October 26, 1981 the Vatican sent more letters to Lima and Managua, providing new figures and confirming that it would not dispose of the little Panamanian companies "without your prior written approval". In other words, Calvi was being told that he, and not the IOR, should unscramble the mess that he had created. Ambrosiano's "Vatican connection" had turned from blessing into curse.

Then there was the pressure upon him to resolve the relationship between La Centrale and Rizzoli. After the Bank of Italy's strong words of August, Calvi had no option but to sell his interest in the publishing group. But any solution would require political backing as well. And so jealously watched was the *Corriere* that any settlement risked winning him as many enemies as friends among the parties and their factions. In the meantime the entire 176 billion lire investment in Rizzoli was becoming an unimagined burden. The Bank of Italy was also pulling the bureaucratic levers to prevent La Centrale winning approval for a long-requested capital increase, to offset the cost of buying 40 per cent of Rizzoli. As a result additional debts were steadily accumulating.

His dilemma was only underlined by the waspish discussions taking place over the future of the *Corriere*. Now that Calvi's shareholding had been neutralized by the Bank of Italy's removal of its voting rights, Angelo Rizzoli and above all Tassan Din had a freer hand to do as they pleased. Their plan was to sell the newspaper to a group of Northern businessmen not noted for any special sympathies with the parties in Rome. One of them was Carlo De Benedetti, the chief executive of the Olivetti office equipment company; another was Bruno Visentini, a pillar of Italy's "lay" establishment, and anxious to replace the prevailing warfare between the political clans by a form of non-party Government.

But as the agreement neared conclusion, the Socialists in Rome— among the most ruthless of the clans—stepped in to veto it, threatening to bring down the Government and put the tax police on to De Benedetti and Visentini if the deal was completed. Mindful perhaps of the fate of the Bank of Italy in 1979, they withdrew. Shortly afterwards a Socialist-inspired attempt to buy the newspaper also failed. Calvi, as he had to, remained on the sidelines all the while. "The *Corriere* was the root of all my difficulties," he would confess later, forgetting for a moment the huge debts on the other side of the world. But in autumn 1981, it was easy to understand his feelings.

The jousting over the *Corriere* was, however, to prove only the opening skirmish of that period. For within a few weeks, financial and political Italy was to be astounded by a separate announcement—that De Benedetti was paying 50 billion lire for two per cent of Banco Ambrosiano, and would become vice-chairman himself.

CHAPTER SEVENTEEN

The Man from Olivetti

MEASURED IN TERMS of days, the union between Roberto Calvi and Carlo De Benedetti was brief. It lasted precisely 65 days, from November 19, 1981 to break-up and De Benedetti's complete withdrawal the following January 22. Nonetheless it is peculiarly revealing, a single snapshot embracing opposite shores of Italian life, and illuminating Calvi at a vital moment. For the deal with De Benedetti marked the banker's last serious effort to win back respect and respectability.

Onlookers had every reason to be surprised by the marriage, for the two partners could hardly have been less compatible. Calvi was more secretive and suspicious than ever, hateful of publicity and frequently ill at ease on social occasions, the most private of Catholic financiers. De Benedetti epitomized the modern, aggressive face of Italian industry, known and admired abroad, and with a natural gift of self-projection. He is glossy and charming; and certainly not "Catholic", coming from an old Piedmontese Jewish family. In 1978, the year Calvi was subjected to the Bank of Italy inspection, De Benedetti was voted Italy's manager of the year for his success in revitalizing the staid and slumbering Olivetti.

So what on earth were they doing together? Enrico Cuccia, the wise old man of Mediobanca, observed to De Benedetti: "I don't think you'll last six months with Calvi. Either you'll have him out in a week, or you'll withdraw. One of you has made a great mistake." In the first aftermath it seemed as if the man from Olivetti had erred; in fact those two tumultuous months probably harmed Calvi much more.

The first contacts occurred in October. De Benedetti wanted to place some bonds of Olivetti and CIR, a holding company he controlled, with Ambrosiano. His representative, Francesco De Micheli, went to see Calvi about the proposal, but came back with intriguing news. Yes, there would be no problem about placing the bonds, but Calvi wished to see De Benedetti personally, about something else. An appointment was made, and the two met in Calvi's office at Ambrosiano. The banker as usual spoke around the issue, crafty and evasive. First he offered a seat on La Centrale's board, but De Benedetti demurred. Then, suddenly, he came to the point.

Despite the conviction, Calvi insisted he was innocent. But he was tired: "I've had enough; there's no point my staying if the politicians, the Bank of Italy and the press are all against me," Calvi said. He wanted to hand over a healthy Ambrosiano, one which he had built into the biggest private bank in Italy. Would De Benedetti buy into Ambrosiano and become deputy chairman, with the understanding that he would take full charge after six months, once the appeal had been upheld?

De Benedetti went away to mull over the proposal. The challenge and the potential rewards were tempting; many believed that he was losing interest in Olivetti, and superficially Ambrosiano still seemed a sound investment. The drawback lay in having to work alongside Calvi for a certain period, for the two instinctively were rivals, temperamentally as different as could be. Eventually De Benedetti concluded that the prize was worth the risk, and terms were agreed. He would pay 50 billion lire for a million shares in the bank. With two per cent of its capital, he would be Ambrosiano's largest single declared Italian shareholder.

Andreatta, the Treasury Minister, upon learning with no small surprise of the deal, remarked laconically that "the ways of capitalism are strange". Ciampi at the Bank of Italy was more enthusiastic. De Benedetti with his entrepreneurial drive and above-board methods might succeed where the central bank had long failed, in throwing light on the hidden foreign parts of Ambrosiano. Ciampi still felt the bank was safe—as the success of that summer's 240 billion lire capital-raising operation seemed to confirm. If De Benedetti wanted to empire-build, then the central bank would not stand in his way.

The public announcement of the deal came as a bombshell. Calvi's motives were obvious enough: the arrival of De Benedetti, after the

Agnellis of Fiat, Italy's best-known businessman, would give sorely needed lustre to Ambrosiano's image at home and abroad. It might even encourage foreign banks to resume lending to the bank—and thus permit the still secret overseas edifice to be shored up. But De Benedetti? What was he about? Was he planning to abandon Olivetti, or was he seeking backdoor control of the *Corriere*? Some of Milan's wiser bankers and brokers were privately dismayed. Too much smoke had swirled around Ambrosiano for there to be no fire; De Benedetti was risking his reputation, they felt—perhaps more besides. One thing was certain: that he would be no sleeping partner and sooner more probably than later the two would be at loggerheads. After just three days that judgement was to be vindicated.

On Saturday, November 21, De Benedetti arrived at Calvi's Drezzo home for a pre-arranged working lunch. He saw at once that his host had been transformed. Calvi seemed to him like a frightened animal, searching to escape the light. Clearly someone or something had warned him off the association with De Benedetti. Calvi nervously told his new deputy chairman that he would have to wait before becoming operational, international reaction would have to be gauged. "What international reaction?" enquired De Benedetti, somewhat mystified. "International financial reaction," Calvi answered.

"But there's no problem there," De Benedetti assured him, referring to an article in the *Financial Times* which pointed out that his entry could only improve Ambrosiano's reputation. No, it wasn't just *financial* reaction, Calvi said guardedly. Were there political problems then? No, came the reply, there were other reasons, "factors of international consensus".

At that stage De Benedetti thought the Mafia, or the P-2, were involved. In any case there was little point continuing there and then, so a new meeting was arranged for the following week. In the meantime De Benedetti asked for an office at Ambrosiano, a secretary, together with annual reports and balance sheets of the bank and its various affiliates. None of these requests was granted: indeed, an Italian journalist who rang Ambrosiano asking for De Benedetti was told that no-one of that name was employed by the bank.

As De Benedetti was to put it in a seven-page letter to Calvi on

December 13 setting out his complaints, he encountered "a wall of rubber" everywhere he turned. Every demand for information was either fobbed off or ignored. The initial understanding was not being maintained, and Calvi seemed personally to be doing his utmost to minimize the importance of the deal. Particularly objectionable, De Benedetti wrote, had been an "incredible" public statement by Pazienza, speaking in the name of the bank itself, and intimating that the secret services could be useful in clinching business deals.

Quite clearly the P-2 and whatever other forces were manipulating Calvi (again, he told De Benedetti his political patrons were Andreotti, Piccoli and Craxi) were signalling that De Benedetti's presence within Ambrosiano was intolerable. As the events of November 21 showed, Calvi too had been told unequivocally that he had made a mistake, and a grave one.

De Benedetti once asked Calvi about his relations with Gelli. The reply was that the two had not seen each other for ages, although Calvi understood that in hiding the P-2 grandmaster had undergone facial plastic surgery, to avoid identification and enable him to return to Italy. In fact Gelli was in frequent contact with the banker, directly and through the intermediary of Tassan Din at Rizzoli.

But De Benedetti too was made quickly aware of the shadowy presence of the lodge. Just before his first Ambrosiano board meeting on December 6, Calvi took him on one side in the corridor. "You be careful," he said, "the P-2 is preparing a dossier on you." But there was no material, De Benedetti protested, he had never had anything to do with the lodge (indeed established private industry in Northern Italy was one of the few areas of national life uncontaminated by the P-2). But Calvi insisted: "I just advise you to take care, because I know."

As the new deputy chairman persisted in his efforts to do his job properly, the warnings became cruder. Someone giving the name of "Ortolani" made several vaguely menacing calls to De Benedetti's home in Geneva, where his family lived. Then at Olivetti's headquarters at Ivrea he received a letter postmarked in Geneva setting out physical threats against himself and his children. In the style of the Mafia, the latter were referred to as "little jewels".

Thereafter, his relations with Calvi steadily worsened. De Benedetti sent Calvi letter after letter complaining of his treatment, and took to insisting that his objections be recorded in the official minutes of executive committee meetings. And as information was withheld, De Benedetti's suspicions about Ambrosiano grew. For if Calvi was behaving so strangely, then he must have something serious to hide, quite distinct from the P-2.

Two other worrying signals reached De Benedetti. First, he read the 1978 Bank of Italy report which had foreseen the causes of Ambrosiano's future downfall. It was three years old, but the complaints of Padalino and his fellow inspectors about Calvi's refusal to supply information might have been his own. Second, the first real word was emerging about massive problems at Banco Andino.

That Christmas Angelo Rizzoli told De Benedetti that the Peru bank could be facing potential losses of $600 million. Later Rizzoli was to say that he had first got wind of the danger from Rosone, who since Calvi's imprisonment the previous May had been thrust into contact with the bank's most delicate affairs. But long before that Gelli himself had told Rizzoli that Banco Andino was engaged in some "extremely risky" ventures. Almost certainly, knowledge of the Achilles heel of Calvi in Latin America was one of Gelli's most potent weapons to blackmail the banker.

In any case De Benedetti was alarmed enough to send Olivetti's chief representative in Venezuela, Paolo Venturini, down to Lima to take a first hand look. His telex back flatly contradicted the bland assurances of Calvi that Andino was a thriving and active bank. Rather, reported Venturini, it wasn't a bank at all, but a specially authorized financial company dealing exclusively in foreign business. The offices were the top four floors of a new office block, but none of its employees seemed to be doing anything.

De Benedetti became genuinely scared. He finally secured a balance sheet of Banco Andino, showing that its loan portfolio had jumped from nothing to $800 million in just twelve months—but with no explanation of how so remarkable an increase had been achieved in the unremarkable Latin American economy of the time, or of what the money was being used for. De Benedetti raised the matter with Calvi. But the chairman gave the familiar assurance: "Don't worry, it's all in the hands of the *sottane nere*." ("The black cassocks", i.e. the Vatican.) "The guarantees are fine."

There was to be no more time for De Benedetti to discover that these "guarantees" were merely the worthless letters of comfort, grudgingly issued by the IOR a few months earlier. For Calvi had decided that this inquisitive, forceful deputy chairman, who seemed the incarnation of both the Consob and the Bank of Italy inside his very boardroom, had to be ejected, and fast.

On January 12, De Benedetti sought to penetrate the ultimate sanctuary, by demanding immediate details of just how the "approval" required for the foreign shareholders was granted, and a copy of the register of shareholders as well as the 1978 report by the Bank of Italy. Three days later he was brusquely informed that he would not be approved as deputy chairman that spring at the annual meeting (further proof, incidentally, of how Calvi controlled Ambrosiano).

After some hasty haggling, terms were agreed. De Benedetti would sell back his shares for the price he paid for them, plus interest and the placement of 27 billion lire of shares in the portfolio of one of his companies. On January 22 the formal announcement of his departure was made, to no-one's great surprise; rumours of profound divisions between them had been rife for a fortnight. Four days later the long-aspiring Orazio Bagnasco was co-opted on to Ambrosiano's board as the new deputy chairman alongside Rosone, after paying an identical price to De Benedetti for a similar two per cent shareholding.

So what can one make of this brief, tumultuous marriage between "lay" and Catholic finance? De Benedetti was criticized subsequently for his behaviour, chiefly on the grounds that he managed to leave with a profit a ship that was to sink with all hands only five months later. To which he retorted that the circumstances of his departure should have been warning, clear enough for those with eyes to see, of the perilous state of Ambrosiano. His own feeling that January 22 was of disaster narrowly avoided. His mistake, he later admitted, was to have been tempted by Calvi in the first place. The same day De Benedetti wrote at length to Ciampi at the Bank of Italy, explaining his decision and the way in which he had been prevented from doing his job at all.

The entire episode only added to Ciampi's apprehensions about Ambrosiano; once again the authorities wondered whether to place the bank in the hands of commissioners, but decided against it. Might not De Benedetti simply have lost an ill-judged powerplay? Instead the central bank multiplied its demands for information, and its insistence that the Rizzoli shareholding be sold.

The harassed Calvi was also under simultaneous attack from Rossi. After waiting in vain on January 19 for Calvi to attend a scheduled meeting to discuss Ambrosiano's bourse quotation, the Consob chairman in his exasperation began the procedure for having Ambrosiano listed in any event. Calvi was horrified, but there was little to be done. A week later, just after the appointment of Bagnasco, he capitulated. On January 28 he travelled to Consob's headquarters in Rome to seal the surrender. Ambrosiano would be quoted as soon as possible on the main market, and the longstanding "clause of approval" for new shareholders would be abolished. In due course the first public list ever of Ambrosiano's main shareholders would also be disclosed.

Whatever judgement is made about Calvi, his life at this time must have been agony. Previous "friends" at the Vatican and the Roman political world were deserting him; at best indifferent, at worst openly manoeuvring to replace him. The pressures of the Bank of Italy, the nagging of the Consob, the pestering of Gelli, Pazienza and the like, the multiplying judicial investigations by magistrates in Milan and Rome, all had to be juggled into some kind of order. Everyone wanted money, promising protection that proved wanting, or solutions to the financial problems that were straws which snapped at the clutching. In the background loomed the appeal, the possibility it might fail, followed by the certainty of four years in a prison perhaps even less accommodating than Lodi.

The liaison with De Benedetti stands out because it was a choice made by Calvi alone, as the pressure upon him to reverse it demonstrates. Did Calvi imagine that he could use De Benedetti briefly and then discard him; that the presence of De Benedetti would somehow placate his enemies in the "lay" establishment, on the left and in the Milan magistrature which he had convinced himself was an instrument of the Communist Party? Or was it one genuine moment of sincerity, when Calvi in his contorted way sought to convey that he wanted to have done with everything, and save the bank he had created from a disaster he knew could not be far away? We shall never know. But if such a moment existed, it was short-lived. For Calvi, as that November day in Drezzo showed, was no longer in command. The pattern was not to change with the arrival of Bagnasco.

CHAPTER EIGHTEEN

Last Illusions

CARLO DE BENEDETTI's departure, though rued by some within Ambrosiano, marked the speedy return of the bank to its appointed place within Italy's political firmament. Orazio Bagnasco was on excellent terms with Giulio Andreotti—the Christian Democrat most expert in the ways of the Church, and the politician whom Calvi held most in awe, even fear. Also, Bagnasco himself was well regarded by the Vatican ("Yes, I know some cardinals and bishops," he once coyly told an interviewer). There was small doubt that he was the chosen successor to the ever more compromised Calvi when he entered Banco Ambrosiano that January 26; Calvi was aware of all this, of course, but he was too weak to put up much opposition.

The ground for the agreement had been carefully prepared. Ever since mid-December, when the improbable partnership with De Benedetti was beginning to fray, Bagnasco had been buying Ambrosiano shares. Terms were settled at one of those weekends at Drezzo, where occasionally Ciarrapico, the publisher whom Calvi now knew, would also be in attendance. Calvi confided to his family that he was unhappy about Bagnasco; and as he left the house on the morning of January 26, he told his daughter that he hoped Ambrosiano's board would not approve the appointment.

In the event, the other directors unanimously endorsed Bagnasco as De Benedetti's replacement. The first stirrings of collective unease by the long submissive board—or merely another example of how Calvi would dispense different truths to different people, including his family? In any case, as he complained back at home that evening, Ambrosiano had become a sort of tramcar, which people got on and off as they pleased. Bagnasco was to ride the tram until the bitter end. Voices, however, were being raised in contrasting places, but with identical urgency, that its driver be changed at once.

A public complaint by De Benedetti on how Calvi had prevented him from carrying out his statutory duties as a director prompted Gustavo Minervini and Luigi Spaventa, two respected deputies from the independent Left, to table a question in Parliament, asking the Bank of Italy to dissolve Ambrosiano's board and send in special commissioners. Given that both had been elected under Communist sponsorship, that might have been construed as politicking. But on March 19 they were to table another question, after a second public tirade by De Benedetti, this time concerning Banco Andino and those inexplicably large loans it had extended.

Did the Bank of Italy have the necessary details about Andino, the two deputies asked? God forbid, they added, that another Sindona affair was in the offing. With timing either sinister or ludicrous, a bland written answer, implying that nothing was critically amiss, arrived from the Treasury Ministry three months later, just as Calvi was packing his bags for flight.

But different worries were surfacing in an almost opposite quarter. A group of small Milanese shareholders in Ambrosiano, all devout Catholics, wrote to the Pope himself protesting at how the bank, for all its vaunted links with Church and IOR, had strayed from the ideals of its founders'. Calvi, they stated, "was the point where Sindona's Mafia legacy and degenerate freemasonry met". The IOR either could remain Calvi's "accomplice", and lay itself open to a new scandal that would last a decade; or it could work with other shareholders for change, by selecting a prestigious outsider to take over as chairman. Rosone, of course, had already had a similar idea, with the unsuccessful effort to bring back Mozzana. Whether the Pope, or anyone else in a position to act within the Vatican, ever read the letter is not known. In any case, it would have been too little, too late; for the Bank of Italy was now closing inexorably upon the truth.

For a man as jealously uncommunicative as Calvi, convinced that every shred of truth revealed was a weapon to be turned against him, the months between February and April of 1982 must have been the purest torture.

One by one, Ambrosiano's secrets were prised from its recesses by inquisition of the central bank. Calvi hoped he had bought at least time, by consenting against his every judgement to a full stock market quotation for Banco Ambrosiano. This would automatically have entailed fully consolidated accounts, *including* the foreign subsidiaries, from 1983. Surely that would satisfy the authorities. But no. Hardly a week went by without the central bank demanding more information. Calvi knew that in months, at best, the terrible flaw in Latin America would be surmised, if not conclusively proved—unless, of course, the debts could be repaid, or transferred on to stronger shoulders than those of the IOR.

Various reasons underlay this offensive by the Bank of Italy. One was the disturbing exit of Carlo De Benedetti, who had written to Ciampi insisting that something had to be done about Ambrosiano. The second was the announcement at the end of January that Ambrosiano Overseas planned to merge with Artoc, and create a single Bahamas bank with deposits of $1,000 million.

De Benedetti's going was one more pointer to advancing putrefaction, while the proposed arrangement with Artoc looked suspiciously like another attempt to avoid the Bank's scrutiny, by expediting an important foreign affiliate into a convenient Arab refuge. On February 5, Calvi was summoned to the central bank in Rome to provide details of his foreign dealings in general, and of the Artoc scheme in particular. His elusive and non-committal answers exhausted Ciampi's patience. Eleven days later he received a bluntly worded letter from the Bank of Italy's Milan office. It demanded comprehensive information on every aspect of Ambrosian's foreign activities; it insisted, moreover, that the matter be submitted to a board meeting, at which every director should confirm that he was being told enough to do his job properly. A copy of the minutes was then to be sent to the Bank of Italy.

The board duly met. One Ambrosiano director, Giuseppe Prisco, head of Milan's bar association, was so angry that he formally tabled comment on the central bank's request as "inopportune, and offensive for individual directors". His colleagues unanimously agreed—but they had no choice but to comply. Finally, the Bank of Italy was showing its real teeth.

Nor had Ciampi's humour been improved by the treatment meted out to two inspectors he had sent informally to Lima, to try and glean some facts about the mysterious Andino. The pair were treated with disdain by the Peruvian authorities, and subjected to a menacing

165

search by frontier police at the airport as they returned to Italy. In the event, though, the setback hardly mattered.

One by one, the veils were being removed in Milan. With as good grace as could be mustered, the *direzione centrale* of Ambrosiano provided first a breakdown of the balance sheet of the Luxembourg holding company, then those of the subsidiaries in Nassau, Nicaragua and Peru. Every number was a tiny stone, with which to reconstruct the financial mosaic Calvi had created across half the world. The Bank of Italy's appetite was insatiable. Once an answer from Ambrosiano even crossed in the post with a new set of demands.

At last, on March 31, the requests halted, but not before the central bank had vetoed the proposed merger with Artoc in Nassau. The last thing it wanted was for Calvi to be able to use the humours of the Arabs, on whose oil Italy heavily relied, as a bargaining counter in his dealings with the authorities in Italy.

Then Calvi dangled before his tormentors a scheme to reorganize his Italian holdings, to overcome the long-standing objection that Ambrosiano's structure was in breach of local banking laws. Instead of it owning the financial company La Centrale, the roles would be reversed. But, he pleaded, the scheme was complex and required time. Time, unfortunately, the Central Bank was no longer prepared to grant.

In the midst of these exchanges with the Bank of Italy, a new passenger climbed aboard the tramcar—though if truth be told, he had been dragged along in its wake for several years. He was Carlo Pesenti, whose own indebted Italmobiliare group was supported in part by large borrowings from Ambrosiano and its various Italian banks, secured by large blocks of shares in companies controlled by Pesenti. At first his arrival seemed to presage the formation of a single Catholic-orientated financial leviathan, adding the banks and insurance companies owned by Pesenti to Ambrosiano's own.

In fact, two enfeebled creatures were clinging together in their hour of trial. Like Calvi, Pesenti was under investigation for certain of his past dealings. Most notable of them was a curious 50 billion lire loan granted to Pesenti in 1972—apparently by the IOR—and indexed to the Swiss franc. The latter's appreciation meant that the sum eventually reimbursed was 185 billion lire. A decade after that loan was signed, magistrates in Milan were still unsure whether the Vatican bank had excogitated a brilliant deal, or whether it had acted as a "fiduciary" once more, this time for an irregular capital export by Pesenti.

On March 10, Ambrosiano announced that Pesenti had joined its board, and that Italmobiliare had become the bank's largest shareholder, with 3.62 per cent of its capital. His advent served a variety of purposes. The million shares sold by De Benedetti would be absorbed neatly, without risk to the market price of Banco Ambrosiano, while a brush of respectability would be given to the list of main shareholders which would have to be contained in the obligatory public prospectus accompanying its listing on the main market. If the Cascadillas and Orfeos in Panama would be displayed in their dubious splendour for the first time, at least the biggest shareholder of Ambrosiano could be demonstrated to be Italian. What was not announced was that Calvi's bank had underwritten a loan for 100 billion lire, with which Pesenti could buy its shares.

The average price he paid, of just under 55,000 lire per share, put a theoretical market valuation on Ambrosiano of almost 2,750 billion lire, or $2,100 million. On paper, Calvi's shaky edifice was now worth more than Chase Manhattan bank—reassurance of a kind before what promised to be a less than usually deferential annual meeting, due on April 17, 1982. For friendly stockbrokers had reported to him that small Catholic shareholders, alarmed by the unceasing bad publicity Calvi was attracting, were selling out. This most unwelcome development was being absorbed and concealed, thanks to the arrival of Pesenti and huge, quite illegal, buying of Ambrosiano shares by the bank's own securities department. But Calvi was nervous of the shareholders' meeting, although he did manage to win postponement of a potentially embarrassing magistrates hearing scheduled for two days before, thus reducing the danger of still more harmful press comment.

In the event, his fears were only partly borne out. A record total of 472 shareholders attended. The little Panamanian and Liechtenstein companies as usual had given their proxies to the chairman, so that he could boast that 43 per cent of the bank's capital was represented. Many doubts were removed by the 1981 results. They were almost the last of Calvi's feats of illusion. Profits had tripled to 43 billion lire, while Banco Ambrosiano's net assets had more than doubled—thanks to the substantial capital increase of the year before (carried out while the chairman was in prison!). Total assets, meanwhile, of the group, including Credito Varesino and Banca Cattolica del Veneto, reached almost $20 billion. The dividend, the last the bank would ever pay its trusting shareholders, rose by 60 lire to 420 lire. And if he was accused of running Ambrosiano too autocratically, then that too, Calvi could claim, was changing. An executive committee was being established, so that important decisions would be taken on a more collegial basis. The intended message was plain: that Ambrosiano's 38,000 shareholders need have no worries. One did however, and most unusually he said so.

Already some eyebrows had been raised by the apparent boycott of the meeting by two Catholic shareholders, the Fabbrica del Duomo, responsible for the upkeep of Milan Cathedral, and Banca San Paolo di Brescia, founded by the same Monsignor Tovini who had established Ambrosiano in 1896. Why, asked one Giuseppe Nicora, were Christian tenets of Tovini being ignored by the present management? Nicora, who held 1,300 shares which had a market value of 65 million lire and probably represented the bulk of his savings, described himself as a typical small shareholder from Lombardy. But he was worried at how Ambrosiano had become a "machine for speculation". And, he warned, there were many others like him, who would show their disapproval at what was happening, "irretrievably different" from what Tovini had intended.

The assembly passed off without further ado. As usual Calvi paid no reference in his closing speech to Nicora's anxious questioning, other than to observe that Ambrosiano had to move with the times. "The facts are in the balance sheet, all the rest is gossip," another, more typical shareholder, proclaimed, and the 1981 accounts were overwhelmingly approved.

But the protest had been noted elsewhere. A few days afterwards Marcinkus gave a rare interview to the Italian press, to declare that beyond doubt, Calvi was "worthy of the IOR's confidence", and that contrary to rumour, the Vatican bank had no intention of reducing its shareholding—then still assumed to be the 1.6 per cent which would appear in the market prospectus on May 1. Marcinkus, in the first of the famous last words which would pepper the last weeks of Ambrosiano's life, said the IOR placed its money where they gave the best return, and that Ambrosiano had been "an excellent investment".

On balance, though, all had gone reasonably well. One newspaper described Calvi's performance at the meeting as "unusually pugnacious". The annual report also contained slightly more information than usual—including the somewhat perplexing revelation that during 1981 Ambrosiano had extended two large credits, for $71 million and $60 million respectively, to its Nicaraguan and Peruvian subsidiaries. He did not elaborate: nor could he. For those two loans were the first and only admission of the process which in less than two months would bring ruin..But announcement of the choice of Coopers and Lybrand to draw up consolidated accounts from 1983 on set the minds of the unsuspecting at rest.

An outward façade of normality still for the most part prevailed, even if Calvi seemed weary, and naturally concerned about his problems with the judiciary, and the appeal now set for late June. But sometimes the mask would slip. On May 15, he ran into Nerio Nesi, chairman of Banca Nazionale del Lavoro, at Ciampino airport, as he made his way back to Milan after yet another sortie to Rome to shore up his collapsing defences. Nesi was off to Egypt, to open BNL's new office in Cairo. "Everyone's exploiting me, it's too much to bear," Calvi told Nesi. He seemed crushed, half-destroyed.

Another such moment had come a few days earlier in Milan, as trading opened on the full market in Banco Ambrosiano shares. Calvi, obviously, had to attend. He wandered morosely down to the *corbeille*, or main ring on the trading floor, where the dealers shouted and gesticulated their transactions. His face pale and expressionless, he watched the price slide downwards: from 50,000 to 45,500 lire at the first call, then to 40,000 lire at the close. Despite friendly support buying arranged in advance, the value of the main asset underpinning the Panamanian folly had fallen twenty per cent in a single day.

Later on there was the routine cocktail party to mark a supposedly happy occasion. Calvi greeted Isidoro Albertini, one of Milan's leading stock brokers, who had known him vaguely since the Bocconi days. Sipping at a fruit juice, Calvi avoided conversation about

169

Ambrosiano, limiting himself to reminiscences about the Russian campaign. He was fatalistic and dejected—for reasons only too obvious.

The importunings of the central bank and the attentions of the magistrates (concerning Sindona, the P-2, and the Genghini affair, to name but three of the most serious) were only two of the vicious interlocking pressures upon him. None had ever shared his power, and now none, beyond his family, could share his ordeal.

To his wife and daughter, Calvi would confide his darkest forebodings. But often pure fantasy must have offered the only release from the stress to which he was subjected. For Calvi the line between truth and fiction was always blurred, but probably never more so than now. The belief that he was being persecuted became an obsession, coloured by deepening fears over his physical safety. He took to carrying to work in his briefcase the pistol he kept in a drawer at Drezzo. Outside his family he was virtually friendless. The calibre of those to whom he turned for help, Pazienza and the flashy Carboni, the courtier with underworld connections, was the measure of the isolation of a man until recently reputed to have been among the most powerful in Italy. The politicians were bothered only insofar as the fate of the *Corriere* was concerned, or a claim might be staked at Ambrosiano itself when Calvi had been forced aside.

But the central difficulty remained financial; and no amount of juggling of money from one corner of his realm to another could plug the leaks opening up from Panama to Luxembourg, as the Bank of Italy peeled away one layer of secrecy after another, and foreign banks remained cold. The IOR would grant no more than the letters of patronage, and the promised deadline of June 30 was approaching. He would describe to his family the unavailing entreaties in the Vatican. "The priests will be our ruin," he told his daughter Anna after one fruitless visit there. "They believe that even if a person dies his soul will survive, so there's no great harm done." The entreaties, moreover, would sometimes be mixed with threats to reveal all, but with equal lack of success.

The foreign banks, on the other hand, were taking less of a long-term view. To fill the gaps left by their defections, Calvi and his two lieutenants, Botta and Leoni, were being forced to siphon money directly out of Milan to the increasingly stretched foreign subsidiaries, irrespective of what the Bank of Italy might say.

A first clue had come in the 1981 report, those $131 million despatched to Lima and Managua. Hundreds of millions of dollars more would be transferred in this fashion in 1982, as the end approached. But in the closing months a further $230 million left Milan less obviously to the same destinations. The device, to cause no little controversy afterwards, was that of "back to back" deposits. Ambrosiano in Milan would borrow money on international markets and deposit the funds with a compliant foreign bank. By prior agreement this bank would lend on an equivalent sum to Peru or Nicaragua, charging a slightly higher rate of interest than it was paying Ambrosiano in Milan, to ensure a profit on the operation. But in the monthly accounts Ambrosiano (like any Italian bank) had to submit to the Bank of Italy, such an ebb of resources down the bottomless wells of Lima and Managua would appear as innocuous interbank deposits.

The foreign bank intermediaries would insist on another point too: they would not repay Ambrosiano until they had first been repaid by the foreign affiliates. Thus the device of the "back-to-back" deposit, not unexceptional in itself, ensured that subsequent default in Luxembourg, Lima and Managua would fatally involve the Milan parent—just as the Bank of Italy's inspectors had feared in the case of Nassau, and set out in their report of four years earlier.

But Calvi knew that even this expedient could not last long. If his affairs were to be unscrambled, only two options, however remote, were left. Either the Banco Ambrosiano and other shares held by the Panamanian companies could be sold for a high enough price for the latter to be able to repay their debts; or he could find a more accommodating partner than the IOR under its present management. For the first task, it seems, he employed Pazienza, for the second his new Sardinian friend Carboni.

There remains only Pazienza's word to gauge how nearly he succeeded. He has said he almost managed to sell one IOR asset held in Panama, by the picturesquely named Laramie Inc. This was a block of two million shares in Vianini, a thriving construction company in Rome, controlled by the Vatican. According to Pazienza, an American group was ready to buy Vianini for $60 million, but the deal never materialized.

171

But if the circle was to be squared, the 5.2 million shares in Banco Ambrosiano itself deposited in guarantee, had to be disposed of a around $200 apiece, compared to a Milan stock market peak o around $40. The only way such a difference could ever be justified was if this ten per cent holding gave control not only of the bank, bu of all its valuable Italian interests as well. And in a sense, of course they did.

Pazienza asked his associate Robert Armao, closely linked to the Chase Manhattan bank and representative in the US of the assets o the Pahlevis, the deposed Iranian royal family, to have Ambrosiano evaluated. The study, carried out by a "foreign affiliate of Chase" was presented on December 9, 1981. It spoke in glowing terms o Calvi's bank, as a first rate investment. A consortium embracing American, Iranian exile and Saudi Arabian interests took shape Armao and Pazienza discussed the matter further with Calvi in Rome the following February. The consortium was apparently ready to pay over $1,000 million for the Ambrosiano shares. In return Calvi would stay on for three years as chairman, while the consortium had the option to withdraw if something went wrong. But Pazienza never was quite clear just how much of Ambrosiano was involved: sometimes it would be ten per cent, then twelve per cent, and on occasion fifteen per cent. When Pazienza asked who owned them, and how much was involved, Calvi would reply only that he could deliver the shares, and that Pazienza would be told "at the appropriate moment".

Pazienza has claimed that even *after* Ambrosiano's demise and Calvi's death, the consortium was still keen to go ahead, and that he had to counsel them against the idea. But little independent confirmation has ever been forthcoming, beyond gossip within the bank from spring 1982 on, that a deal was ready to sell a major interest in Ambrosiano. It would have been only too easy for Pazienza to play on Calvi's fascination with the Arabs and their wealth, in those fraught times. For who would pay five times the going market price for shares in a bank as controversial as Ambrosiano, without even knowing who was the seller? Possibly, the deal was a desert mirage, conjured up by Pazienza and Calvi himself as comfort when all else failed.

And beyond doubt Calvi had other irons of rescue in the fire, of which he did not inform Pazienza. From January, he curiously seemed to lose interest in the consortium idea. The reasons for his cooling were probably not unconnected with the endeavours of Carboni.

CHAPTER NINETEEN

Carboni and Flight

FLAVIO CARBONI IS perhaps the key figure in the final stages of Calvi's life. From January 1982 onwards, he would with increasing frequency visit Calvi in Milan, or for weekend consultations at Drezzo. The small Sardinian, who once boasted to his family he would become the richest man in Italy, would be companion and paid counsellor to the chairman of Ambrosiano, right up to the end. Vaunting contacts among the Roman politicians, the press and the highest echelons of Italian freemasonry, Carboni took over the role that Gelli had once assumed for Calvi—and more besides.

For Carboni was not only on good terms with Armando Corona, who in March 1982 was to become the head of the Italian Grand-Orient. He could also enlist the services of such as Ernesto Diotallevi and Danilo Abbruciati, notorious bosses of the Rome underworld. Magistrates would later charge that Carboni's building and property businesses were used to recycle the proceeds of organized crime and maybe right-wing terrorism also. In most of the subsequent discoveries which seemed to link Calvi's Ambrosiano with common crime, the name of Carboni would be a constant thread.

Calvi was attracted to Carboni, as he was to Pazienza, by his promised access to hidden, and therefore real power. Precisely to what extent his helpers were in collusion it is hard to establish. But Calvi feared Carboni, just as he was afraid of Pazienza with his vaguely threatening *braggadoccio*, and well-advertised secret service connections. Reading of *The Godfather* was not only instructive of the advantages of hidden power, but also of the fate which might befall those who offended it.

Calvi was by this stage scared not only for his own safety (his retinues of bullet-proof Alfa Romeos and bodyguards were costing

174

his bank four million lire every day) but for that of his family as well. From February on, he was imploring his wife to leave Italy for somewhere less dangerous. In May, and with some reluctance, she finally yielded to his urgings and went to join their son Carlo in Washington. And with good reason, for the violent undertows gripping Ambrosiano's affairs had broken dramatically to the surface.

Roberto Rosone, despite his lofty rank of general manager and deputy chairman of Banco Ambrosiano, had lived for many years in a modest first-floor flat in a corner block of Via Olofredi, close to the central station in Milan. On the ground floor of the same building was the branch office No. 18 of Ambrosiano in Milan. It was protected round the clock by armed private guards, as indeed are bank premises up and down Italy, as a matter of routine.

On the morning of April 27, 1982 Rosone left as usual for his office shortly after 8 a.m. Suddenly, as he turned into the street, a man with a pistol stepped forward and fired wounding him in the legs. But the guards had quickly noticed the danger and shot back, killing the assailant outright. To their great surprise police identified the corpse as that of no ordinary Milanese delinquent, but the important Rome gangland figure Abbruciati.

Abbruciati's links with Carboni, and indeed Carboni's intimate dealings with Calvi, were not yet public knowledge. Even so, the episode raised more questions than it answered, casting a yet more sinister shadow over Ambrosiano. What was a high-ranking gangster from Rome doing carrying out a task that would normally fall to a minion? Was the attack a botched attempt at murder, to punish Rosone for some affront to the underworld; or was it a deliberate warning and no more, delivered in classic fashion? But what had Rosone done to merit such punishment? Or was the warning intended not for him but for Calvi himself? Later, after Calvi and Ambrosiano had perished, a still darker possibility emerged—that Calvi himself, through Carboni and Abbruciati, was directly or indirectly responsible for the attack on his own vice-chairman, suspected of plotting against him.

What is certain, is that Carboni was already receiving money from Calvi. In Italy, Ambrosiano lent large sums to companies owned by Carboni, and Calvi even provided finance to help the campaign of

Corona to become the new head of Italian freemasonry. Abroad, Ambrosiano was more generous (and more desperate) still, if a bizarre incident involving Ambrosiano Overseas in Nassau was anything to go by.

On February 9, 1982 the bank received instructions from Europe to credit $14 million to six numbered accounts in Switzerland, through four different correspondent banks. Siegenthaler was away at the time sailing. But Calvin Knowles, the treasurer of Overseas, was uneasy enough to cable back to Milan asking for more details, to ensure that the transfers were not "against correct banking practice". But Ambrosiano's head office ordered the money to be paid over, offering only a vague undertaking to make good the sum in 48 hours. It was not.

Swiss investigators found afterwards that the $14 million had ended up as part of $20 million held in personal accounts by Carboni and a girlfriend. Carboni was later to insist that the payment was to settle an earlier loan *he had made to Calvi*. According to another version, the money was to pay for a fabulous consignment of stolen jewels passing through Carboni's and then Calvi's hands: in other words, that the chairman of Banco Ambrosiano was by this stage also an underworld fence. Carboni was also preserving for history others of his dealings with Calvi by secretly taping some of their conversations.

And what was Carboni offering in return? Above all promises of help in finding escape from the approaching financial disaster, of which Calvi was receiving almost daily reminders. Not only was the Bank of Italy piecing together the truth about Nassau, Managua and Lima, but periodically staff from Banco Andino or Ambrosiano Services in Luxembourg would visit Milan. Their demands never varied: that he should start making good his undertaking to reduce debts which had now become to all intents and purposes unmanageable.

One project, mentioned by Calvi, and in which Carboni seems to have been instrumental, was of scarcely believable proportions. No less than 80 billion lire would be paid out to buy a package solution to Calvi's difficulties with the Milan magistrature and the central bank, and over the future of the *Corriere*. There was another idea too, and hardly less remarkable. Agreement would be sought from that obscure Catholic organization, the Opus Dei, for it to shoulder part, at least, of the debts of the IOR towards Ambrosiano.

Whether a serious plan was drawn up, or whether the scheme extended little further than Calvi's own tortuous mind, we do not know. Such obscurity is entirely appropriate. Opus Dei and its 72,000 members were once described as "executive class Catholics", whose ideal member is rich, "with sharp suits, a snappy briefcase and steel-rimmed lips". Equally important, it is secretive even by the Vatican's own standards. Pope Paul VI disliked Opus Dei and tried to curb its influence within the Church, especially in Spain where the movement had originated, and was most strongly rooted. John Paul II, on the other hand, was more sympathetic, and in November 1982 bestowed upon the organization the status of a "personal prelature", increasing its independence, and its standing within the Vatican.

Calvi recounted to his wife that he had met the Pope in early 1982, who agreed to entrust him with the task of sorting out the financial troubles of the IOR. The Vatican has flatly denied that any such meetings took place, and that Opus Dei admits to no dealings whatever with Calvi. Nonetheless, through the offices of the ubiquitous Carboni and his masonic ally Corona, Calvi did meet with Cardinal Palazzini, one of the Curia figures most strongly supporting the Opus Dei. He also sought the aid of Hilary Franco, an Italo–American prelate in the Curia. Calvi's motive, plainly, was to get around the obstacle posed by Marcinkus.

However, as he told his wife, these manoeuvres had drawn him into a fierce power struggle within the Vatican. The price of the putative support of the Opus Dei in making good the errors of the IOR was control of the Vatican's finances, and with it a much more conservative diplomatic stance on the part of the Church. This would imply less truck with Communist regimes (including the Pope's own Poland) and a setback for the Vatican's established Ostpolitik towards Eastern Europe. As such, the scheme—according to Calvi—was being resisted by both Marcinkus and by Cardinal Agostino Casaroli, the Holy See's secretary of state, in a sense its "Prime Minister". His version to his family was that the rescue of IOR/Ambrosiano, sponsored by the powerful financial interests the Opus Dei could mobilize, was about to go ahead, until thwarted at the last by Marcinkus and others. The truth of all this would remain obscure; the Vatican, it should be recorded, has denied all. In any case, moreover, the debate would soon be academic.

On the other side of the world, far from the subterranean eddies of ecclesiastical politics, another of Calvi's final illusions was being enacted.

On April 26 Ambrosiano House, the vulgar but opulent new headquarters of Ambrosiano Overseas, on whose board still sat Archbishop Marcinkus, opened for business for the first time out on Nassau's East Bay Street. That business now ranged from the long-standing exchanges of secret telexes and letters with Milan, Monte Carlo and Managua, to a new retail or "high street" banking service for ordinary customers. For these last, a special car park, capable of holding 150 cars, had been extravagantly provided behind the building.

The Bahamas banking community, as it watched Ambrosiano House take shape, was quite baffled by the motives for so lavish an investment. For the tiny size of the domestic market, already dominated by the Royal Bank of Canada, meant that ordinary domestic banking was never likely to be a money spinner. But for Calvi, image and credibility were now all. Anything which might camouflage the real nature of his business was justified. Siegenthaler (incidentally chairman of Astolfine, the tiny Panamanian Company which on its own had by now borrowed nearly half a billion dollars from Banco Andino) was back from his sailing holiday for the opening. He showed off to the press Ambrosiano House's ornamental internal staircase in Italian marble, his own palatial suede-wallpapered office, and an electronic security system surpassing anything in Nassau. "The style of this organization is to do things with taste and to do them well. We're not looking to the next five years, but to the next fifteen,' he declared. "We're going to be here a long, long time." As disingenuous last words go, they rivalled Marcinkus' almost simultaneous pronouncement in Rome that Ambrosiano was an "excellent investment". The grandiose new premises were built on the flimsiest foundations. For within three months Ambrosiano Overseas had lost its banking licence, and within four was in voluntary liquidation. The Bank of Italy now had the evidence it needed. For Calvi it was checkmate.

On May 31 as usual, the Bank of Italy's annual meeting listened respectfully to the dismal verdict of Ciampi on the country's financial and economic performance the previous year. That was in Rome. While Ciampi was speaking, the deputy head of the Bank of Italy's office in Milan was writing a far more destructive missive, to Calvi in person.

The letter from Michele Bonaduce, standing in for Alfio Noto, the director of the Milan branch, bore the serial reference number 30671. But everything else about it was exceptional, above all the crucial paragraph at the foot of the second of its four pages. Documents so far submitted by Banco Ambrosiano, it said, showed that the group's lending to unspecified "third parties" exceeded $1,400 million. This exposure was abnormally high, and worse still was concentrated on three banks, Banco Andino in Lima, Ambrosiano Group Banco Comercial in Managua, and Ambrosiano Overseas. Of the total sum, more than $650 million was provided directly by Ambrosiano Overseas and Banco Ambrosiano Holding of Luxembourg. The last-named, moreover, had given its guarantee for a further $300 million of loans.

Conceivably Calvi, when he had read that far, still thought that the issue could be fudged as before. But any such illusion vanished at the bottom of page three. The central bank ordered him to issue a separate copy of the letter to every director, to be discussed at a forthcoming board meeting. Once again, as in February, each board member would have to separately confirm that he had sufficient information to perform his duties. Finally, a copy of the minutes to that effect should be sent back to the Bank of Italy. Calvi realized the long deceit was about to end. The most useful service Carboni could now render was to organize his escape.

May 31, the day the letter was sent, was a Monday. He spent almost all the week in Rome, in a last effort to persuade the Vatican bank to honour its debts. But on his return from the Papal journey to Britain on June 2, Marcinkus told Calvi flatly there was nothing to be done. Desperately, Calvi worked on contingency plans with Carboni. He also saw Pazienza a last time, to see if the famous consortium, supposedly ready to pay $200 a share for the ten per cent of Ambrosiano in Panama, could be mobilized *in extremis*. By Friday evening he was back in his Milan flat, alone with his daughter Anna, waiting anxiously late into the night for a call from Carboni.

At dawn the next day Calvi woke his daughter, ordering her to pack a suitcase in readiness to leave the country. He too would probably be leaving. "Events are getting out of hand. I can't stay here any longer," Anna was told by her father. "I've got to continue my work outside Italy where it's safe." Calvi prepared two suitcases for himself, loaded them into the boot of the chauffeured Alfa Romeo his daughter usually used, and the two left for Drezzo. What remained of the weekend, the banker spent anxiously. For the following day, Monday June 7, the board meeting was due, and by this stage Calvi nursed few illusions about its probable outcome.

The meeting bore out his worst fears. In small groups, the thirteen other directors present filed into the room, each taking from a trolley by the door a thick envelope containing the complete recent correspondence between Calvi and the Bank of Italy. They listened in silence as the chairman hastily read out the text of the letter of May 31, identifying the $1,400 million risk concealed in the foreign affiliates. Only Pesenti, long in poor health, was missing.

Calvi made one last effort to buy time, proposing that full discussion be postponed and that in the meantime the documentation be kept within the bank building. But it was too late. Bagnasco, worried and impatient, suggested that each director be allowed to take his envelope away with him, to peruse at his leisure. "I'm not going to closet myself away here, going over papers line by line," he told Calvi. A vote was taken, and only Rosone and two other directors supported the chairman. Even Prisco, who less than four months before had criticized the Bank of Italy's hectoring as "offensive", now sided with Bagnasco.

The defeat outwardly seemed on a technicality, and Calvi bore it without expression. But at that moment his eleven years of undisputed rule at Banco Ambrosiano ended. For the first time he had found himself in a minority in his own boardroom, previously so subservient to his every suggestion. The real tragedy, of course, was that had Ambrosiano's directors ever dared such a display of independence earlier, the calamity about to engulf them all would never have happened. Now at a few seconds short of midnight, the long-kept secret was out.

Drained and depressed, Calvi returned home with the ever-present Carboni to eat a cold supper prepared by his daughter. Afterwards Carboni left, taking with him the two prepared suitcases. The next day the banker again urged Anna to leave Italy. He too was probably going abroad, "to continue the operation in hiding". But if the situation became worse he told his daughter, he would start to reveal everything he knew. The following afternoon, of Wednesday June 9, she left for a hotel in Switzerland, where she had already booked a room. A few hours later Calvi himself left Milan on a private plane for the last time, bound for Rome.

That evening, he stayed at Carboni's Rome flat until 2 a.m. reviewing with him the dwindling options still open. Almost certainly at this point the decision to spirit Calvi abroad was taken, the only remaining doubt was when. Almost incredibly, however, even at this hopeless juncture, Calvi could still maintain the façade of normality.

On Thursday morning, after a wretched night's sleep, Calvi went to Ambrosiano's representative offices in the capital, in Via del Traforo. He gave no clues of his real intentions. Nor did he to Giorgio Gregori, the criminal lawyer who for eighteen months had been acting for Calvi in the multitude of legal proceedings in which he was embroiled. In the months before Calvi had spoken vaguely of leaving the country, if everything became too much. But during the two hours they talked that morning, Calvi intimated nothing to his lawyer. Gregori was pleased to have had a tricky interrogation put back a couple of days; if anything, the press attacks against him had abated somewhat lately.

At 1 p.m. he left, to see Carboni again, and then Emilio Pellicani, Carboni's "secretary", who would be responsible for the execution of the imminent flight. Finally, at nine in the evening, Calvi returned to his tiny flat in central Rome. He told his personal chauffeur of nine years, Tito Tesauri, to switch off the flat's elaborate alarm system, and dismissed him with the instruction to pick him up at 6.30 a.m. the following morning. But when Tesauri returned early the next morning, Calvi had vanished.

Just what was finalized during the discussions with Carboni and Pellicani, or whom else Calvi may have seen or called, is not known. But that evening he went home to wait for a summons, which seems to have come around 10 p.m. For when Tesauri came back the next day, he found Calvi's bed lightly crumpled but unslept in, the habitual bottle of mineral water untouched. Where Calvi spent that night is an equal mystery; for his odyssey only began in earnest the following afternoon when, accompanied by Pellicani, he left the capital for the last time bound for Trieste.

The chauffeur swiftly informed Gregori and Costanzo Zugaro, Ambrosiano's Rome representative and an old friend of Calvi's from their cavalry days in the war, of the disappearance. Whatever had happened, it had been urgent enough to make Calvi miss an appointment arranged for 8.30 a.m. with Luigi Mennini at the IOR. Mennini called Zugaro asking what had happened to Calvi: "Where's your chairman, he was due here two hours ago?" After urgently consulting Zugaro, and then Rosone in Milan, Gregori reported to the Rome magistrates that Calvi had been missing for fourteen hours; as he had to, for his client was only free on provisional bail and was without a passport. But hardly had Gregori called the magistrates, than the vanished Calvi was back in contact—with Rosone.

The Ambrosiano vice-chairman told Calvi that his disappearance had already been reported to the judiciary and the police. Calvi replied that they must go back to the magistrates and tell them everything was all right. He couldn't say more, but was conducting "top secret" talks, crucial for the bank. He would be back in Milan on Saturday, and wanted Botta and Leoni from the foreign side to be put on standby.

Rosone was reassured enough to leave for a planned weekend's relaxation in Sardinia. It was much-needed convalescence, for the leg wounds of April 27 were still painful. It was the last time Rosone was to speak to Calvi. For instead of heading back to Milan, his chairman was leaving the country.

Upon his arrival with Calvi in Trieste, Pellicani transferred him to the keeping of Silvano Vittor, a petty border smuggler. Vittor's association with Carboni was reinforced by the fact that their girlfriends were sisters, two pretty Austrian girls called Manuela and Michaela Kleinszig, who lived in Klagenfurt. Vittor's usual clandestine trafficking from the frontier port of Muggia, seven miles from Trieste, involved coffee and blue jeans, commodities much sought after in Yugoslavia but rather cheaper in Italy.

On this occasion, however, Carboni entrusted him with the task of carrying out the illegal export from Italy of Calvi himself, whom Carboni described as a friend of his who needed to go to Austria. From Trieste, Calvi travelled northwards through the night to Klagenfurt. He crossed the frontier bearing a falsified passport which the Sardinian had arranged for him. The passport, bearing the number G116847, and issued in Rome on March 12, 1981, was genuine in all respects other than the name of its bearer. "Roberto Calvi" had been crudely but simply adjusted to "*Gian* Roberto Calv*ini*."

At dawn Calvi was delivered to the house of the Kleinszig sisters. Exhausted, but temporarily at least in safe refuge, he rang his daughter at her hotel in Morcote, just across the Italian border into the Ticino region of Switzerland. Calvi for once sounded relaxed and confident. He said he would have a bath and then get some sleep. "I think we can sort everything out, and I'll probably be back in Italy soon. You'll see, on Monday everyone will know that I've gone away."

There he was mistaken. By Saturday evening the news was on the television. Giovanni Spadolini, the Prime Minister, declared that the affair was "extremely serious". Police and customs posts were placed on full alert. But no-one was more alarmed by the disappearance of Calvi than the Bank of Italy. After the letter of May 31, everything was plain. Although the central bank indicated that it was not planning immediately to send a commissioner to take charge of Ambrosiano, a team of inspectors was alerted to move into the Milan head office of the bank, first thing on Monday morning. Both Ciampi and Dini knew that the edge of the abyss was close indeed.

But the Ambrosiano board, which by now had read the fateful letter, must have been at least half-expecting something of the kind. Bagnasco realized that Calvi's dramatic departure gave him the opportunity to assert his claim as the natural successor much sooner than he had expected. Rosone cut short his own break in Sardinia to rush back to Milan, where he had called a board meeting that Sunday afternoon.

But rapidly, what should have been a concerted effort for survival turned into a battle between the two deputy chairmen, each believing himself the heir apparent. The rivalry was as grim as it was grotesque, two captains wrestling for the wheel of a ship, whose keel was already out of the water, heading for the bottom. Instead of serious deliberation, that hot Sunday in a deserted Milan saw Bagnasco and his entourage encamped at the Principe e Savoia hotel (belonging to CIGA chain which Bagnasco owned), arguing at one remove with Rosone, up in the fourth-floor command centre of Ambrosiano itself. Ferrying messages between them was Giuseppe Ciarrapico, based in Bagnasco's quarters. That night Rosone won the Pyrrhic victory of being named the temporary chief executive of the bank, in Calvi's absence.

In the next few days, Bagnasco would try to portray himself as the trusted contact of the Bank of Italy at Ambrosiano. Unfortunately, an aide unwisely put it about that Bagnasco had personally discussed the problem with the Governor of the Bank of Italy. The embarrassed denial he was forced to issue did little to enhance the credibility and reputation of Bagnasco. But his discomfort was but a footnote to the most dramatic week in the recent experience of Italian high finance.

CHAPTER TWENTY

Week of Fire

EVEN BEFORE FINANCIAL Milan had rubbed the sleep out of its eyes that Monday morning, Calvi's disappearance was creating a stir in time zones ahead of Italy. A big Far Eastern bank was rung up by its subsidiary in Bahrain: should the latter try to wriggle out of delivering $5 million it had already promised to Ambrosiano's foreign department? The bank's representative in Milan was rung up at home in the small hours for advice. His view was that if Ambrosiano opened its doors for business, then they had to go ahead.

And Ambrosiano did open its doors, in an atmosphere of electric expectancy. The dimensions of the bank's foreign problem was still a secret, but the feeling was widespread that the key to Calvi's flight lay not in Italy, but abroad. And there were enough other uncertainties. Would Calvi return? If he did not, who would replace him at the head of the country's largest private banking group? What would the Bank of Italy do—and what about the appeal, due in seven days' time? But the most immediate question was the stock market. A year before, Calvi's arrest for those currency offences, against which he was to appeal now, had been the boulder which started the landslide of prices that culminated in the three-day market closure. What would happen now?

As trading began at 10 a.m., there was no doubt about the answer. A new landslide had started, against which it was pointless for even the practised traders in Ambrosiano's securities department to attempt to erect barriers. That day, shares in Banco Ambrosiano fell by over fifteen per cent, nor were its various subsidiaries like La Centrale spared.

But for the next 48 hours an uneasy respite prevailed, favoured by the absence of any news, good or bad, about the missing Calvi. Police swiftly discarded the idea that he had been seized by the Red Brigades or some other terrorist group. They were suspicious, if not yet sure, that he had left the country; at his exact motives they could only guess. And, as a little timid support buying protected Banco Ambrosiano itself, the pressure turned towards the companies controlled by Carlo Pesenti, Ambrosiano's biggest shareholder, and whose problems at first glance still seemed rather greater than those of Calvi.

But on Thursday, June 17, came the *coup de grâce*. The usually cautious *Il Sole 24 Ore*, Italy's leading financial newspaper, published virtually the complete text of the Bank of Italy's decisive letter of May 31 to Calvi. The paper presented its huge scoop with circumspection, on an inside page; but however guarded, the very mention of a $1,400 million risk was sufficient to explain why he had departed.

On what was to prove the last day in the life of both Calvi's Ambrosiano and Calvi himself, its shares tumbled another eighteen per cent. For a while no market could be made, but finally a few intrepid bargain hunters stepped gingerly in. The closing price was 25,950 lire, just half the level of a month and a half before, when Rossi had won his battle to have them quoted on the full market.

The shares were never traded officially again. That evening Consob ordered their suspension after a wretched 43-day Odyssey, which had been the worst possible advertisement for the Milan stock exchange, and for the judgement of Italy's financial authorities. And within a few days even that closing price of 25,950 lire was to look ludicrously over-generous. For Ambrosiano's directors, barricaded in almost permanent board meeting on the fourth floor in Via Clerici, were discovering that the true worth of the bank was less than nothing.

"Banks deal in confidence," Rosone would remark long after the tempest had blown itself out, "and we just ran out." In a sense, that is a succinctly exact description of the apocalyptic events of that third week of June 1982. No bank in the world—Barclays, Rothschilds, or Chase Manhattan—could survive on its own if every depositor decided simultaneously to withdraw his money. In the year since Calvi's arrest, Ambrosiano had retained, somehow, enough confidence to survive such a threat, in the vague general belief that whatever the shadows abroad, its substance in Italy and its prosperous subsidiaries there would cover any eventuality. Now that fragile confidence ran out. As Aneurin Bevan would have put it, the organ-grinder had fled and only the monkeys remained. Ambrosiano was to reap the bitter consequences of Calvi's lifelong habit of divide and rule, of surrounding himself with people who asked no questions and obeyed his every word. When the crisis at last broke, no-one was equipped to deal with it.

Rosone, general manager and now acting chief executive, knew full well that the only means of satisfying creditors and depositors who wanted their money back would be to recover over $1,200 million by now lent out by the foreign affiliates. From Calvi's references earlier, he had quickly understood that the IOR was involved. Leoni, more than anyone in Calvi's confidence and aware of the nature of the foreign problem, confirmed that indeed most of the money had gone to companies controlled by the Vatican bank. But, he added, everything was guaranteed.

With honest acknowledgement of his own limitations, Rosone realized that he desperately needed expert outside help to cope. The only person he could think of who qualified was Leemans at La Centrale. Leemans rushed round to the bank, where Leoni explained that the guarantees were in Luxembourg, in the form of letters of comfort.

The next day, Angelo De Bernardi, deputy chairman of Banco Andino and head of Ambrosiano Services, the company managing Andino's accounts, arrived in Milan carrying the fateful documents. Leemans took one look and realized they were virtually worthless. The two letters, he saw, merely confirmed that the IOR controlled the eleven companies, and "was aware" of their indebtedness. As an enforceable guarantee they might not have existed. The only possibility lay in a direct appeal to the Vatican bank, that it face up to a moral, if not a legal, obligation.

As desperation gripped Ambrosiano, besieged by creditors and its share price crumbling, Leemans effectively assumed command. Through Alessandro Mennini, he fixed an appointment at the IOR for 8 a.m. the next morning, June 16, with Alessandro's father Luigi. Only with difficulty did he convince Rosone that he should go to Rome as well, but finally that evening the two, together with De Bernardi, flew down to the capital on a private plane. They stayed the night at the Grand Hotel. First thing the next morning, Rosone was once more protesting nervously that his place was in Milan.

But Leemans overcame his doubts, and at 7.40 a.m. they left for the Vatican in a car driven by Alessandro Mennini. When they arrived at the IOR's offices in Sixtus V courtyard, Leemans and De Bernardi were told to wait. Rosone went in to see Mennini and De Stroebel alone.

With customary forthrightness, Rosone demanded that the companies owned by the IOR start paying back the money. Ambrosiano in Milan could not borrow any more, and the Luxembourg company needed urgently the small sum of $7 million. Otherwise it would show a loss for its financial year to June 30, in just a fortnight's time. In that case, it would be forced to speed up repayment of its borrowings, and probably go into default.

Mennini and De Stroebel listened impassively. Then they produced their trump card—the original letter from Calvi asking for the letters of patronage, discharging the IOR from any responsibility. Rosone was dumbstruck. "That was the moment the world fell in," he said afterwards. What he had obstinately refused to believe was true: Ambrosiano was bankrupt.

Leemans was summoned, to see if some device might be elaborated to stave off disaster. He jotted down on a scrap of paper the assets held in Panama. There were the 5.2 million shares in Banco Ambrosiano, 10.4 per cent of its capital. Then there was 5.5 per cent of La Centrale (held in the name of a couple of Liechtenstein *anstalts* called Zwillfin and Chatoser), six per cent of Banca del Gottardo, 5,500 shares in Suprafin (the Milan company which began the buying of Ambrosiano shares back in 1974), the two million shares in Vianini, 189,000 shares in Rizzoli, and 300 shares in Ambrosiano Overseas of Nassau. Last but not least, Leemans noted down 520 shares, equivalent to 52 per cent, of *Sorrisi e Canzoni TV*. That this was a frothy Italian counterpart of the *TV Times* had not prevented its employment to secure $40 million lent by Ambrosiano Nicaragua to World Wide Trading Corporation of Panama. In all these sundry shareholdings secured exactly $1,287 million worth of debts.

Leemans argued that Ambrosiano had to have at least some of the money there and then, but the two IOR officials again refused, insisting that the debts were not theirs. "But what about the Ambrosiano shares?" Leemans asked. "*Sono vostre*," "they're yours," came the cold answer, "take them back." But Leemans still retained a fraction of hope and came up with what was to prove the final scheme to save Banco Ambrosiano.

Whether it liked it or not, he insisted, the IOR had to co-operate, or else find itself involved in a colossal scandal. Probably Ambrosiano's valuable Swiss subsidiary, Banca del Gottardo, together with other odds and ends, could be sold for, say, $250 million. That left roughly $1,000 million to be found. Leemans suggested that the IOR raise this sum through an international loan, with a life of six or seven years. This would be used to settle the debts to Ambrosiano's Latin American banks. The IOR would find the money to repay the loan when it fell due by selling the 5.2 million Banco Ambrosiano shares. This meant that Leemans had to find someone to buy ten per cent of Ambrosiano in six or seven years' time at a price of almost $200 per share. True, this was five times more than their highest ever level on the Milan Stock Exchange, but conceivably, with share splits and capital issues, the trick could be pulled off. But the IOR, which after all *was* involved, had to pay the interest on the $1,000 million loan, and accept the exchange risk.

The meeting broke up. Rosone at last could return to Milan, while Leemans threw himself into the hopeless task. He could think of only one possible buyer for the Ambrosiano shares—Carlo De Benedetti. In the next few hours he went back and forth to De Benedetti at Olivetti's head office, in Ivrea, near Turin. But De Benedetti would only consider taking an option to buy the shares, without committing himself further.

Leemans made a new appointment in the Vatican for 8 am the following morning, June 17. His deadline was noon that day, when Ambrosiano's board was due to meet again in Milan. In all likelihood it would throw in the towel and place the bank in the hands of the Bank of Italy. This time Marcinkus was there, along with Mennini and De Stroebel. His terms were impossible.

The IOR, said Marcinkus, had to have a firm *promise* to buy the shares; nor could the Vatican bank meet either the interest payments (around $100 to $150 million a year) on the loan, or the exchange risk. "We just don't have that kind of money."

Well then, Leemans replied, "I'll just have to call Milan and tell them to ask for a Bank of Italy commissioner. Everything's going to collapse, and there'll be an almighty scandal."

"I know," said Marcinkus wearily. "I did all this to help a friend, and look where we are." Leemans made one last bitter joke: "When there's that much money involved, it's hard to have any friends." He left the IOR, and phoned Rosone with the grim news. The Bank of Italy would have to be called in.

In Milan, on the fourth floor of Banco Ambrosiano's headquarters, turmoil reigned. Apart from Calvi himself, four other directors did not attend what was to prove the final board meeting of the 86-year life of Ambrosiano. But the panic of those who were there more than made up for any absences; as they argued, exchanged accusations, and frantically called their lawyers for advice. At noon proceedings were finally under way.

First Calvi was by unanimous vote stripped of all his powers at the Bank. Then Rosone proposed that the board be dissolved, and the bank placed in the hands of a commissioner from the central bank, whose inspectors were already in the building anyway.

Then it was the turn of Leoni. He explained to the dumbfounded directors how the Panamanian and Luxembourg companies controlled by the IOR owed the foreign subsidiaries, above all Banco Andino, almost $1,100 million, while the Vatican bank directly owed them $200 million. But the IOR was refusing to help. Ambrosiano in Milan was being pressed to repay loans. It had already directly transferred $380 million to the beleaguered foreign subsidiaries, quite apart from the indirect "back-to-back" operations through intermediaries. But no more money could be provided. Rosone then disclosed how the bank had (illegally) spent over 60 billion lire buying up its own shares in the final months, to support their price before and during the brief quotation on the main Milan market.

But even at this hopeless juncture, the struggle for power between Rosone and Bagnasco continued. The acting chairman should resign, Bagnasco accused Rosone in fury. He had known the truth and lied about it, saying nothing at board meeting after board meeting. Rosone equally angrily rejected the charges. At 2.30 p.m. the meeting was suspended for half an hour, to permit tempers to cool and yet more calls to lawyers.

Rosone produced a new draft motion requesting the Bank of Italy to step in; but Bagnasco remained adamant. He would agree to nothing until he had had more time to study the true situation of the bank. Meanwhile Botta, the head of the foreign department warned that unless Banco Andino received $15 million to repay a loan by the end of June, the group would be thrown into default by other creditors. Finally the vote was taken. By nine votes to nil, and the abstention of Bagnasco, the board of Banco Ambrosiano voted to dissolve itself. Hardly had the news begun to clatter out on wire service printers just after 6 p.m. than the Bank of Italy activated its contingency plan.

The most senior of the team of inspectors in Milan, Vincenzo Desario, was named provisional commissioner. Only hours later he was telexing all the foreign and Italian banks which had dealt with Ambrosiano, pleading for their "widest possible" co-operation, and promising that the regular administration of Ambrosiano would be guaranteed. Nothing however would again be regular or normal in the affairs of the bank.

Every one of Ambrosiano's 4,200 employees must have been bewildered and fearful at the upheavals of the week. None more so than Graziella Corrocher, the 55-year-old personal secretary of Calvi, and before that of the previous chairman Mozzana. She was a spinster who had given her life to the bank. In recent weeks she had been worried not only by the ill health of her sister, but at the evident irritability and dissatisfaction of Calvi himself. Not even with his personal secretary could he form a relationship of trust and warmth. Towards the end, he would complain to his lawyers about her performance; maybe in some obscure way he saw Corrocher too as part of the great conspiracy against him.

Shortly after the directors had agreed to ask the Bank of Italy to take over, she took a red felt-tipped pen and wrote a short note. She apologized for what she intended to do. Her work with Calvi though had been miserable. How much coldness she had endured, how little satisfaction Corrocher had derived from her work; "I stand by the decision taken by the board," she wrote, "but I cannot stand by Calvi any longer . . . what a disgrace, to have run away. May he be cursed a thousand times for the harm he has done to everyone at the bank, and to the image of the group we were once so proud of."

Then, just before 7 p.m., she climbed on to the windowsill of her fourth-floor office and threw herself to her death. Her body landed with a thump on the ramp leading down to Ambrosiano's underground garage in the inside courtyard. Rosone was talking to a journalist on the phone, telling what had happened that day. The caller heard a din in the background, and Rosone broke off the conversation. Then he returned to the phone. "My God," he said, "Calvi's secretary's just killed herself."

Some have been tempted to see Corrocher's death as murder, not suicide, that she did not jump, but was pushed to her death. The motive, presumably, that she should not divulge the secrets she must have known. But to have devised a suicide note of such despairing intensity would surely have taxed the most cynical assassin. In that overcharged moment, it was more probably a gruesome, but melodramatically fitting, end to a day when the last illusions died. Or at least it *seemed* the end.

CHAPTER TWENTY-ONE

Death in London

ROBERTO CALVI NEVER did return to Italy. Perhaps, in his initial relief at successful escape to Klagenfurt, he really thought he could. His family in Washington had already learnt of his flight; both from Pazienza, who mysteriously visited London briefly on Friday June 11 before taking the Concorde back to New York on the morning of Saturday June 12, and from Giorgio Gregori, their lawyer in Rome. On her father's instructions, Anna relayed on Calvi's reassurances to his wife and son, telling them to go as planned on a trip to Los Angeles.

That weekend the participants in the last journey gathered at the house of the Kleinszig sisters. Vittor drove up from Trieste, while Carboni flew in from Rome. Calvi spent the weekend making phone calls and burning documents he had brought with him in the fireplace in the sitting room. It is not known whom else he telephoned from Klagenfurt, or what were the documents he destroyed. Presumably they related to his links with the Vatican and the P-2. Maybe he was still in touch with the IOR, or trying to mobilize what allies he had left, in a final attempt to save Ambrosiano. But his room for manoeuvre was fast vanishing. That Sunday his disappearance was on the front page of Italian newspapers: by Monday it was news all over Europe.

Roberto Calvi was now the most sought after man in Europe and his last four days of life were to be spent dodging furtively, under a transparent alias, halfway across Europe. Not least of the riddles of this period is why, if Calvi had to run, he did not go to join his family in America—or travel to South America, a traditional refuge for runaway Italians, and where he had such strong connections, both business and political. Perhaps he was unable to face his family, and present them with conclusive evidence of his failure; perhaps intermittently he still was able to persuade himself that salvation was possible; perhaps he was no longer physically free to decide. We do not know. It is impossible to be sure.

True to his love of the shadows, Calvi travelled mostly by night. Late in the evening of the Sunday, June 13, he and Vittor left Klagenfurt for the drive across the mountains to Innsbruck, where they arrived at dawn on Monday. Carboni himself that day travelled on to Zurich, where he was joined by Ernesto Diotallevi, his underworld associate who is believed to have procured the false passport for Calvi.

Calvi, however, did not stay in Innsbruck long. He and Carboni agreed that their next rendezvous would be at Bregenz, a small town close to the border with Switzerland and West Germany, on the shores of Lake Constance. There Calvi spent the night of Monday, June 14, and there he met Hans Kunz, the Swiss businessman and friend of Carboni, and who was to be the main organizer of the last stage of the journey to London.

The decision to go to London may have been in doubt right up to the last moment. That night Calvi called his daughter telling her that Kunz was arranging a flat for her in Zurich, adding cryptically that perhaps he would be coming to join her. In the event he was not to see Anna again, nor was she to have the promised flat.

The following morning, of Tuesday June 15, Calvi and Vittor abruptly returned to Innsbruck. The banker still seemed in good humour; again we do not know whom he spoke to by phone, or what promises he received. He can hardly have been unaware, however, of developments in Italy, above all the savage run on Ambrosiano's shares. As his daughter travelled to a hotel in Zurich, waiting for Kunz or his wife to get in touch, and as Leemans and Rosone in Milan prepared for their fateful trip to the IOR in Rome, Calvi left for London.

Accompanied by Vittor, he travelled in a private jet, which had been arranged by the Swiss businessman. The pilot of the plane was told his two passengers were executives of the Fiat motor company. At sunset that Tuesday evening the plane touched down at Gatwick airport. Calvi's false passport aroused no suspicions at Gatwick's immigration controls. Together with Vittor, he went straight to the

194

lodgings Kunz had arranged for them at Chelsea Cloisters in Sloane Avenue. Vittor, both guardian and Calvi's last bodyguard, signed in for both of them, and they were assigned apartment 881.

Foreigners are often misled by its name, for Chelsea Cloisters is no romantic, luxurious hideaway in bohemian Chelsea, but a vast barracks like building, containing innumerable apartments and small rooms for short- or longer-term letting. Here, in the anonymous circumstances of the fugitive, the man who until a few months earlier had been Italy's most powerful private banker was to spend the last two days of his life.

Calvi's mood changed to match his new surroundings. He became, Vittor said, agitated, depressed, and again frightened. Most of Wednesday he spent in the room stretched on the bed, staring at the television, or making phone calls. Vittor, whenever he went out, had to call him every twenty minutes. During the day, Carboni arrived with the Keinszig sisters from Zurich via Amsterdam, and booked into the Hilton Hotel on Park Lane. From there he phoned Calvi, who protested strongly about the conditions under which he had to live, demanding to move somewhere else. The two met that evening, with Vittor, in Hyde Park, and Carboni promised to make new arrangements. It was, he maintains, the last time he saw Calvi alive.

But why London? As far as can be established Calvi contacted none of his previous business associates in the city, neither De Savary, nor others in the banking world, with whom the Calvis were on friendly terms after that visit to London in February 1981. Calvi's knowledge of London was that of the occasional business visitor; his command of English was adequate but no more. True, Pazienza had been in London a few days earlier; but practised antennae in the City had picked up no signal of unusual activity indicating that the improbable deal, to sell the Panamanian shares in Ambrosiano for $1,000 million or more, was nearing completion.

Perhaps the key lay in the shadowy "*Loggia di Londra*", a "London Lodge" of freemasons of which Calvi would sometimes cryptically admit membership. Those to whom he spoke of it gained the impression that Gelli had put him in touch with it; Calvi would imply that it was of enormous financial influence and had helped him in

195

many of his dealings. The "*Loggia di Londra*" would fit in with Calvi's love of secret clubs and cabals, with his preference for the back rather than the front door. The fact, however, was that Calvi was rarely financially active in London—Ambrosiano did not even have a representative office in what is, after all, Europe's financial capital.

Conceivably, London was chosen because it was so huge a metropolis, where identity checks were minimal. A fugitive could easily go to ground, and connecting flights abounded to every corner of the world. What can be said is that if there did exist a premeditated plan, then the arrangements devised by Carboni and his fellows, and their behaviour, bore little sign of it. Rather, a nervous improvisation was the order of the day.

Early on Thursday June 17 Carboni appears to have made a call from the Hilton to Wilfredo Vitalone, a Rome lawyer enlisted by himself and Pazienza to help persuade Italian magistrates to take a gentler line towards the banker. Afterwards he spoke to Calvi himself by telephone and then checked out of the hotel.

Carboni then contacted an English acquaintance called William Morris, a local Government officer from West London, whose Italian wife was aunt to Carboni's mistress of many years. Morris insisted he had previously met Carboni just twice, while on holiday in Italy. And so, as the Kleinszigs spent that Thursday shopping, the Sardinian enlisted his help to find more satisfactory lodgings for his unhappy charge.

For all the while Calvi was becoming more restless and depressed. At some point on June 16 or 17 (the accounts of Carboni and Vittor differed) he shaved off the thin moustache he had always worn. He spent the whole of Thursday in his room, his only contact with the outside world, apart from his faithful Vittor, the telephone. Even his family, to whom he had seemed cheerful in the days before, noticed the change. In one of the last conversations with his wife, he was still talking of the "wonderful thing" that was going to change their existence. But that Thursday morning he spoke three times with his daughter Anna in Zurich, insisting on the danger she faced, and that she should leave Europe for the US: "Something really important is happening, and today and tomorrow all hell is going to break loose."

Anna booked a flight the next day from Zurich to New York, and her father called again to tell her that the Kunz would provide the money required to buy the ticket. He added he would be in touch the following morning to make sure she was on her way. Early on Friday the Swiss businessman's wife arrived at the hotel to give Anna 50,000 Swiss francs in cash. By that time, of course, her father was dead.

The state of Calvi's mind that last afternoon can only be guessed at. It is hard to believe that he did not learn of the tumult in Milan: the removal by Ambrosiano's board of his power to sign documents, which banished what hopes there were of the rescue deal, the decision to place Banco Ambrosiano in the hands of the Bank of Italy, and finally the death of his secretary Corrocher. And it is inconceivable that in one way or another they did not bear on what was to happen that night. Back in Italy, the events at Banco Ambrosiano's head-quarters (though not those within the Vatican earlier) were the top item on the evening news at 8 p.m., or 7 p.m. London time.

Only later was Carboni, who had meanwhile booked into the Sheraton Hotel near Morris's home, back in touch with Calvi and Vittor at Chelsea Cloisters, saying he was on his way at last. Not until about 11 p.m. did he arrive in Sloane Avenue. But instead of going up to Calvi's room, he asked Vittor to come down. They then left, to collect the Kleinszig girls, who had long been waiting in a nearby bar. Both assert that from that moment, they never saw Calvi again. Vittor's version was that Calvi earlier had refused to go down and meet Carboni. When he returned to the apartment, after leaving Carboni and the girls, he found it locked and empty. Calvi had left on the last journey of his life. After having himself let into the room by a porter, Vittor spent an anxious night before taking the first flight the next day for Vienna. The Kleinszig sisters also left for Austria.

Carboni, however, seems to have been much less perturbed. On the next morning, Friday, he took Morris's 21-year-old daughter Odette to lunch in Chelsea, and then suggested they went to call on a "friend" of his who was staying at Chelsea Cloisters. There was of course no-one, since Calvi was dead and Vittor already out of the country. The two then went back to Morris's home in Heston, close to London airport. The next day, for reasons unexplained, Carboni and Odette caught a plane to Edinburgh, from Gatwick, not Heathrow. They stayed in Edinburgh just 24 hours, before Carboni completed his erratic European odyssey by taking a private plane to Austria on the Sunday morning. He was arrested in a villa close to Lugano at the end of July.

At any given time, there are between 70,000 and 80,000 Italian citizens in the greater London area, under the jurisdiction of Italy's consul general in London. Problems with the police are inevitable. Once a fortnight on average he receives notification that one of them has been arrested, or worse. And so it was on Friday, June 18. But Teodoro Fuxa, the consul, swiftly suspected that something really important could be afoot.

At 10.30 that morning came a call from the City Police. The body of a man with an Italian passport, in the name of Calvini, had been found three hours earlier hanging from scaffolding under the North side of Blackfriars bridge. Fuxa had read the Italian papers, and the similarity of the name with that of the banker missing for almost a week was enough to make him curious. Even more curious, had he known of them, were the detailed circumstances of the death.

The alarm was given by an unsuspecting City clerk walking to work along the embankment. Tall enough to see over the parapet, he noticed to his horror a corpse dangling from the second rung, and quickly gave the alarm. The body was cut down by the River Police.

The soggy Italian passport bore the name of Gian Roberto Calvini. The pockets of the expensive-looking suit contained the equivalent of almost £7,400 in cash, but chiefly in dollars and Swiss francs. There was just £47 in sterling, and only 58,000 Italian lire. The police also discovered two watches on the body; a badly corroded wrist watch which had stopped at 1.52 a.m., and a pocket watch which had run until 5.49 a.m. In the pockets, and stuffed down the trousers, were lumps of stone weighing over ten pounds to act as ballast, plus various slips of paper.

Some bore incomprehensible figures, one was a torn out page, No. 47/48, of Calvi's address book, with various names under the letter "F": Rino Formica, the Socialist Finance Minister, Alberto Ferrari once of the Banca Nazionale del Lavoro and the P-2, and Hilary Franco from the Vatican, were just three of them.

There was the Washington address of his wife and son, and—inexplicably—the business card of a prominent City solicitor, who told the police he'd never met Calvi in his life. The body was suspended from a yard-long nylon rope, fastened at the neck by a simple noose, and to the scaffolding by two half hitch knots.

Nothing was to hand in the London police or Interpol records to suggest who the victim might be, so the city of London police wired off to their opposite numbers in Rome for help. Fuxa meanwhile went to the City of London police, in whose jurisdiction Blackfriars bridge fell, and a glance at the photo in the falsified passport heightened his own suspicions further. When he saw photos of the corpse, the suspicions became virtual certainties. But the last doubts were removed by the laconic answer from Rome: "You've got our banker."

At 4 a.m. the next morning Domenico Sica, the magistrate investigating Calvi's disappearance, arrived from Rome with senior police officers aboard a special military aircraft. But before that, and formal identification of the corpse by Leone Calvi, the dead man's brother, those most closely involved in Italy had decided for themselves. Rosone was watching the late Friday night news. "They only said the body *might* be . . . but I knew."

The delicacy of the case was evident, and the police trod with suitable care. William Whitelaw, the Home Secretary, was given a briefing, and the investigations went on much longer than would have been the case in a clear-cut suicide. For although the City of London police tended to assume from the beginning that Calvi took his own life, the peculiarities were endless.

In Italy public opinion was convinced that it was a case of murder. Calvi, after all, was "God's banker", with a special relationship with the Vatican—indeed, indication of just how special was emerging every day at home. Ambrosiano had been the greatest banking disaster anywhere since 1945. Its chairman had been a member of the P-2, and were there not "masonic" trimmings to his death—the stones in the pockets, the choice of the bridge of Blackfriars (also, of course, the name of a British lodge), and the washing of Calvi's feet by the river tide? There is even a "Blackfriars" lodge, number 3,722, in the "List of Lodges Masonic", the official register of European freemasonry. Rumours abounded that Ambrosiano was involved in Latin American arms trading. The Falklands war had just ended, and might it not be significant that the bridge was painted pale blue and white, Argentina's national colours?

199

Finally the inquest was fixed for July 23, more than five weeks after the discovery of Calvi's body. A jury was duly appointed. The hearing finished only at 10 p.m., but the final verdict was as the police had maintained. Dr David Paul, the coroner, emphasized to the jurors that to return an open verdict would be an evasion of their responsibilities; a majority, probably anxious to be home and rid of this ghoulish Italian mystery, wearily concluded that on the basis of the barrage of evidence they had heard, suicide by strangulation was the cause of death. But was it *really* suicide?

By and large Italians have much respect for the English legal system, encrusted with the ritual of centuries and, unlike their own, traditionally free of political interference. This time, however, it was the object of incredulity and even derision. How could it be, everyone in Italy and more than a few in Britain wondered, that in so obviously complex a case, so much of whose background was beyond understanding in London, the court chose to ignore the safer option of an open verdict? Dark talk of a cover-up did the rounds, of how the jurors had somehow been "nobbled".

More serious perhaps was the degree of incomprehension between the British and Italian authorities. The London police officers on the case did not conceal their frustration at the conditions under which they had to operate within Italy, and the scant co-operation, especially in Rome. Particularly irritating was the inability to interrogate directly suspects and witnesses; under the Italian system, this job is done by magistrates.

Faced with such hurdles, it would not be surprising if the London police were sometimes tempted to wash their hands of the whole messy affair. In fact the investigation continued, although by early in the New Year the unexplored leads had dwindled to next to nothing.

Long before that, however, the Calvi family, deeply distressed and unbelieving of the suicide verdict, opened their own campaign to have it overturned. As summer turned into autumn and winter, his widow and son in Washington let hardly a week go by without publicly insisting that Calvi had been murdered.

Magistrates, journalists and the Italian parliamentary commission probing the P-2 affair, paid visits to the US. Every one produced fresh, sensational allegations. Clara Calvi named the politicians, likely and less likely, who her husband said had received money from himself or Ambrosiano. She spoke of his private desperation at the Vatican's refusal to bail him out in the last year, and the attempts he recounted of how he had tried to enlist the Opus Dei to replace the IOR. She accused the Bank of Italy of secretly aiding, and then betraying, Ambrosiano, and told of her meetings with Andreotti, Craxi and Piccoli to try and secure their intercession. The denials and retaliatory lawsuits flew thick and fast; but few, it seemed, could escape the vengeful wrath of this frail, tiny woman with her bright gipsy clothes, and her delicate face beneath a bouffant of wispy blonde hair. Few too could be completely unimpressed by the resolute way in which she fought her cause. If the reliability of her principal source, her husband, was much to be questioned, especially in those final twelve months of his life, it was hard to doubt that she was at least faithfully relaying what she had been told. And whatever the variations, her theme remained constant: that her husband would not, could not, and had not committed suicide.

Nor is there any denying that the murder theory has stronger foundations than mere fantasizing and obsession with conspiracies, real or imagined, of which Italians are so often accused. Reasons, both subjective and objective, exist for believing that Calvi could not have taken his own life.

In the first place relatives and friends have testified that he suffered from vertigo and could not have managed to climb 25 feet down a ladder from the embankment parapet, and then clamber across the scaffolding to the point of his death. Then again, where did the banker find the stones, and above all the rope with which Calvi is supposed to have hanged himself? Why should he have gone to Blackfriars bridge, five miles from Chelsea Cloisters? He had in his room enough barbiturates to kill himself quite painlessly. In any case, Calvi had never mentioned suicide to his family at any stage, right up to the end. On the contrary, he was convinced that not only he himself, but also his wife and children were in physical danger.

In a rare interview†, just before he vanished from Italy in early June, Calvi set out his fears. The climate was that of "a religious war", he declared. "Now it's almost the order of the day to attack me,

†*La Stampa*, June 15, 1982.

and in this sort of atmosphere, any barbarity is possible. A lot of people have a lot to answer for in this affair. I'm not sure who, but sooner or later it'll come out."

This in turn leads to the key question: just who was threatening Calvi? Of whom was he so frightened? For if he was murdered, it was surely to silence him for ever. Those last two sentences above may even be taken as the thinnest of warnings that Calvi was readying himself to tell all. Carlo Calvi has, moreover, sworn under affidavit that his father had told him that he planned to speak out at the appeal hearings, due four days after he died. And with Banco Ambrosiano by that stage in ruins, Calvi would have had little left to lose.

Broadly, Calvi's fears appear to have sprung from four quarters. The first derived from the magistrates in Milan, those front line troops of an imagined assault mounted by the Communist Left, and who were implacably uncovering the truth about his affairs. But it is obviously preposterous to suppose they had anything to do with his death.

His second constant, obsessive, source of worry was the Vatican— and the consequences of the obscure but momentous power struggle that his search for agreement with the Opus Dei is supposed to have detonated between "Left" and "Right" within the Holy See and beyond. Clara Calvi maintained† that her husband's murder was sponsored by the anti-Opus Dei faction, alarmed at the consequences for the Vatican's carefully nurtured dealings with Communist Eastern Europe. Calvi would tell his lawyers that he had channelled $50 million to Solidarity; and that there was more to follow. "If the whole thing comes out," he would say, "it'll be enough to start the Third World War."

At this point, Calvi's death would become an ingredient in the rivalry between East and West; it could even seem connected with the attempt to kill the Pope, alleged to have been mounted by Bulgaria and the KGB.

The third, more prosaic, shadow of violence was cast by Carboni, his confidant and associate for the last six months. Carboni's underworld connections were not unknown to Calvi, who had paid him $20 million, including that $14 million almost extorted from his bank in

†*La Stampa*, October 7, 1982.

Nassau. One of these connections had been killed when shooting at Rosone, deputy chairman of Ambrosiano, on April 27. Calvi in that last interview maintained that the attack was a warning for his bank and himself: Rosone later insisted that Calvi himself had organized the ambush. Either way, however, the odour of crude physical threat was heavy in the air.

The fourth and last basic origin of Calvi's fear was perhaps the least tangible, but most potent of all. It stretched from Gelli, with whom Calvi had long done his utmost to avoid contact, through the now disbanded P-2 freemasons' lodge and the Italian secret services into Latin America and international freemasonry, arms trafficking and right-wing terrorism. London, as a string of arrests since the late 1970s has proved, is a favourite refuge of Italy's neo-fascist extremists.

Sindona, that other bankrupt Italian financier, who believed himself a martyr, claimed—for what it was worth—that "left-wing South American freemasons" were responsible. Somewhere in this mosaic must have lain those "factors of international consensus" which so troubled Calvi in his short-lived dealings with Carlo De Benedetti.

Of course, none of these ingredients, probably partly real and partly the product of Calvi's tortured and tortuous mind, can be kept separate. He was, after all, convinced that Carboni was influential within freemasonry and within some quarters of the Vatican. Gelli and Ortolani too were points where the normally antagonistic forces of Catholicism and masonry overlapped. They are all pieces in a kaleidoscope which can be shaken into endlessly tantalizing theories—some of quite numbing implication.

There remained, moreover, one last mystifying circumstance, the disappearance of the briefcase from which Calvi was never separated. Many documents were apparently burnt that Sunday in Klagenfurt, but other papers must have gone with Calvi to London. Like the key to the room in Chelsea Cloisters, and the rest of his address book, they were never recovered. Did they depart on the private plane chartered by Kunz which travelled from Geneva to Gatwick and back on the evening of June 18?† Did Calvi destroy his most sensitive papers himself, or was their destruction the completion of the cover-up which began with his murder?

†*Sunday Times*, November 14, 1982.

But the arguments for a suicide, however unlikely the method could not be wholly dismissed. In the first place, neither the first autopsy in London, nor a second one carried out in Italy, revealed any trace of violence upon Calvi's body, or that drugs had been administered to make him unconscious. The medical evidence at the first hearing in July was decisive in securing the suicide verdict. In March 1983 three Italian forensic experts concluded, on the basis of the exhaustive examination, that it was "probable", although by no means certain, that Calvi had taken his own life.

Furthermore, if Calvi was murdered, not one firm clue has emerged of the identity of his assassins. Police appeals for help from anyone who might have heard or seen something suspicious either around Blackfriars bridge or on the river that night drew no response. Admittedly, that area of London is almost completely deserted in the small hours. The fact remained that nobody came forward.

Moreover, the circumstantial evidence in favour of suicide was considerable, at least no less than the grounds for believing in ritual masonic executions. That afternoon Banco Ambrosiano, to which Calvi had given the best 35 years of his life, had to all intents and purposes collapsed. His secretary had killed herself, leaving behind her bitter imprecation against him. He was a fugitive from justice, whose appeal against imprisonment was to be heard in just four days' time. Calvi and Ambrosiano, moreover, figured in no less than 32 lawsuits back in Italy. The events of that June 17 in Milan would have done little to improve the chances of his appeal being upheld, and of his escaping four crushing years in prison.

He was depressed by his strange lodgings in a city far from home. To the end Calvi had insisted to his family that all would be well; but now there could be no concealing the disaster he had brought upon himself. To his wife and children, the last who had faith, the truth would finally have to be revealed. The miraculous agreement that would save him—if indeed that was the reason for Calvi's furtive presence in London—was now out of the question, for Ambrosiano's board had stripped him of any power to negotiate. And although it is not known how, Calvi surely learnt from someone of what had happened in Milan that afternoon.

The inner despair of the man must have been immense. And so was it completely beyond possibility that he took advantage of Vittor's absence from the room to escape, walking south from Chelsea Cloisters until he reached the river, and then turning leftwards along its bank until Blackfriars? None of this, of course, satisfactorily explains the stones and the rope. But such a reconstruction is no more implausible than the elaborate theory of the motor launch, chartered and manned by expert criminals, slipping on a night tide under Blackfriars bridge and hanging Calvi's body from the scaffolding—leaving no trace of violence.

If it was a strange way to commit suicide, it was an equally odd method of murder. Moreover, the suggestion that Calvi was killed in such a way as to look like suicide may be countered by the argument that perhaps it was a suicide dressed up as murder. For Calvi had prepared a 4 billion lire ($3 million) policy on his life in favour of his family. Insurance companies do not often pay in the case of suicide.

Many months after the event, investigators in both Italy and England seemed little closer to solving the conundrum, with no great immediate prospect that they would. Silvano Vittor and Flavio Carboni, the two most obvious suspects, had been under interrogation in Italy since autumn 1982. But the formal charges against them, in direct connection with Calvi's death, did not extend beyond organizing the banker's illegal flight abroad. The choice remained between a perfect murder and a most unusual suicide.

But on March 29, 1983, Latin imagination and Anglo-Saxon phlegm were at least partly reconciled. Lord Chief Justice Lane ordered that the July 23 verdict be quashed, on the grounds that the coroner had improperly rushed through so complicated a case in a single session, and had inadmissibly leant upon the jury to avoid returning an open verdict. Furthermore, it was wrong that Flavio Carboni, the most important witness, had not been called to give evidence. The Calvi family had won a first concrete victory, and a new inquest would be held later in 1983 to attempt to elucidate the baffling mystery of Roberto Calvi's death.

CHAPTER TWENTY-TWO

Clearing up the Mess

IF THE CHAIRMAN of Banco Ambrosiano had few friends in his life, he had fewer still after his gruesome death. Usually, when a prominent figure dies in Italy, the obituary columns are filled with the condolences of those who knew and worked with him. Quite fortuitously, a strike prevented Italian newspapers from being published on either Saturday June 19 or Sunday June 20. And so the country had to rely on radio and television alone to learn that the missing Calvi had been found dead, hanging beneath a bridge in London.

Only on the Monday could the papers proclaim the news in banner headlines. But the *Corriere*, the paper Calvi partly owned, and the voice of the Milanese *bourgeoisie* to which—however uneasily—he belonged, carried just one four-line notice. It was placed by Goffredo Manfredi, the Roman builder who had joined Ambrosiano's board earlier in the year, and who had been one of the three directors to side with Calvi when it voted against him a fortnight earlier. The next day, two more appeared. One was from Marino Mariani, a small shareholder who had stayed with Ambrosiano to the end. He remembered Calvi's "hardworking and talented" life. The other came from the family of Umberto Ortolani, Gelli's lieutenant in the P-2 but on much warmer personal terms with Calvi than was Gelli. And that was all.

The politicians who had received much from Calvi were silent. Even before the last Ambrosiano board meeting and Calvi's death, Banca del Gottardo in Lugano announced that he was being removed from its board. Former colleagues at the bank insisted that Calvi alone had known what had gone on. A scapegoat for the disaster was to hand. Calvi could be blamed for everything, and as quickly as possible forgotten. Even the Vatican, through those elusive "reliable sources" who profess to speak for it at awkward moments, was letting

206

it be known that it was "extraneous" to the Ambrosiano crisis, underlining that its shareholding was just 1.6 per cent. But just how reliable those sources truly were, was to be proved in a matter of hours.

For on the morning of Monday June 21, the economic and financial weekly *Il Mondo* carried a remarkably detailed account of the events of the previous week in Milan, and the visit *in extremis* to the IOR by Leemans and Rosone. Above all it identified the colossal loans advanced by Ambrosiano's affiliates in Peru and Nicaragua to companies controlled by the IOR, and revealed the existence not only of the letters of comfort, but also of Calvi's own earlier letter absolving the Vatican bank from responsibility. The scandal of which Leemans had warned Marcinkus just four days earlier was out in the open, in all its tawdry splendour.

Events were now to move at an astonishing pace. Whatever may be said of the authorities' legalistic approach to Ambrosiano before, they now acted with lightning speed. Vincenzo Desario was in charge of Banco Ambrosiano for hardly 24 hours. By the weekend three permanent commissioners had been named. Technically the central bank had a fortnight to choose, but the risk of political meddling and the urgency of Ambrosiano's plight meant that no time could be lost.

The three made an oddly contrasting, but nicely complementary group during the 46 days of life left for Banco Ambrosiano. Youngest of them, at just 42, was Alberto Bertoni, Professor of Corporate economics at Milan's Bocconi university, an expert in accounting, and, as the following weeks were to prove, an indefatigable optimist. Giovanni Arduino was different, a courteous commercial banker of an older school, with a distinguished career at Credito Italiano stretching back to 1936, primarily on the international side. To him fell the ticklish task of dealing with the 250 foreign banks desperate to recover their money from the stricken Ambrosiano. But most senior and most redoubtable of the three was Antonino Occhiuto, a stocky 70-year-old Neapolitan who until the Ambrosiano affair thought he had seen all there was to see of the dark face of Italian banking.

Occhiuto belonged to Baffi's generation at the Bank of Italy, a stickler for discipline. "A law, even if it's a bit mad, must be obeyed or else you have anarchy," he once typically remarked. At the central

207

bank he had been head of the vigilance department between 1969 and 1976, the predecessor of the unfortunate Sarcinelli. As one who had handled the death-throes of Sindona, he knew more about collapsing financial card castles than almost anyone.

From the first, it was obvious that the bank would take some saving. Only Bertoni, mindful of the valuable Italian assets of the Ambrosiano group believed that the line could be held. Occhiuto was the gloomiest, feeling privately that the old Ambrosiano board should not have asked for the Bank of Italy to take over on June 17, but applied directly to go into liquidation. Nor was Arduino hopeful, but he felt that something could be saved. But what all three instantly realized, as had Leemans a week earlier, was that salvation lay only in agreement with the IOR.

For despite the soothing reassurances issued daily by the commissioners, an old-fashioned run on the bank was under way. The confidence of depositors, and of the Italian and foreign banks who had lent money to Ambrosiano, had all but disappeared when Calvi vanished from Italy on June 12. His death and the placing of the bank in the commissioners' hands destroyed it completely. Everyone wanted their money back.

And as the commissioners and Ambrosiano's staff juggled desperately to meet the claims as they fell due, Occhiuto and Arduino sought an appointment with the IOR. Marcinkus stalled, but finally on July 2 the encounter took place. With the difference only of the shorter patience of the commissioners it was to be a repeat of the vain efforts of Leemans and Rosone to sway Marcinkus, Mennini and De Stroebel a fortnight before. Predictably, no detailed information about the IOR's overall finances was forthcoming. Occhiuto turned to the letters of comfort. The debts were the Vatican bank's, he insisted, and it had to help. Marcinkus replied that the letters of comfort had been issued *after* the debts had been contracted, as a favour to Calvi. Then he produced the standard trump card, the disclaimer from Calvi.

Occhiuto, however, was not one to be easily persuaded. As far as he was concerned, the "counter-letter" simply proved that the IOR had collaborated with Ambrosiano's chairman in perpetuating a fraud. Not only that, but the absolving letter was in Calvi's capacity as chairman of Ambrosiano Overseas in Nassau, of which Marcinkus

208

had been a director. And what about the letter, dated October 26 1981, from the IOR giving Calvi full powers of attorney for the debts to Lima and Managua?

Arduino then tried a gentler approach. For two weeks, he told Marcinkus, he had given no formal confirmation to creditor banks pressing for payment that the IOR was involved, despite the reports in Italy. He had spoken merely of "an important debtor through various affiliates". But from Monday July 5, the IOR's name would be on the desk of every foreign bank in London, Paris and New York.

Marcinkus gave a resigned shrug. "Too bad," he said. Well then, Arduino retorted, "All I can say is that I'm awfully sorry. For this bloody mess is your responsibility."

The meeting ended, and with it, to all intents and purposes, hopes of a peaceful solution to the Ambrosiano crisis. The commissioners were to have other contacts with the IOR, but with similar lack of success. What exactly happened inside the Vatican during that fortnight between the final detonation of the Ambrosiano crisis, and the blunt refusal to help on July 2 can only be guessed at: the Holy See is not generous with information. One must presume, however, that Marcinkus had managed to satisfy Cardinal Casaroli, and through him the Pope himself, that the IOR was guilty only of naïvety, that it had been deceived by Calvi. That line of argument, indeed, was to remain basically the same through the stormy months ahead.

Ironically, some believe that Ambrosiano could perhaps have been saved for much less than the full $1,287 million outstanding. If $300 or $400 million had been available to satisfy creditors, that might have been enough to restore confidence—had it been provided at once. Instead, confident of its case, the Vatican played for time, with the habit born of a long contemplation of eternity.

Only on July 13 did it announce appointment of its own three "wise men", to examine relations between the IOR and Ambrosiano. The three were Philippe de Weck, a recent chairman of UBS, one of the largest Swiss banks, Joseph Brennan, from the Emigrant Savings Bank of New York, and Carlo Cerutti, a senior executive at STET, the Italian state telecommunications company, as well as a trusted financial counsellor of Popes since Pius XII. The decision was unprecedented and was partly the consequence of something hardly less

209

unusual—a Christian Democrat Minister who spoke out against the Vatican.

One reason, perhaps, why the Vatican had escaped comparatively lightly in the Sindona affair, was that the Government was firmly in the hands of sympathetic Christian Democrats. This time, however, things were different. Spadolini, a Republican not a Christian Democrat, was Prime Minister. Andreatta, meanwhile, had watched Ambrosiano with growing concern since his arrival as Treasury Minister in October 1980. But not even his visit to the Vatican to warn about Calvi in April 1981 had produced much effect. And that July 2, as the commissioners were receiving their decisive rebuff, Andreatta made a Parliamentary statement on the affair. The IOR, he declared, had in some instances been Calvi's business partner. The Italian Government was therefore expecting "a clear acceptance of its responsibility". Such forthrightness was typical of Andreatta; at around this time he seriously considered going to see the Pope in person about the IOR's behaviour. Ambrosiano, however, was rapidly moving beyond deliverance.

The run on deposits was growing worse, and the bank alone could no longer cope. At that point the commissioners took two crucial decisions. On July 5, following the peremptory refusal by the IOR, the Milan parent bank stopped helping its affiliates to meet their own debts as they fell due. The enfeebled children were left to die, and they did so rapidly. On July 16 Ambrosiano Overseas in Nassau had its banking licence suspended, after failing to repay $8 million due that month.

A week earlier the board of Ambrosiano Holding of Luxembourg met for the last time, to vote to place the company under special administration. For Ruggero Mozzana, the 79-year-old predecessor of Calvi at Banco Ambrosiano itself, the occasion was understandably heart-breaking: "I've been alive too long," he said in tears. "Why are *you* crying," replied Carlo Olgiati, still on the Luxembourg board: "You don't have to worry, you're too old to go to prison."

Such was the human dimension of disaster. More important by far, however, were the international implications of that first decision of July 5. Deprived of the support of the Milan parent, the foreign affiliates of Ambrosiano were forced to default on their own repayments to the international banks which had lent them money. The Bank of Italy's arguments for withdrawing support were two: first, that only by adopting an uncompromising policy could it exert pressure on the IOR; and second, that the Rome authorities could not be responsible for debts contracted by offshore subsidiaries of Ambrosiano, beyond all control. For the ambiguous "Basle Concordat" of 1975, agreed by leading central banks at their "club", the Bank for International Settlements in Basle, to deal with such circumstances, obliged a central bank to come to the aid of a bank on its own territory. It was not necessarily obliged to act as "lender of last resort" for subsidiary holding companies like Ambrosiano Luxembourg, and their further appendages. From a legal viewpoint, the Bank of Italy may have been correct, but the decision was to draw a venomous response.

The second decision of that week would also not be without controversy. Discreetly the Bank of Italy had started to sound out leading Italian banks about taking part in a "lifeboat" arrangement to prevent Ambrosiano going under. On July 6, the three commissioners warned Ciampi that Ambrosiano could no longer manage on its own. The choice, they said, lay between a huge injection of new capital, or immediate liquidation. Rapidly, it became clear that the price of the first was the second. Other Italian banks were not prepared to commit unspecified sums without certainty of compensation. And the most obvious compensation was the two highly attractive banks controlled by Ambrosiano; Credito Varesino and above all Banca Cattolica del Veneto, the most profitable single bank in the country.

On July 9 representatives of more than 50 banks belonging to the Italian Banking Association (ABI) met in Milan, but could not agree. In the meantime, however, a select group of major banks had drawn up their own rescue-cum-takeover scheme for Banco Ambrosiano, with the tacit prior endorsement of the Bank of Italy. On that same evening of July 9, after the Milan meeting produced no solution, the plan was launched.

That evening the chairmen and general managers of the six (later to become seven) banks in this secret second group were summoned by Ciampi to the Bank of Italy. The banks involved were a carefully balanced assortment. From the public sector there was the Banca Nazionale del Lavoro (BNL), the largest commercial bank in Italy, the Istituto Bancario San Paolo di Torino, and Istituto Mobiliare Italiano (IMI). The much smaller private sector was represented by Credito Bergamasco of Bergamo, Banca Popolare di Milano and— most fitting of all—Banca San Paolo from Brescia.

History had come full circle, for the Brescia bank was founded in 1889 by that same Monsignor Giuseppe Tovini, who later set up Banco Ambrosiano. Like Ambrosiano, San Paolo di Brescia was profoundly Lombard and "Catholic". Its deputy chairman, Giovanni Bazoli, shared a law practice with Lodovico Montini, the younger brother of the former Pope Paul VI. Tradition, even in this grim hour, had to be respected.

A sombre reception committee awaited the group at the Bank of Italy. It consisted of Andreatta, Ciampi, his deputy Dini, and the commissioners and special auditors down from Milan. The Treasury Minister led off with a stark warning. Without immediate help, Ambrosiano could collapse. But even such aid might not be enough. Ambrosiano could well have to be placed into liquidation—in which case it was essential that a new bank be ready to take its place at once, to avoid the disruption that complete closure would cause for depositors, borrowers and staff of the old Ambrosiano.

For six hours the discussions dragged on, interrupted only by a break for sandwiches. To make matters worse the heat was stifling, as for some reason of "austerity" the central bank's air conditioning had been turned off. The two commissioners Occhiuto and Arduino did not hide their opinion that Ambrosiano was doomed. Bertoni, ever the optimist, argued, however, that conceivably the bank might be salvaged. Some were inclined to believe him, most were more than doubtful.

At last, close to midnight, agreement was reached, and the "pool" was born. The Bank of Italy issued next day a laconic communiqué, recording the guarantee given by the "pool" banks to make available resources to meet the "possible" short-term needs of Banco Ambrosiano. The statement also noted their readiness to "safeguard the continuity of the bank's activities."

Everyone, with the possible exception of the cheerful Bertoni, knew in fact that liquidation was well-nigh inevitable, and attention shifted to the shape of its successor, to be called Nuovo Banco Ambrosiano. No more than 50 per cent of the new bank's capital would be held by the three state banks, to preserve as much as possible Ambrosiano's tradition of private ownership. The number of the private banks involved meanwhile rose from three to four. Banca Popolare di Milano would hold twenty per cent of the new Ambrosiano, and the other three (including San Paolo of Brescia) ten per cent apiece. The blend was as subtle as the forces which previously played upon both Ambrosiano and the *Corriere*, in the eyes of the politicians its most important asset. The Christian Democrats' say was assured primarily through the private banks, above all Banca Popolare di Milano and its chairman, a formidable lawyer called Piero Schlesinger. The other parties had a voice through the state banks. The Social Democrats were represented through San Paolo di Torino, by its deft chairman Luigi Coccioli; the Socialists in the person of Nerio Nesi, admired for both his political and banking judgement as chairman of Banca Nazionale del Lavoro.

But the agreement did little to lift spirits at Calvi's dying Ambrosiano. The mood was of bleak bewilderment. Ordinary staff were fearful for their jobs; middle and senior management, who had always believed they were employed by the soundest of banks, now found that that remote, rarely glimpsed figure deferentially referred to as *Signor Presidente* had tricked them, like a husband who cheats on his wife. Even those who knew, like Leoni, Botta, and in the last stages Rosone, had probably deluded themselves—as maybe Calvi had—that with "the priests' guarantee", everything would be all right. But what God giveth, he can also take away.

For the priests were becoming if anything still more uncompromising. In the early stages there were signs that the Vatican might at least accept responsibility for the $200 million apparently lent by Calvi's banks in Nassau and Lima directly to the IOR. But on July 23, when the commissioners met for the last time with de Weck, Brennan and Cerutti, even that small comfort was removed.

The three investigators appointed by Cardinal Casaroli made clear that the IOR disowned not just the indirect borrowings through Panama, "covered" by the letters of comfort, but the apparently direct ones as well. More letters had been discovered from Calvi, dating from 1976, confirming that the IOR would act merely as a

213

nominee for such deposits from Calvi's banks. The Vatican bank would lend on an equivalent sum to that other Panama shell company, the United Trading Corporation, established back in November 1974. Once again, the Vatican was maintaining it had been duped.

All of this only added to the difficulties facing Arduino, the commissioner who was dealing with the foreign creditor banks. Severance of the financial life support system for Ambrosiano's offshore subsidiaries had its first international effect on July 12, when the Midland Bank in London called Ambrosiano Luxembourg into default on its $40 million loan of 1980, after the first repayment of principal was not met. Under the standard "cross-default" clauses contained in such loans, Banco Ambrosiano Holding was automatically held to have defaulted on the $75 million financing arranged by National Westminster in 1981, and other borrowings as well.

On July 29, Arduino went to London to tell representatives of more than 200 creditors gathered in the Tower Hotel just how $1,287 million had vanished through a trapdoor in Panama. The fortunate banks who had lent to the Milan parent were clearly protected under the 1975 Basle agreement. But he could offer no assurance that the Bank of Italy would cover the debts of Ambrosiano's foreign affiliates—still less that the IOR would.

His audience was not pleased. They reminded Arduino they had always dealt through Milan, and that the same people ran Banco Ambrosiano, Banco Ambrosiano Luxembourg and Banco Andino. The Luxembourg company even had the word "bank" in its name. How could the Italian authorities pretend it was a mere holding company, outside its jurisdiction? The central bank's attitude, someone from a leading Swiss bank warned, could damage Italy's financial reputation. The threat, given the country's need to borrow abroad to help cover a current payments deficit which would reach $5,500 million in 1982, was not to be entirely dismissed.

Arduino listened, and then politely suggested, with appropriate metaphor so soon after the Falklands, that the creditor banks form a task force to handle talks with the Italian authorities. The task force was duly formed, and was to pack no little fire-power. On the other hand, his own wearying stint at Ambrosiano was about to be ended. The very same day, the new auditors reported from Milan that the bank's plight was hopeless; and on August 4 the three commissioners transmitted their formal request that Ambrosiano be liquidated at once. Even Bertoni the optimist had had to give best. The "pool" banks had provided 457 billion lire, but there was nothing to be done. The only question remaining for students of such matters was: which would be liquidated first, Banco Ambrosiano or the Government of Giovanni Spadolini?

In the event, the bank won the race, but narrowly. The torrid Friday of August 6, 1982 was a remarkable day. For the unusually long period of thirteen months, Spadolini's five-party coalition had survived intact. Now, however, at the start of the holiday month, when Italian Governments traditionally are made, not unmade, the Socialists withdrew from the Government, after a Parliamentary defeat. Spadolini had no choice other than to resign. But he delayed his going until Saturday—long enough for Andreatta to summon the meeting of the Interministerial Credit and Savings Committee, which had to take the momentous decision on Calvi's Ambrosiano, for early on the Friday afternoon.

It was for the Treasury Minister to pronounce the death sentence. But first the Governor of the Bank of Italy read out the prosecution's unanswerable case.

Banks may suffer from two fatal diseases: a crisis of solvency, when liabilities exceed assets, or a crisis of liquidity—in other words a run on deposits—when the demands for customers for their money back cannot any longer be met. Sometimes insolvency can be masked (as it long was in the case of Ambrosiano) if the confidence of depositors and lenders is maintained; sometimes, too, a liquidity crisis can be overcome, if a bank can realize enough of its readiest assets to cover withdrawals and convince other depositors that it is sound. But Ambrosiano was terminally ill on both counts.

The bank on its own could meet neither the demands of its foreign creditors, thanks to an unrecoverable $744 million lent to its subsidiaries abroad, nor those of depositors at home. In just two months since May 31, deposits had fallen by 25 per cent, and the pace of withdrawals was quickening. The liquidity crisis, Ciampi declared, was irreversible. Simultaneously the bank's balance sheet showed an overall deficit of 480 billion lire, even after taking into account the reserves of over 500 billion lire accumulated by the old Ambrosiano.

Nor was $744 million the end of the problem. Ambrosiano's shareholding in its Luxembourg holding company was now without value, while its provisions against bad debts were insufficient. Also to be written off was the total of 70 billion lire spent on buying shares in itself to prop up the price before the stock market listing. These too were now plainly worthless. Almost superfluously, the Governor of the Bank of Italy recorded two criminal offences committed by the old management: concealment of the fact that $1,287 million had been lent to a single group of overseas borrowers, and the unauthorized purchase of Ambrosiano shares. Truly they were operations, in Ciampi's words, "beyond every bound of banking logic".

There was little left to be said. That hot Friday afternoon, near the end of the 86th year of its life, the old Banco Ambrosiano died. The declaration of insolvency by a Milan bankruptcy court on August 26 was the merest formality. The scale of the world's most spectacular postwar banking failure was underlined by the final accounts of the Luxembourg holding company for the year to June 30 1982, showing a loss of almost $1,000 million. But the controversy over the disposal of Roberto Calvi's unhandsome legacy still lay ahead.

CHAPTER TWENTY-THREE

Aftermath

THE COMPLEXITY OF Italy, and the division of power between a myriad competing interest groups, can so often make procrastination seem a way of life. But when the eleventh hour is about to expire, and real emergency beckons, then decisions can be improvised and taken with conjuror's speed. So it was with the birth of Nuovo Banco Ambrosiano.

As the old Ambrosiano of Roberto Calvi slowly perished, its successor was being readied at hectic pace. The seven pool banks agreed to put up an initial capital of 600 billion lire for the new bank, a colossal figure given that Ambrosiano's deposits had dwindled to little more than 2,000 billion lire. A new statute was drawn up, and a board chosen, while lawyers finalized the terms of the transfer of activities from Banco Ambrosiano to Nuovo Banco Ambrosiano. Not least important, a chairman was found, in the appropriate person of Giovanni Bazoli, a devout Catholic, and vice-chairman of Banca San Paolo di Brescia, the pool bank which had the closest historical links with Calvi's Ambrosiano.

Bazoli agreed to take the job on August 5. The following day, as Andreatta signed the fateful decree in Rome, and a summer thunderstorm fittingly swept over a half-deserted Milan, the new bank was formally registered. Its first board meeting was held the same afternoon, in the offices of the Banca Popolare di Milano.

That weekend, punctuated by a symbolic closedown of a single second, Calvi's Ambrosiano physically became Nuovo Banco Ambrosiano. Officials spent Saturday and Sunday almost without sleep, going over the books of every one of the 107 branches of the old bank. Miraculously the new Ambrosiano opened for "business as usual" at 8.30 a.m. on Monday, August 9. In fact, an uninterrupted transition was essential, for had the bank been shut even for a week, everything might have been lost.

As it was, difficulties abounded. The withdrawal of deposits was only slowly stemmed and the 4,200 staff of the former bank were almost twice as many as its smaller successor warranted. For only those most heavily compromised with Calvi—the previous board, and senior foreign officials like Leoni and Botta—had been dismissed. To their surprise, moreover, the new directors found that even in Italy where it had seemed so profitable, Ambrosiano left much to be desired. Its branches were poorly sited, its methods unenterprising, and even the record 1981 profit had only been achieved thanks to the proceeds of share dealings. For Calvi's neglect of the ordinary activities of his bank, Ambrosiano had also paid a price.

The pool had additional teething problems of its own. Strains sometimes would arise between its participants, public and private, Socialist and Christian Democrat, and between banks which were direct competitors in Milan of Ambrosiano and those which were not. Not surprisingly, despite advertisements portraying it as "the bank made of banks", Nuovo Ambrosiano expected to lose 30 billion lire in its first year.

And then, pervading everything, there was the past. Bazoli himself wondered long whether "Ambrosiano" should disappear from the new bank's title. In the event, continuity at home was deemed more important than opprobrium abroad. It fell to Bazoli, too, to step into the shoes, or rather the office, of the dead Calvi. Above him, on the fifth floor, the liquidators of the old bank sifted through the documents of the past. But in those first days, he would occasionally shiver to find himself alone in that huge, half-empty office below, that had once been Calvi's. Early on, Bazoli decided to turn the room over to committee meetings, while he would work in what used to be a waiting room. But little time was to spare for the contemplation of lingering ghosts.

First, the authorities in Luxembourg, piqued at the discredit thrown upon its tax haven status by the Ambrosiano scandal, ordered Italian banks with similar subsidiaries there to provide full guarantees within 48 hours for these latter—or risk losing their local banking licences. The ultimatum was duly met. But the episode betrayed an initial

218

unhappiness felt by more than one foreign central bank at the conduct of the Bank of Italy, and the absence of earlier intimation of its longheld suspicions about Ambrosiano.

But this discontent was modest, compared to the resentment felt at the principal ruling of August 6: that La Centrale, which controlled the choicest Italian interests of the old Ambrosiano, be transferred not to its liquidators, as normal practice would have seemed to dictate, but to its successor. The new bank paid just 350 billion lire for the good will. The liquidators, who would have to pay off the foreign creditors were left with only Banco Ambrosiano Holding in Luxembourg and its mostly worthless appendages. As the implications sunk in many were upset—but not the seven pool banks whose reward would be La Centrale and its banking and insurance subsidiaries.

The 39,000 small shareholders of the old Ambrosiano who had lost everything, Leemans at La Centrale, Rossi at the Consob, and above all the creditors of the foreign banks of Calvi, felt cheated or worse.

The decision was justified on the grounds that it would prevent such important assets being put to chancy auction, with the risk that the highest bidder might prove another Calvi or Sindona. The true reason, more probably, was the political requirement to keep Rizzoli and the *Corriere* within their existing orbit, something so carefully ensured by the composition of the original pool, which was now the owner of the new Ambrosiano. In vain did irate small shareholders bring legal actions to try and reverse the decision. The promise of success was small; and to placate them, Nuovo Ambrosiano announced that it would issue warrants, enabling subscription on favourable terms to a capital increase planned for 1985. In the meantime Leemans, who had described the transfer of La Centrale as "the steal of the century", had been forced to resign as its managing director.

Far more revealing, especially of the inbuilt institutional rivalries within Italy, was the departure from the Consob of Guido Rossi. The Ambrosiano collapse was a most embarrassing setback both for the stock market and for the regulatory body trying to change its ways. True, Rossi had by his insistence forced Ambrosiano to issue a prospectus naming Cascadilla, Orfeo and their like in Panama. But it was another Pyrrhic victory in a story full of them. By its omissions, the prospectus was a fraud: and daylight of the main market was far too bright for Ambrosiano to withstand.

In truth, Rossi had been wondering for some while whether to leave. But the Ambrosiano affair was the last straw. Had the Bank of Italy let the Consob know of its suspicions about Ambrosiano, he felt, the quotation might never have happened; as for the decision to liquidate a quoted company, Rossi had learnt of it only after it had been taken. Four days later, he resigned with bitter words for the Bank of Italy and the Treasury Minister for their lack of co-operation.

His going was variously received. Some took it as a ploy to protect himself from the wrath of small shareholders, for many of whom Consob's admission of Banco Ambrosiano to the main market had been a guarantee of soundness. Others simply put the episode down to frayed nerves in the heat of a banking crisis without recent precedent. But not a few were quietly relieved to see the back of Rossi, in the hope of a less prickly, more malleable successor.

But most awkward—and most serious—of all for the Italian authorities were the objections of the foreign creditor banks to the liquidation procedure. At that London meeting in July they had been told in effect that only the IOR could ensure repayment of the $450 million lent to Calvi's Luxembourg holding company.

Now they were learning that the most valuable assets of the bankrupt Ambrosiano were not to be sold off, and the proceeds distributed to creditors. To disappointment was added injury, which observations that the banks had been guilty of professional misjudgement of a risk did nothing to assuage. Indeed, such suggestions only strengthened their resolve to prove through the courts that the Italian authorities were as bound to underwrite the debts of Ambrosiano in Luxembourg and Lima as they were those of Ambrosiano in Milan—whatever the Basle Concordat might or might not say.

The creditors advanced three main arguments. First, Ambrosiano had always been presented as a group. Second, although the loans were made to different companies, they were all negotiated by the same few people at Ambrosiano, to disappear in an identical conspiracy down an identical drain. For the liquidators to discriminate against some creditors was therefore unfair and inadmissible. Thirdly, the Bank of Italy's inspection of Ambrosiano showed that it had formed a very shrewd idea of what Calvi was up to as long ago as 1978.

The Italian authorities, the creditors maintained, should have acted much sooner.

Curiously, it was some while before they managed to look closely at Padalino's report, which since late 1981 had been circulating secretly in photocopy form among those in the know in Milan. At one stage a creditor bank in London found itself being offered a copy for £250; happily, one mysteriously arrived for free under anonymous cover, a few days later.

In reply, the Bank of Italy submitted three arguments of its own. Firstly, it had no duty to make good money borrowed by foreign subsidiaries, operating from offshore banking centres impossible to monitor. Secondly, much of the responsibility for the Ambrosiano affair belonged not to Italy, but to the Vatican and the IOR. Thirdly, and more generally, the skill of banking lay in judgement of risk. If all loans were automatically guaranteed by a central bank, it maintained, one of the main disciplines of banking would be removed, increasing the danger of unwise lending.

Thus the opening positions were staked out for what would be lengthy three-way jousting between the Italian state, the IOR and the foreign creditors. The weapons were study groups, task forces, and mixed commissions.

Above all, however, there were the lawyers and the lawsuits, stretching from Europe to North and South America. Many might face losses at the hands of Calvi, but the lawyers with certainty would profit handsomely. By the end of April 1983, the creditor banks had brought 93 separate lawsuits, claiming over $500 million from the liquidators in Milan and Nuovo Banco Ambrosiano. In reply the Bank of Italy signalled its irritation with those twelve foreign banks which had obliged Calvi with $230 million of risk-free "back to back" loans from late 1981, by suing two of them for the return of $17 million lent them by the old Ambrosiano.

But even richer legal extravagances were conceivable. Theoretically, Banca Nazionale del Lavoro, simultaneously one of the main creditors of Ambrosiano Luxembourg and a leading shareholder in Nuovo Banco Ambrosiano, could end up suing itself.

Most tantalizing of all was the possibility that someone might sue the IOR. The Vatican bank filed claims in December 1982 with the liquidators of Ambrosiano Overseas for the return of $73 million

221

deposited in Nassau. But those same liquidators considered legal proceedings against the IOR—for the return of $90 million Ambrosiano Overseas had in turn deposited with the Vatican bank. Many of the creditor banks, understandably, felt like doing the same.

In fact though, despite their public insistence that nothing less than a 100 per cent settlement would suffice, a compromise did not look impossible. Early in the year, the liquidators of Ambrosiano in Milan, with the blessing of the Bank of Italy, sent a secret emissary to see representatives of the creditors in a Paris hotel. He made a "take-it-or-leave-it" proposal: 30 per cent or nothing.

The banks went away to mull the offer over. Alas, however, news of the meeting was swiftly leaked to the press. Ciampi, the Governor of the Bank of Italy, was initially so angry that he wanted to stop all bargaining there and then. But both sides had an interest to settle. Italy as a borrower needed the good will of potential lenders; the banks for their part knew that it could be years before they won any lawsuit—if they won at all.

More clear-cut, if less eyecatching, were the consequences of the Calvi disaster at home. Directly and indirectly, the Ambrosiano affair would cause great changes in the country's financial landscape.

Under the August agreement Nuovo Ambrosiano agreed to dispose of the insurance and publishing interests which Calvi had defied the law to obtain. The first to go was the 56 per cent interest in the Toro insurance company, sold for 270 billion lire in March 1983 to a consortium led by IFI, the holding company of the Agnelli family and the dominant shareholder of Fiat. The fate of Rizzoli, however, was inevitably a rather more complicated matter.

Now that Calvi—both its paymaster and effective owner—had gone, the old Rizzoli seemed as surely doomed as the old Ambrosiano. Even the 176 billion lire provided by La Centrale in 1981 had failed to set it to rights. That year, imaginative accounting had limited Rizzoli's declared loss to 13 billion lire, although Angelo Rizzoli was to admit publicly that the real loss was five times greater.

Most important of all, neither La Centrale, losing 60 billion lire a year itself thanks to its involvement with Rizzoli, nor Ambrosiano under its new management, was prepared to put up with this state of affairs any longer. During August and September, the various banks

222

of the Ambrosiano group refused to extend 120 billion lire of loans to Rizzoli as they fell due for repayment. The consequences were immediate. On October 7, Rizzoli applied to be placed under *amministrazione controllata*, meaning that a moratorium would be placed upon its debts, while expert outsiders went through the books.

At last, the unintelligible balance sheet of years past, and the mysteries of its ownership were made clear. A small discovery was that, partly through the Banco Andino in Lima, Calvi controlled 100 per cent of the *Corriere* itself. A larger one was that between 1980 and 1982, Rizzoli was estimated to have lost 300 billion lire, including 142 billion lire in 1982 alone. It was a monument worthy of the follies of the past. Angelo Rizzoli withdrew from his company's affairs, philosophical but morose, to contemplate the virtual loss of both his business and his fortune. Only Tassan Din attempted to resist, twisting and turning to find an escape from the maze he had helped construct. But in mid-February of 1983 he was forced to resign from the post of managing director.

The worst, however, was yet to come. Rizzoli's special administrators and the *Guardia di Finanza* had discovered that payments totalling 28 billion lire had not been recorded at all in the company's previous balance sheets. Not only was the group close to bankruptcy; fraud was suspected as well. Just after dawn on February 18, Angelo Rizzoli, his brother Alberto, and Tassan Din were arrested at their Milan homes, and taken to prison for questioning by magistrates about the missing money. Alberto Rizzoli, less heavily implicated, was released in mid-March. Angelo Rizzoli and Tassan Din were only freed just before Easter.

Admittedly, Milan in recent years had grown used to the spectacle of financiers in handcuffs: Calvi himself had spent two months in jail in 1981, and the ritual of the dawn arrest had become familiar enough to earn the nickname of the *assegno delle sette*, the "Seven o'clock ticket"; many, moreover, had suspected that it would be the turn of Rizzoli and Tassan Din before long. Even so, it was a sad way for the old Rizzoli to go. Once it had been Italy's most prosperous publishing group, an advertisement for Milanese enterprise. Now the company was discredited and of uncertain future.

Only for the *Corriere*, perhaps, was this miserable dénouement a kind of liberation, putting conclusive end to its association with Gelli and the P-2, to which both Rizzoli and Tassan Din—as well as Calvi—had belonged. There were hopes that the issue of its ownership might be at last resolved to the satisfaction of itself and that of the politicians, after the general election of June 1983.

Less vivid, but perhaps of greater implication for Italian finance, were the repercussions of the Ambrosiano bankruptcy for Carlo Pesenti, oldest of the Vatican's financial allies. Italmobiliare had been the largest single Italian shareholder in the liquidated Ambrosiano. By all accounts, many of its assets had been mortgaged to Calvi's banks, to secure loans helping Italmobiliare finance debts of some 1,000 billion lire.

The bankruptcy had meant that Pesenti lost 100 billion lire on his four per cent shareholding in Ambrosiano alone, and action could be put off no longer. Six weeks after Calvi died, Pesenti sold his biggest bank, Istituto Bancario Italiano, to Cariplo, the savings bank representing the provinces of Lombardy, for 550 billion lire. The transaction further enlarged the presence of the public sector within the Italian banking system. But many doubted that it alone would suffice to free Pesenti from his difficulties. A greater political adroitness than Calvi and the ownership of some sound industrial companies had for years enabled him to confound predictions of financial demise. However, Pesenti was now not only a victim of Ambrosiano's downfall, but also 75 years old and suffering from heart troubles.

There was an additional discomfort too. Milan magistrates were again scrutinizing that peculiar 50 billion lire loan of a decade earlier from the IOR, so suspiciously indexed to the Swiss franc. For Marcinkus and the Vatican bank, on the other hand, that was the least of their worries.

CHAPTER TWENTY-FOUR

Vatican Disarray

THOSE WHOM PAUL Marcinkus numbered as his friends received at the end of 1982 a small postcard of Christmas greetings. On one side there were images of the Madonna and child, on the other a brief message, speaking of the ups and downs of a "difficult" year. But that was to put his problems mildly; nor was there much sign that they would disappear with the old year.

Marcinkus could hardly have imagined that his blunt refusal of assistance to the three Ambrosiano commissioners on July 2 would have closed the affair. Indeed, far from blowing itself out, the storm in Italy and abroad was only gathering. Cardinal Casaroli had already seen enough to realize that outside expertise would be needed to help sort out the muddle, and had appointed his own three "wise men" to assess the IOR's involvement.

From the Italian press, meanwhile, Marcinkus had learnt to expect little sympathy, and he received none. "The super-Calvi in the Vatican", read one headline of those days. "Marcinkus: angel or devil?" ran another. More seriously, those stern magistrates in Milan evidently felt the same.

Formal notification was issued to Marcinkus, De Stroebel and Mennini (along with a score of senior former officials of Ambrosiano) at the end of July, warning them that they might face charges arising from the collapse of Ambrosiano. The Vatican refused on procedural grounds to take delivery of the three *comunicazioni giudiziarie*, arguing that since the Holy See was a foreign state, they should first have been channelled through the Italian Foreign Ministry and the Italian Embassy to the Vatican.

Little more was heard of the episode—but for months afterwards Marcinkus would remain a virtual prisoner within the square mile of the Vatican city state, apprehensive that the notification would be delivered if he crossed on to Italian soil. He was forced to abandon his flat in Villa Stritch, the traditional residence of American priests in Rome, for the spacious but impersonal apartments which fell to him as Governor of the Vatican city.

Nonetheless, in those early weeks, as Casaroli's appointees began their work, Marcinkus appeared comparatively cheerful. The Vatican's position remained his own—that everything should be denied, not least because the slightest concession would be taken as admission of guilt. Even the normally restrained *Osservatore Romano*, the Vatican newspaper, was moved to complain vehemently at the harassment from the Italian press. From mid-August on, however, Marcinkus became steadily more isolated.

Casaroli, just back from a ten-day visit to the United States (during which he was suspected of contacting informally leading American banks about assistance for the IOR) gave an interview resounding with faint praise. More outspoken was Cardinal Giovanni Benelli of Florence, among the most powerful voices in the Italian church and long an opponent of the American Archbishop within the Curia. If the IOR had been imprudent, Benelli remarked, then that was due to "incapacity and inexperience". Marcinkus, in other words, had been a fool.

Next came the loss of his job as organizer and unofficial bodyguard on Papal journeys abroad. The attentions of the magistrates were, of course, one reason. At least an equal consideration, however, must have been the unflattering publicity Marcinkus would have received, distracting attention from the pastoral and spiritual purpose of a Pope's travels. For the Ambrosiano affair had made him a most unspiritual celebrity around the world. When John Paul II went to Spain that October, Marcinkus for the first time was absent from his shoulder.

Marcinkus was paying the price, not only of his indiscretions with Calvi, but also of the jealousies held by many within the predominantly Italian administration of the Vatican, who had never come to terms with a forthright, demanding, but so successful outsider. In the past this resentment had been stifled by unswerving support from the Pope. But now Marcinkus would attract criticism aimed at John Paul

II himself; of his unquestioning trust of the American archbishop; and of how his travels had prevented him from listening to more sober counsel at home—especially about the bad name of the IOR's financial partner.

The person of the Pope was soon to be drawn into the Ambrosiano scandal again—this time by Andreatta, the Treasury Minister. On October 7, in a second parliamentary statement on the scandal, he once more made no bones about the involvement of the Vatican bank, but pointed out that the Italian authorities were powerless to act against a foreign bank on foreign soil. On the other hand, Andreatta observed, the Pope could intervene, if he wished, to oblige the IOR to "behave in a specific fashion".

He had stated no more than the obvious; but to some in his own Christian Democrat party the words appeared unacceptable *lèse-papauté*, and talk of a "trial" by his party peers was briefly heard.

Fortunately, the hubbub quickly faded, and the inquisition never materialized. In any case the Vatican in its secretive fashion was hinting at possible accommodation. An understanding had evidently been reached to set aside the judicial threat to Marcinkus, for that Christmas he flew back to Chicago to see more trusted friends. And in the quiet of Christmas Eve, Italy and the Vatican announced that they had established a joint commission to evaluate responsibility for the Ambrosiano bankruptcy.

The Vatican's new found willingness to talk reflected several considerations.

Firstly, it was aware that serious breach with Italy would endanger what chances there were of an agreed revision to the Concordat, on which negotiations had been laboriously proceeding for five years. Secondly, its researches had suggested that the IOR's innocence might be less clear-cut than earlier maintained. Nothing more was heard, for example, of the notorious "counter-letter" given by Calvi in August 1981, the most glaring evidence of connivance in the continuation of a fraud.

Finally—and most important—an assembly of Cardinals would gather in Rome in November, to discuss, among other things, the Church's precarious finances. And already complaint was widespread among Catholics about the IOR's links with Calvi, and the failure of the Vatican's statements to keep pace with evident facts. A much fuller account would have to be provided, along with proof that the IOR's house was being set in order. Meanwhile, a propitious occasion to prepare the ground further was offered by a meeting between John Paul II and President Sandro Pertini.

In the middle of October the two lunched together at a hunting lodge once of the royal house of Savoy, but now for the use of the Republic's Head of State. The meeting was a deliberate demonstration that relations between Italy and the Vatican, at the highest level at least, were in excellent order. It also allowed John Paul II to tell Pertini of his intention to make 1983 a Holy Year.

The announcement was made only at the end of the Cardinals' meeting on November 26. It drew some surprise, not least because of the shortness of the notice, and because only eight years had elapsed since the last Holy Year. The Jubilee would be dedicated to "Redemption", and mark the 1,950th anniversary of the death of Christ. On spiritual grounds, this latest "extraordinary" Holy Year in Catholic history could be amply justified as a sign of the Church's commitment to peace and justice at a time of much tension in international affairs.

But it almost certainly had secular meaning as well—as a sizeable olive branch from the Vatican in the Ambrosiano dispute. The pilgrims who would travel to Rome in search of indulgence would spend foreign currency, perhaps many hundreds of millions of dollars, for the benefit of the Italian economy. In this elegantly indirect way, both the IOR and its "debts" to the Ambrosiano of Roberto Calvi might be redeemed.

For the Vatican was now forced to admit publicly what the Italian authorities, Ambrosiano's old directors in Milan, Nassau and Lima and the world's press had long been insisting: that the IOR owned the tiny companies which owed almost $1,100 million to Ambrosiano.

The six-page statement with which Casaroli explained the *imbroglio* to the College of Cardinals on November 26 constituted the Vatican's one and only detailed account of the fraud since it was exposed five months before. It should therefore be studied carefully.

First, Casaroli listed the five main conclusions reached by the experts appointed in July.

They were 1) the IOR had received nothing from Calvi or Ambrosiano, and therefore had nothing to repay; 2) the IOR had never run the companies which owed so much money to Ambrosiano, and had no idea of what they were doing; 3) all the money was made over to these ten companies *before* the letters of patronage were issued; 4) for this reason the letters had no bearing on the loans themselves; and 5) the IOR had documentary evidence to support these assertions. So what did happen? Casaroli gave his version.

The IOR, he said, had always trusted Ambrosiano, believing it to be a serious Catholic bank, of undisputed soundness. But when its troubles started, the Vatican bank found out that this trust had been abused, in a long series of apparently unconnected operations. Each on its own seemed perfectly normal, but from them had been built a "secret project" for which the IOR's name had been used as cover.

"In particular," said Casaroli, "the bank found itself the *direct owner of two companies, and the indirect owner of eight more*." But, he repeated, the IOR had never run them, and knew nothing of what they did. In July 1981, the IOR learnt it had the "juridical control" of all ten companies. Therefore the IOR issued the letters of comfort to the directors of Ambrosiano's Lima and Managua subsidiaries "to freeze their debt position", while the IOR disposed of the ownership. Apart from interest accrued, the debts had not risen since the issue of the letters of comfort in September 1981. The IOR, therefore, was technically blameless. It was accepted in the international banking community, Casaroli added, that letters of comfort had no legal value.

Thus did Casaroli set out the Vatican's starting position for the discussions with the Italian authorities. In a word, the IOR was maintaining that Calvi had taken it for a colossal ride. Its sins, if any, were those of naïvety and inexperience.

The 107 Cardinals returned home still rather bemused. But they were reassured by the Pope's promises that the Vatican would rely less on the IOR, and more on the "St Peter's Pence" offerings of the faithful to balance its books, and that the bank would be more tightly supervised. For Marcinkus the outcome was a setback, even though he would still insist to visitors, fretful and more downcast than in August, that he "would see this thing through".

In January came another indication of the disfavour into which Ambrosiano had led him. His was the most conspicuous missing name from a list of fifteen new cardinals appointed by the Pope. For traditionally, Marcinkus' position as pro-president, or Mayor, of the Vatican city would have entitled him to that rank. In the meantime Casaroli's lengthy explanation in November began to look less convincing, as the liquidators unearthed evidence of a decade of complicity between Calvi and the IOR. Yet again, the Vatican was paying the price of its failure to be frank.

CHAPTER TWENTY-FIVE

The Vatican and the Money

THE RELATIONSHIP BETWEEN the Vatican bank and Ambrosiano was the perfect illustration of the Italian illusionist's art. A carnival mask could be stripped away—to reveal another mask. In other words, was the IOR acting for its own interests? Or was Ambrosiano acting behind the façade of the IOR; or was the IOR behind Ambrosiano behind the IOR—or even Ambrosiano behind the IOR behind Ambrosiano behind the IOR? Rarely has the technique of the fiduciary or the nominee in high finance been so dazzlingly employed. But then the two had been practising their skill a long time.

The relationship, after all, dated from August 1971, when Marcinkus joined the board of the newly formed Cisalpine Overseas (later to become Ambrosiano Overseas) in Nassau, and a vital part, as we have seen, of Calvi's scheme. He remained a director until June 14, 1982, three days before the end.

Thereafter one may list just a few salient episodes. From 1972 the IOR was involved in the Italian dealings of Calvi, including its sale to him of Banca Cattolica del Veneto and his acquisition of Credito Varesino. In 1974 the Vatican bank set up United Trading Corporation, the Panamanian company which would long remain the most impenetrable of all of them. In 1975 (or 1978), it lent its name to Suprafin, the company which carried out the huge initial purchases of shares in Banco Ambrosiano.

In 1976, Calvi wrote to the Vatican bank asking for money deposited with the IOR to be passed on to UTC. But was this ploy devised by Calvi himself, so that he could operate the company as he wished? Or was it devised by the Vatican, to pass on to Calvi responsibility for what it knew was being done on its behalf? Later Cisalpine in Nassau, on whose board sat Marcinkus, was doing its best to prevent Coopers and Lybrand, its increasingly uneasy accountants, from revealing the extent of the relationship with the IOR. Then 1981, and the Vatican bank's discovery of the size of the mess which it had helped create, the letters of comfort, the absolving letter from Calvi, and the climax in June 1982. Other evidence is in the hands of liquidators in Milan, Luxembourg and Nassau.

Certainly the IOR never administered the Panama and Liechtenstein companies; but is it really to be believed that it knew nothing of or did not at least strongly suspect, their true activities before the summer of 1981? From that moment on, of course, the documents accompanying the letters of patronage show that the IOR was aware that the debts were secured by shares worth only a quarter of them. Quite understandably, it extracted the exonerating letter from Calvi.

Many, moreover, were unconvinced by the finding of the Vatican' lawyers, and relayed by Casaroli to the Cardinals, that the IOR had received nothing from Calvi or from Ambrosiano, and therefore had nothing to repay. The matter may be left aside of who was the final recipient of the dividends paid each year on the Ambrosiano shares, held through the Panamanian front companies owned by the IOR, and totalling nearly $2 million for the financial year of 1981. More indicative perhaps was the case of Vianini, the last Italian company in which the Vatican held a controlling shareholding after Sindona began the disposal of its Italian interests at the end of the 1960s.

In 1980, the IOR agreed to sell six million shares in Vianini to Laramie, one of the clutch of Panamanian front companies in three annual tranches of two million shares, each for a total of $20 million. The first payment went through, and indeed two million shares in Vianini appear in the letters of comfort as the asset securing the final debt of Laramie outstanding to Ambrosiano in Nicaragua. But since the IOR already owned Laramie, *it was in effect selling the shares to itself, in return for money provided by Calvi* (and rather more than they were really worth). No wonder the Vatican had little choice but to sign the letters of comfort.

There was, moreover, an interesting footnote to the Vianini affair. According to Francesco Pazienza, who claimed to have found an American buyer willing to pay $60 million for Vianini, the deal fell through at a "Kafkaesque" meeting between himself, Marcinkus and Calvi at the Vatican. Pazienza simply could not understand whether it

232

was the IOR, or Ambrosiano, which controlled the company. On this occasion, one could sympathize with Pazienza.

Probably the full truth about the Vatican bank's relations with Calvi would never be known—except maybe in the confessional box. Indeed it was possibly in too many people's interest that it would not be. Documents abounded to prove many things, but not the spirit in which they were written. Undoubtedly, Calvi tricked the Vatican; the question remained: where did negligence and naïvety end, and collusion begin?

What the unfortunate outcome of its dealings with Calvi certainly did show, was how the concern of the Vatican with financial secrecy had been its own worst enemy. If the IOR's activities had been properly scrutinized by outside accountants, if it had dealt with banks less underhand than the Ambrosiano of Calvi, such an affair would never have happened.

In that respect at least the scandal might bring benefit. The pressures to reform the IOR had never been as great as after the Ambrosiano affair. They derived not only from the Italian Government, which would like to see the Vatican bank open a branch on Italian soil, and be treated exactly as are the Italian branches of Barclays Bank or Chase Manhattan bank. Many within the Catholic Church also decided that clarity, even at the price of truly "lay" management of the IOR, is preferable to the impenetrable methods of the past, with all their damaging consequences.

These questions would perhaps be resolved by the mixed commission established on the Christmas Eve of 1982. Less certain of complete solution was another of the mysteries at the heart of the Ambrosian scandal, the final destination of exactly $1,287 million.

"All I can say," Marcinkus would shrug to visitors who afterwards pressed him on the matter, "is that it's a heck of a lot of money." And so indeed it was. Almost $1,300 million—a sum, he may have estimated while ruing the day he first set eyes on Calvi all those years earlier, to match the entire proceeds of St Peter's Pence since the donations to the Pope began in 1860, and enough to cover the Vatican's total declared expenditure for a decade.

Close Italian observers of Ambrosiano, including the Bank of Italy, had a similar reaction. Certainly, they had suspected that

Calvi's secrecy was a sign that he had something unpleasant to hide behind the screen of Latin American affiliates. It was not the nature of his difficulties which surprised; rather the sheer extent of them. Where *did* so vast an amount of money disappear?

Nearly a year after the demise of Banco Ambrosiano and the gruesome climax in London, the answer had not been established with any certainty. But thanks to the endeavours of the magistrates, liquidators, and the police (by 1983 the *Guardia di Finanza* alone was conducting eight separate investigations into the affair), a picture was beginning to emerge.

By far the largest single culprit, as this book has made clear, was the purchase of shares in various companies of the group Calvi controlled. The process began with Zitropo and Pacchetti in 1972, but most important was the holding, between ten and fourteen per cent, built up in Banco Ambrosiano itself.

The shares were mostly bought at inflated prices in the first place, and then passed on with even higher theoretical value, from one tiny company to another. By this device the new loans required to finance their purchase and pay for interest could be justified, on paper, to the banks of Ambrosiano in Nassau, Managua, and then Lima which would provide the money. In this way Manic and Astolfine, the two companies which near the end were holding between them 5.8 million Banco Ambrosiano shares, booked them at a value of $509 million— compared with a historic maximum worth on the Milan stock market of only $207 million. That latter valuation, moreover, had only been achieved by massive illegal support buying by Ambrosiano itself.

The case of Astolfine was most instructive of all. The 2.1 million shares it had pledged were ascribed a book value of $200 apiece, compared with an actual price, at the moment of Ambrosiano's full quotation, of about $36. By the end Astolfine had borrowed no less than $486 million from Banco Andino in Lima, although its own capital was just $10,000.

Then there were the shares in Banca del Gottardo, Pacchetti, Credito Varesino, La Centrale, TV Sorrisi e Canzoni, Vianini and Rizzoli, Suprafin, Montreal Holding and Banco Ambrosiano Overseas, which featured either in the letters of patronage of autumn 1981, or at the moment of reckoning nine months later.

Other money was spent for undeclared shareholdings, most notably the 30 per cent of Banco Ambrosiano Holding in Luxembourg which the Milan parent did not own, but which it undoubtedly controlled. Some of these shares, with a face value of $50 million, were held by the United Trading Corporation of the IOR, others by Banco de la Nacion, Calvi's ally in Lima. By the end, moreover, Banco Andino there had a capital of $75 million, subscribed almost entirely by Ambrosiano in Luxembourg.

All in all, the Italian authorities reckoned that $800 or $900 million might have been used for these purposes, in other words about two thirds of the total debt. But that still left $400 million or more to be accounted for—one of the largest puzzles outstanding after the collapse of Banco Ambrosiano.

A broad subsidiary category of losses may have been money provided to companies and individuals which had earlier been doing business with Ambrosiano at home. In 1978 the central bank had identified a potentially dangerous concentration of loans within Italy to customers such as Rizzoli, the Genghini construction company, and Voxson, the electronics company owned in part by Umberto Ortolani, all of them of course in one way or another within the orbit of the P-2. If inspection by the Bank of Italy had prompted Calvi to increase concealment of the true ownership of his bank, what more natural than that he should also seek to hide the extent of his lending to such favoured but suspect customers?

One piece of evidence suggesting financial links between Ortolani and Calvi abroad was the $37 million loan provided by Erin, one of the Panamanian companies, which in turn had received the money in 1980 from Banco Andino in Lima. It was made over to an emanation of Bafisud, the bank in Uruguay owned by Ortolani. Then there was the puzzle of the two transfers in spring 1981, of $95 million and $48 million from Bellatrix, one of Erin's Panamanian sisters, to those peculiar Zirka and Recioto accounts held at Rothschild Bank, Zurich. That the operations were in some way connected with Rizzoli seemed beyond doubt; Tassan Din, the former managing director of Rizzoli, as well as Leoni, Botta and Costa, the senior Ambrosiano executives on the board of Banco Andino at the time, would later be arrested and charged over the financings. Possibly they were to pay for a subsequent transfer, into Panama or elsewhere, of the 40 pe cent of Rizzoli acquired by La Centrale, Ambrosiano's holdin company in Italy, shortly beforehand. But as we have seen, tha transfer never took place—probably because of Calvi's sudden im prisonment in May 1981. So what did happen to the money? Did pa of it at least go to Gelli, to Ortolani, or somewhere else within th labyrinth of the P-2? Some $30 million, it was later discovered, wa held in a proxy account at a bank in Dublin—of all places—on behal of Bruno Tassan Din.

Indeed, Gelli and Ortolani were surely prominent among the ne group of likely recipients of the money of Ambrosiano: those whor Calvi paid, willingly or less willingly, for the protection from which h believed he might benefit, or without which he might be endangere Some $55 million, which Gelli tried to retrieve in person from a Swis bank account, probably originated at Ambrosiano. And how muc more did he receive? Pazienza was another whose services did nc come cheaply; nor did those of Carboni. As we have seen, more tha $20 million was found in Swiss accounts of Carboni, including thos $14 million despatched from Ambrosiano Overseas in Nassau i February 1982. Nor was it hard to imagine that political parties withi Italy were also among the beneficiaries; if not directly, then indirectl through intermediaries like Rizzoli.

In Latin America too, where the P-2 was active, Calvi must hav been generous; both locally, and for the benefit of favoured associ ates back in Italy. How much money oiled the wheels in Peru an elsewhere in Latin America (or indeed if any was employed, a frequently rumoured, to finance the purchase of arms) had not bee established with certainty. But Calvi would always take precaution against any eventuality. Anastasio Somoza, the late dictator o Nicaragua, was said to have received money from Ambrosiano i Managua. Calvi himself would claim to have provided later muc financial assistance to the left-wing Sandinistas who overthrev Somoza in 1979.

Then there were a host of smaller outlays. They included the $ million spent on those unnecessary new headquarters in the Baha mas, the $10 million or so which may have disappeared with th collapse of Banco Occidental in Spain in 1981, as well as $16 millio lost through a company called Capitalfin which burnt its hands badl

236

after the shipping collapse of the mid-1970s. The Ambrosiano group held 25 per cent of Capitalfin. Nor could the personal use of funds be ruled out entirely. It was not known what money Calvi had accumulated for himself abroad; but the precedents established by other Italian financiers of little scruple suggest it would be strange if he had accumulated none.

Last, but not least, there was the Vatican itself. Its denial that it received any money from Calvi or his bank had to be weighed against the consideration that there would seem little reason other than that of profit, for the IOR to have worked with Calvi so unquestioningly and so long. The Vianini transaction alone would suggest it benefited, quite apart from whether Ambrosiano helped finance Solidarity— which the Vatican strongly denied. A great deal remained unclear, many months after the disaster; but all in all, it was not so difficult to imagine how over a period of ten years and in such a variety of fashions, so much money could have been squandered; the precise purpose of its going obscured by a tracery of front companies and nominees.

In any case, much of the $1,287 million quite clearly was beyond recovery, without a change of heart on the part of the IOR. The calculation of Leemans on that last desperate day in the Vatican, that the realizable value of the assets which secured the debts in Panama was $250 million or so, was hasty but probably not very wide of the mark.

The most valuable of them all by far was the 51 per cent holding in Banca del Gottardo, whose gradual disengagement from Calvi's affairs from 1980 left it little damaged by the downfall of Ambrosiano two years later. Several potential buyers were showing cautious interest in early 1983, although the risk that Gottardo might find itself at the wrong end of a lawsuit over the missing money was plainly a deterrent. Some of the other shareholdings moreover, like Vianini and even TV Sorrisi e Canzoni might fetch useful prices; but the total would probably not differ much from Leemans' guess in June 1982, when the game was about to be lost.

CHAPTER TWENTY-SIX

Epilogue

EARLY ON A cold, damp Saturday in mid-November, the physical remains of Roberto Calvi were laid to rest at last. The ceremony in the little parish church of Drezzo was simple. Journalists and photographers outnumbered the mourners. From his family there was his daughter Anna, closest in many ways of all to him, his two brothers and his aged mother. A wreath of red roses had come from his wife and son in Washington. The old Banco Ambrosiano, to which, for better or worse, Calvi had given his life, sent nobody. Just a few loyal ex-colleagues were there in a personal capacity. His driver Tito Tesauri went; so did Costanzo Zugaro from the representative office in Rome, who had first known him as a promising young cavalryman leaving for Russia more than 40 years earlier.

Locked and silent on the hillside stood the modest villa, the weekend refuge where he had played host to the powerful. Its gates were now sealed by order of the magistrates, who had confiscated all Calvi's assets in Italy.

By 9.30 a.m. Calvi had been buried in Drezzo's tiny cemetery, and the cortège was on its way back to Milan in the rain. In the *Corriere* next day just four of those little obituary notices appeared to mark his final going. One was from his wife and family, lamenting the "countless injustices" inflicted upon Calvi in the final years of his existence. Even after death, it read, "there is no peace or comfort, only resignation".

As 1982 gave way to 1983, and 1983 to 1984, that sadhearted and bemused reflection proved exact. The Ambrosiano affair and its varied ramifications seldom left the headlines of the Italian, indeed the world's, press. But all the while a sense of resignation grew, that the truth about how Calvi met his death in London, or about the

238

whereabouts of hundreds of millions of dollars, would not be exactly established.

Not that there was any lack of endeavour to do so. Carboni, Pellicani, Vittor and others connected with the last days in London were at different times detained, questioned and arrested. In Rome, the parliamentary commission examining the P-2 scandal conducted its own parallel, if cumbersome, enquiries.

Carboni did consent in the autumn of 1982 to be extradited back to Italy, but only to answer the comparatively minor charges of abetting Calvi in his illegal flight abroad, and of being party to the bankruptcy of Ambrosiano. For the Swiss magistrates had quickly found out all about those $14 million extracted from Calvi's bank in Nassau the previous February. Their Italian counterparts meanwhile were discovering much else about the dealings of Carboni.

Gradually a most unattractive picture was emerging from about a dozen separate investigations up and down the country. Carboni, his name unknown until Calvi's death, was one who appeared to mix political influence-peddling with common crime, ventures in the press with involvement in an illegal cocaine traffic and right-wing terrorism. With little doubt, Carboni was a crossroads of wrongdoing of many kinds, and the Italian authorities sought his extradition for other offences also.

Most serious of all was the charge that Carboni—and thus by implication Calvi himself—had inspired the attack in Milan on Roberto Rosone, deputy chairman of Ambrosiano, which had been carried out the previous April by Danilo Abbruciati, the underworld acquaintance of Carboni.

Nor did it seem entirely a coincidence that Carboni had been a friend of Giuseppe Pisanu, the junior Treasury minister who had read out in Parliament the astoundingly innocuous answer about Banco Andino on June 8, when the final collapse of Ambrosiano was only nine days off. In January Pisanu was forced to resign, insisting that it was pure accident that it fell to him to reply. Then there were odd tales of dinner parties given by Carboni for the likes of Ciriaco De Mita, the new Christian Democrat leader, Armando Corona, grandmaster of Italian freemasonry, as well as Carlo Caracciolo, proprietor of *La Repubblica*, the Rome paper long among Calvi's severest critics. Truly Carboni was a man for many seasons.

From Switzerland meanwhile, news had come quickly of an even bigger prize. Staff at a Geneva bank were instantly suspicious of the tall dark-haired man with glasses who appeared at the counter one mid-September day in 1982, seeking to withdraw no less than $55 million from an account connected with the Ambrosiano affair. They made time, politely telling the somewhat impatient gentleman to return in the afternoon. In the meantime they alerted the police. When he came back he was challenged and found to be travelling on a false passport. Quickly his real identity was established. It was none other than that most venerable of grandmasters, Licio Gelli himself, sought for eighteen months and facing accusations ranging from espionage to fraud and common extortion.

Italy, once again, demanded his extradition, but at first the chances of success seemed slender. Gelli engaged some of the most expensive lawyers in Europe on his behalf. From the comfort of the modern, supposedly escape-proof, prison of Champ Dollon on the edge of Geneva, he proclaimed himself a victim of political persecution and intimated that he was writing his memoirs.

But as the summer of 1983 wore on, Gelli's defences were patiently broken down. A court hearing was set for the middle of August in Lausanne, at which—it was universally assumed—the request of the Italian authorities would finally be granted. The prospect was tangible that decisive light might be thrown not just on the disaster of Banco Ambrosiano, but on other dark episodes of recent Italian history also.

It was not to be. On a hot summer night between August 9 and 10, Gelli escaped from Champ Dollon, taking his secrets with him. His cell was left in disarray, with smears of blood on the floor, as if to indicate that he had been forcibly abducted. In fact he vanished with the complicity of a prison guard, bribed for just 20,000 Swiss Francs— and evidently of others as well. A van carried him at dawn across the border into France. Gelli travelled southwards to Monte Carlo and thence, with little doubt, to the well-tried refuge of Latin America.

Yet again, Gelli had shown how the ordinary constraints of law did not apply to him. Just who else had had a hand in his flight could not be said with certainty. But a few months later a mightily embarrassed Swiss Government made diplomatic complaint to Rome about the unfettered activities of the Italian secret service upon its territory; a pointer perhaps that an organisation once so heavily infiltrated by the P-2 had once again served the grandmaster of the lodge in his moment of need.

Gelli, none the less, was most unlikely ever to return to face Italian magistrates or an Italian court—to the profound relief, it could safely be observed, of many of power and influence within the country. His case, as did that of his old friend Michele Sindona, merely proved a rule of modern Italy: that somehow potentially embarrassing defendants never managed to be called to justice at home.

In March 1983, the formal trial relating to the bankruptcy of Sindona had begun, eight and a half years after the collapse of Banca Privata Italiana and his own escape to the United States. But negotiations were proceeding between Rome and Washington for the inmate of Otisville to be temporarily "borrowed" by the court in Milan. The trial was accordingly adjourned. A year later the negotiations were still in progress, with no indication of when they might be successfully completed.

Long before that, however, the machinery had been set in motion, which one day would lead to a trial covering the fraudulent bankruptcy of Ambrosiano itself. The most important defendant, of course, was long since dead. But in the winter of 1982 the magistrates in Milan confiscated the passports of those who seemed most closely implicated in the calamity, including Rosone, Leoni, Botta, Costa and Mennini. Almost 30 others had also been initially notified that they might be facing criminal proceedings. In the meantime personal assets of board members of the old Ambrosiano were placed provisionally under official seizure.

Subsequently, Rosone, Leoni and a few more would be arrested—but not before the former deputy chairman of Ambrosiano had secured picaresque revenge on his foes in the judiciary. He was, he had established, entitled to severance pay of 470 million lire for his three decades and more of service at the old bank; his property might have been confiscated, but Rosone was determined to get his due. Payment, he insisted, should be in cash. A date was agreed in early November 1982 for Rosone to collect the money from the headquarters of what was now Nuovo Banco Ambrosiano, in 100,000 lire denomination banknotes.

Naturally the magistrates had been told too. On the appointed day, police were waiting outside the main entrance of the bank to intercept Rosone and appropriate his spoils. Rosone, however, was too quick for them. He slipped out of a side door, drove off, and lost his pursuers at a red light. By all accounts, the money was not recovered. Thus did yet more assets of the old Ambrosiano of Roberto Calvi vanish into thin air.

Rosone was to return to the Ambrosiano story a little later, but in somewhat more sinister circumstances.

On the second floor of the block where he lived at Via Olofredi, in Milan, directly above his own flat, there operated an obscure import-export agency called Stibam. On November 24, 1982 police arrested Stibam's proprietor, a 70-year-old Syrian called Henri Arsan, on the grounds that his seemingly innocuous company was in fact engaged in illegal arms and drugs trafficking, of enormous proportions, between Italy and the Eastern Mediterranean. The coincidence that Stibam's offices were next to Rosone's home, and that the building was owned by Ambrosiano itself, appeared to suggest another possible explanation of that mysterious shooting of April 27, when Rosone was wounded in the legs.

Matters soon became even more complicated. Other Italian magistrates claimed to have uncovered a link between Stibam's dealings and the supposed Bulgarian conspiracy against the Pope. The connection was the person of Bekir Celenk, a Turkish businessman resident in Sofia, held to have been involved in both episodes. It was another odd coincidence, in a story full of them.

Yet again that kaleidoscope of theories could be agitated; and the pieces were if anything more numerous than when Calvi died. They included Banco Ambrosiano and hundreds of millions of missing dollars, international arms trading, and the so-called "Bulgarian connection", with the shadow of the Soviet Union in the background. In early 1983 evidence was unearthed of an apparent attempt by the Bulgarian secret services to assassinate Lech Walesa, leader of Solidarity, when he was in Rome to visit the Pope in January 1981. Some would recall the claims of Calvi to have given large sums to the independent Polish trade union. With a pinch of imagination, Banco Ambrosiano and its Vatican connection could again be seen as part of the secret struggle between East and West.

Such considerations, however, are beyond the scope of this book. Nor, despite the wealth of hints, pointers and coincidences, did the year and a half after his death produce any irrefutable evidence that Calvi—consciously or unconsciously—was a player in such a struggle. A similar uncertainty would continue to surround the way in which he died.

The second inquest into the death of Roberto Calvi opened at the City of London Coroner's court on June 13. From the outset it was clear that it would be a far more painstaking affair than its predecessor. Most of the main witnesses to that strange last journey to London were heard. Two, however, were missing. Flavio Carboni, by now in prison on very serious charges in Italy, did not attend; nor did Hans Kunz, the Swiss businessman who arranged the flight from Innsbruck, and the booking at Chelsea Cloisters.

The two weeks of hearings produced no conclusive new evidence bearing directly on how the chairman of Banco Ambrosiano met his end. But they provided a wealth of extra detail on the circumstances leading up to it, including such trivia as the correct combination required to open the numerical lock of Calvi's overnight case: it was 0-0-0-0. More serious, many of the grey, and still darker, aspects of the affair, left unexplored in a single day's inquest of July 23, 1982, were given a thorough airing. Those most responsible were Dr Arthur Davies, the mediculous and most inquisitive Coroner, and Mr George Carman QC, engaged by the Calvi family in their campaign to demonstrate that the banker had been murdered.

First, Mr Carman concentrated on showing how difficult it would have been for Calvi to have committed suicide in such a place. The banker was 62 years old, portly and cumbersome. He would have to climb over a parapet and down a ladder, then clamber across a scaffolding and fasten the rope—all the while weighed down by ten pounds of stones. Professor Keith Simpson, the chief pathologist at Guy's Hospital, was obliged to concede that it would have been easier for Calvi to have been taken by professional criminals to the spot in a boat, and his body then suspended from the scaffolding.

Professor Simpson, whose forensic evidence was so important in securing the first suicide verdict, maintained that he had found no trace of drugs or foul play during his original autopsy. He reiterated that the medical evidence was consistent with suicide by hanging. But he admitted that Calvi could have been immobilized, or mad unconscious, by a drug which left no trace, such as ethyl chloride, or curare-based drug of the kind used in abdominal surgery.

Furthermore, Mr Carman demonstrated how the night entrance t Chelsea Cloisers was effectively unguarded, so that Calvi could hav been taken from the building by other people, without being noticed Donald Bartlett of the Thames River Police, who had taken dow Calvi's corpse on the morning of June 18, confirmed that it woul have been simple, when the Thames tide was high, for an experience boatman to take a small craft in under the bridge, and from it hang body to the scaffolding. But in the absence of hard confirmator evidence, these remained hypotheses; possibilities but no more.

The second avenue explored by the inquest was the behaviour, o occasion bizarre to say the least, of those who accompanied Calvi i his flight. Sustained questioning exposed discrepancies and contra dictions between the testimony of the Kleinszig sisters and of Vittor and earlier statements made by himself and Carboni to magistrates i Italy. There were also curious lapses of memory about importar episodes during that last week of the banker's life. The exact timing c movements during the most crucial period of all on the Thursda night, between Vittor's leaving Calvi in apartment 881 at Chelse Cloisters at roughly 11 p.m., and his return between an hour and tw hours later to find Calvi gone, remained unclear.

Few seriously believed that Carboni and Vittor, neither of ther English speakers or familiar with London, actually carried out murder as skilful and well planned as that which the questioning of M Carman was intimating. But, as he put it to the court on June 15: " have never sought to suggest that if Calvi was murdered, Carboni wa physically involved. Whether he was aware of it is another matte entirely." So was Calvi left unguarded deliberately, at a pre-arrange moment? On the other hand, if that was so, then there has been no one firm pointer to the identity of the third party (or rather parties who intervened at that point to set their murder plot, complete wit masonic ritual, into motion.

There was also the question of Carboni's peculiar return on June 2 to Austria, via Edinburgh; and then his meeting the following day i Zurich with Vittor. Was this to work out an agreed version of event before Vittor turned himself over to the Italian police in Trieste o

June 23? And if so, why?

The key was still Carboni. Only he could tell exactly why he went to London, and on whose, if anyone's, behalf he was engaged. Only Carboni, moreover, could explain the payments made by him before and after Calvi's death: including one of $100,000 into the Swiss account of his mistress, Laura Concas, niece of the wife of Morris; and another, far larger, of $530,000 in favour of his underworld acquaintance Ernesto Diotallevi, whom he had seen in Zurich shortly before leaving for London on June 16. For what services was that money paid? Diotallevi, who had been on the run for many months, was another whom police and magistrates were particularly anxious to question.

But Carboni was not there; and in his absence the questions raised by the second inquest outnumbered the answers. Maybe the balance of probability had shifted away from suicide and a little closer to that of murder. But of certainty there was none. The verdict of the coroner, given at 4 p.m. on Monday June 27, 1983, was an open one: as it had to be, and as it should have been at the first inquest eleven months earlier. Italy, it is often said, is a country where everything is possible. That judgement remained as true of the death of Roberto Calvi as it was of his extraordinary life.

CHAPTER TWENTY-SEVEN

Conclusions

ON THE AFTERNOON of Friday February 17, 1984 a group of sober-suited men left the Hotel des Bergues in Geneva, well satisfied with the outcome of their discussions. Less than 24 hours later, and some 600 miles away to the south in the graceful Renaissance setting of Villa Madama on a pineclad hillside overlooking Rome, Bettino Craxi, the first Socialist Prime Minister of modern Italy sat down with Cardinal Agostino Casaroli, the Vatican's Secretary of State for a solemn ceremony. That afternoon they signed into effect a new Concordat governing relations between the two States, 55 years after Mussolini and Pope Pius XI had concluded the first such agreement in 1929.

For all their different character, the two events were most closely connected. The meeting in Geneva was the culmination of a search which had begun a year and a half earlier, for agreement between the Vatican, the Italian authorities and 120 foreign creditor banks on a settlement of the debts left by Banco Ambrosiano. And for many months it had been clear that without such a settlement, the new Concordat which had been under negotiation for almost a decade, could not be ratified.

Often during 1983 it had seemed that an understanding would be impossible. The joint commission of experts representing Italy and the Vatican, set up on Christmas Eve 1982, worked through most of the subsequent year. Its six members, three from each side, travelled to Luxembourg, Nassau, Latin America and beyond, to sift through the records of the dealings between the IOR and the foreign subsidiaries of the Ambrosiano of Roberto Calvi. In the autumn they presented their conclusions. But these brought little enlightenment.

The dispute which had sealed the collapse of Ambrosiano in June 1982 remained. The three Italian members of the commission were convinced that the Vatican bank was a knowing accomplice to fraud. But the representatives of the Holy See insisted as all along, that the IOR and Marcinkus had in their naïvety been tricked, and could not be held responsible for the *débâcle*.

Gradually however it became clear that even the secret work of the commission was merely elegant camouflage for real negotiations taking place elsewhere.

A settlement was in everyone's interest. The Vatican might affect studied unconcern; in fact it wanted at all costs to close the affair, to protect its relations with Italy and to prevent further embarrassing details of its financial behaviour being aired in court actions which were growing steadily more probable. The creditor banks quite simply wanted their money back—or as much of it as possible. For its part, the Italian Government was as keen to remove a lingering irritant in its own financial dealings abroad as it was to force the Vatican to honour its own obligations.

As 1983 wore on, contacts intensified between the main interested parties: the liquidators of the old Ambrosiano, Pasquale Chiomenti, a wise old Italian lawyer trusted by all parties, emissaries from the creditor banks, as well as representatives of Touche Ross, the London accounting firm which now managed Ambrosiano Holding of Luxembourg, and as such was seeking to trace the money dissipated by Calvi. In the background, both the Bank of Italy and the Vatican authorities monitored proceedings intently.

The pieces in the settlement jigsaw gradually fell into place. To raise money, the Vatican sold its interest in the Vianini construction group for $41 million. Next, Ambrosiano Luxembourg disposed of its controlling interest in Banca del Gottardo for $144 million to the Sumitomo Bank of Japan. These proceeds too would help towards the overall settlement. Most important of all, the IOR consented to provide $250 million as its contribution to a lasting peace treaty. The Vatican would emphasise that the payment, which would have to be raised in large measure by an international loan, did not amount to an admission of responsibility. For most interested onlookers however, it was precisely that.

And so, that February day in the Hotel des Bergues, agreement in principle was sealed. Ratification was still required from the 88 main creditor banks of Ambrosiano Luxembourg, and from 32 other smaller creditors of banks in the Ambrosiano group, most notably Ambrosiano Overseas in Nassau and Banco Andino in Lima. The procedure might take two months or more; but at that late stage, few were likely to cavil.

In all Touche Ross would have up to $475 million available. The "group of 88", which had fought so hard for recompense, would see its efforts rewarded by repayment of 70 per cent or more of the money its members had so injudiciously lent to Calvi's Luxembourg holding company. Smaller sums would go to the minor creditors, and to the liquidators in Milan. In return, the foreign banks would drop all outstanding lawsuits against the Italian authorities, Nuovo Banco Ambrosiano—and against the IOR. Lending to Italian borrowers, in so far as it had been disturbed by the Calvi scandal, would be resumed normally.

But even this laborious settlement threw no light on the ultimate destination of much of the vanished money. The search would probably continue for years, with little guarantee of success. Nor would the Vatican do much to help. After a meeting in March, which estimated that the budget deficit for 1984 of the Holy See might reach an unprecedented $32 million, the cardinals who superintended its finances stated cryptically that the role of the IOR in the Ambrosiano affair would be explained "in due time". As a synonym for "never", the phrase was as polite as any other.

But the puzzle over the money, even the hints of entanglement in global conspiracy, are mere stepping stones towards the mystery at the heart of this story: Roberto Calvi himself.

The modest son of a modest bank official in Milan had brought about, if not entirely singlehanded, at least principally by his own endeavours the greatest bank scandal in living memory. He had exposed the ease with which a natural deceiver could exploit the opportunities offered by the international banking system, and how that deception could be maintained for so long. Indeed in May 1983 the leading central banks had revised their own "Concordat" of eight years before—a revision specifically designed to eliminate the uncertain division of responsibilities exposed by the Ambrosiano crisis.

The career of Calvi had laid bare the extent to which the ingrown ways of the government of Italy had become aberrant; and how expensive such aberrations could be. The financial cost, to be met in the end by the ordinary taxpayer, would run into many hundreds of billions of lire. The politicians also perhaps paid a price. By suitable irony, the open verdict at the second inquest in London was delivered at almost the very moment that the Christian Democrat politicians in Rome were learning of their worst ever defeat in 38 years of power at the general election of June 26 and 27—a defeat to which the scandal of Calvi and Ambrosiano had probably contributed. Then there were other, less quantifiable considerations.

One was the subtle damage that the exploits of Calvi may have inflicted upon the status of Italy in international financial markets, between summer 1982 and the spring of 1984 when settlement with the creditor banks was reached. Another was the wider impact of the Ambrosiano affair upon the Bank of Italy.

The argument would extend well beyond whether a host of foreign banks should have an error of lending judgement made good. Just how deeply the central bank had been marked by the story of Roberto Calvi, only time would reveal. Sureness of touch, self-confidence and prestige are qualities difficult to measure. For a while, and in foreign eyes at least, the Bank of Italy perhaps lost a little of all three.

In retrospect, the "Bank of Italy affair" of 1979 would stand out even more vividly as the most miserable episode (at least to one who was not Italian) in a miserable tale. It had neither the gruesome fascination of Calvi's end, nor the baroque seediness of the way in which $1,287 million vanished. But rarely before or since has the dark underside of Italian life been so vividly illustrated. It was easy, when all was done, to argue that the central bank should have acted more vigorously and far sooner to cut short Calvi's enterprise—certainly after his conviction in 1981. But that was to ignore the pressures, unspoken but in Italy no less real for that, upon it. And, in the end, it *was* the central bank which finally exposed Calvi. Perhaps the knock-out should have been a clean blow in an early round, rather than a messy affair at the end of the fight; but a knockout none the less it was.

What is more, those pressures would remain. In December 1982 Rinaldo Ossola, another distinguished product of the Bank of Italy, where he had been general manager until the summer of 1976, was left with no choice but to resign as chairman of Banco di Napoli.

Ossola had been sent to what was notoriously a bank conditioned by the Christian Democrat political establishment in Naples, in the hope of bringing greater clarity and modernity to its workings. In the event, his ability and his reputation counted little against the entrenched political interests with which an outsider had to contend. Before he left, his deputy chairman and fierce critic Aristide Savignano publicly stated that the real Mafia "was not to be found in Palermo, or even Naples but at the Bank of Italy". The turn of phrase was over-theatrical—but another sign of how the philosophy of the central bank was not universally shared. Later however Ossola would win redress of sorts. Early in 1983, he was appointed chairman of Credito Varesino, the bank which Calvi had dubiously acquired with the complicity of the IOR in 1972, and which would probably be sold by the Nuovo Ambrosiano group during 1984. There could be no greater symbol of changed times than the presence of Ossola at the helm of a bank once controlled by Calvi.

And finally, even the laborious renegotiation of the Concordat first signed in 1929 by Pope Pius XI, a relative of an earlier chairman of Banco Ambrosiano, could not escape the consequences of the deeds of its last one. All in all it was no mean legacy for a quiet diffident man from Milan.

And so we return, as we are compelled, to Calvi himself, elusive to the last. His story has made depressing, even tragic reading at times—quite apart from the horrible manner of his dying. All that was heroic about his fraud was its scale and its duration. The methods and ends of it were furtive, defensive, and in a curious way, second-rate.

In the financial dealings throughout his life Calvi was unprincipled and ambitious. But in that field he was beyond doubt a genius, however distorted, and whatever the social and human limitations to his character. In the early days the shortcomings did not matter; but later they did, as the need grew to protect financial spoils by non-financial means as well. Those to whom he was forced to turn, the politicians, Gelli, Pazienza, and at the end Carboni, trapped Calvi in a mechanism in which the plunderer became the plundered, the master the slave—and in some ways a most ordinary one. "Someone like Calvi simply could not be behind a mystery like this," Carlo De Benedetti, his unlikely colleague of two months, would remark after it was all over. And many shared the perplexity of De Benedetti. Calvi appeared to lack the dimension of the scandal he had brought about.

And yet such was the aura of financial infallibility which surrounded him that many, especially within his bank, were beguiled, trusting until the end. Italians can occasionally be as gullible as they are usually realistic; Calvi's own habit of giving little away only added to his mystique. *Più uno non si fa capire, più viene considerato intelligente*, was how Rosone, the last chief executive of Banco Ambrosiano, summed him up afterwards. "The harder someone makes himself to understand, the cleverer they're thought to be." Thus it was of Calvi, so long considered one of the most powerful men in Italy.

He also shared Gelli's gift of playing on both sides at once—the Fascist and Socialist party cards after return from Russia, the good relations with both Somoza and Sandinistas in Nicaragua, the employment of Pazienza and Carboni for apparently different schemes. A double reality persisted to the end in his banking group as well; the seemingly prosperous Italian part, and the cracked mirror of it in Latin America.

So where did the key lie? Just conceivably, we should go back to before the beginning, to the Valtellina, those foothills of the Alps. *Scarpe grosse, cervello fino*, runs the Italian saying about people from such parts. Clumsy boots but a subtle mind. The aphorism fitted easily upon Roberto Calvi.

His humour was mostly that of the mountains; at best wry and understated. He knew the price of everything and of everyone, and yet the value of very little, beyond his family and the country weekends at Drezzo. Even his bank may have been only a vehicle for a purpose, a vehicle of which all the doors by the end were locked.

And then there were "the priests". A banker from Rome, with all the ancestral cynicism of that city about the Church, would surely not have trusted the Vatican and the IOR as Calvi did. For in his way, and despite his cunning, he undoubtedly did trust them, and felt betrayed when they did not stand by him as crisis deepened. In Calvi's eyes, the

Church was not only of huge power and influence, and as such a secret key to the doors of success. It was also to be looked up to and relied upon, even vaguely feared, much as the peasant regards the village priest. Here again we are left with the two conflicting images of the man: suspicious yet ingenuous, untrusting, yet trusting to the last.

And so-for now the story ends. The fortunes of the various members of its cast differ considerably. In August 1983 Andreotti, the great survivor, returned to Government as Foreign Minister, his reputation intact as the shrewdest of the Christian Democrats. Craxi, the Socialist leader whose party had benefited so much from the largesse of Ambrosiano, became Prime Minister. Carboni was in prison in Italy; so was Tassan Din, whose health was reportedly giving way. Rosone, Leoni, Botta and Costa, all of whom had worked closely with Calvi, had been arrested. Angelo Rizzoli too spent 1983 in and out of prison. The magistrates in Milan were sifting through tens of thousands of pages of statements, documents and transcribed tape recordings to try and establish the truth.

Baffi would spend much of his time in Switzerland, working on a study of the Bank for International Settlements. Sarcinelli was director general of the Treasury Ministry in Rome, not entirely without prospect that one day he might become Governor of the Bank of Italy. In early 1984 Mennini and de Stroebel had taken refuge within the Vatican walls to escape the attentions of the magistrates. Marcinkus was still chairman of the IOR, but talking of his desire to end his career as a working parish priest, perhaps in a neighbourhood of the Chicago he had left for Rome in 1950.† Sindona was reading Nietzsche in upstate New York, while De Benedetti announced in March 1984 a rise of 73 per cent in the profits of Olivetti. From the Bahamas, Clara Calvi was persisting, bravely but increasingly for-lornly, with her campaign to clear her husband's name.

Roberto Calvi, of course, was no longer there. The successor to his Banco Ambrosiano was carefully feeling its way. It was a middling-sized Milanese bank of no great pretension—which the old Ambro-siano would have been to this day, had not Calvi entered it all those years ago. Afterwards many would still rub their eyes, and wonder

† Chicago Tribune, March 13, 1983

whether he really had, whether the whole story had really happened at all.

But it did happen; and the ways of Italy have not greatly changed. Sometimes even now, as the cold fog of a Milanese winter's evening settles on those narrow streets behind La Scala, and a light burns smokily on the fourth floor above Via Clerici, it is easy to imagine Calvi still there; talking enigmatically of priests, and of strange banks without substance half a world away.

Bonn, March 25, 1984

APPENDIX

Gentlemen:

This is to confirm that we directly or indirectly control the following entries:
- Manic S.A., Luxembourg
- Astolfine S.A., Panama
- Nordeurop Establishment, Liechtenstein
- U.T.C. United Trading Corporation, Panama
- Erin S.A., Panama
- Bellatrix S.A., Panama
- Belrosa S.A., Panama
- Starfield S.A., Panama

We also confirm our awareness of their indebtedness towards yourselves as of June 10, 1981 as per attached statement of accounts.

Yours faithfully,

ISTITUTO PER LE OPERE DI RELIGIONE

One of the notorious letters of comfort

254

MESSAGE NO. 352 APRIL 23, 1979

TO CALVIN

RE.: AGBC : PAYMENT VALUE 25 APRIL

FURTHER TO OUR VARIOUS TELEXES ON THE MATTER I HAVE BEEN
INFORMED BY MR LEONI THAT VALQE 25 AGBC HAS TO MAKE THE
FOLLOWING PAYMENT:

DLRS 3,000,000
TO NORDEUROPA
C/O BANCA DEL GOTTARDO (ATTENZIONE MR BOLGIANI)

THE PERIOD OF THE LOAN IS 25TH APRIL - 25TH OCTOBER 1979,
RATE 11.1/4

THESE 3 MILLION WILL BE GIVEN TO AGBC BY CISO UTILIZING
3,000,000 OF THE 7,500,000 RISED BY YOU AND MARCO, RATE 11.1/8.
THE REMAINING FUNDS (DLRS 4,500,000 PLUS THE 15,000,000
RECEIVED FROM BCV AND CV) PLUS ANY OTHER AMOUNT WE CAN
RISE (...?) WILL BE PAID OUT (INSTRUCTIONS WILL FOLLOW)
WITH VALUE 30TH APRIL.

PLEASE SEND THE PAYMENT INSTRUCTIONS FOR THE A/M 3,000,000
TODAY.

I HOPE ALL IS IN ORDER. THANKS AND REGARDS.   46638
LICIA

One of the telexes from Montecarlo to Nassau

Lists of main shareholders in Banco Ambrosiano SpA
(percentage holdings)

1. 1973 (Bank of Italy inspection)

Locafid AG (Zurich)	6.93
Kredietbank SA (Antwerp)	3.33
IOR (Vatican City)	1.37
Banca San Paolo (Brescia)	0.50
B.B.B. Ind. Tessili SpA (Milan)	0.50
Invest SpA (Milan)	0.50

2. 1978 (Bank of Italy inspection)

Finprogram, Cascadilla, Lantana, Orfeo La Fidele, Marbella (all Panama)	9.79
Sapi, Ulricor, Rekofinanz, Sektorinvest, Finkurs, Sansinvest, Ecke (all Liechtenstein)	6.80
Toro, Italfid, Italtrust (all of Ambrosiano group)	5.80
Suprafin (Milan)	4.02
Kredietbank (Antwerp)	3.09
IOR (Vatican City)	1.85
Veneranda Fabbrica del Duomo (Milan)	0.42
Infidfin (Lugano)	0.40

3. 1979 (Guardia di Finanza inspection)

Credito Overseas, Lantana, Cascadilla, La Fidele, Finprogram, Orfeo, Marbella (all Panama)	9.54
Sapi, Rekofinanz, Ulricor, Ecke, Finkurs, Sektorinvest, Sansinvest (all Liechtenstein)	7.03
Toro Assicurazioni (Turin)	5.11
Kredietbank (Antwerp)	3.09
IOR (Vatican City)	1.82
Cogebel (Luxembourg)	1.00
Crédit Commercial de France (Geneva)	0.46

4. 1982 (as listed in Bourse prospectus)

Italmobiliare SpA (Milan)	3.62
Kredietbank SA (Antwerp)	3.20
Credito Overseas (Panama)	2.72
IOR (Vatican City)	1.59
Fiduciaire La Tour SA (Panama)	1.59
Crédit Commercial de France (Geneva)	1.37
Rekofinanz (Liechtenstein)	1.22
Ulricor (Liechtenstein)	1.18
Interpart SA (Milan)	1.10
Cascadilla SA (Panama)	0.93
Lantana (Panama)	0.93

The main companies backed by the IOR's letters of patronage, the debts and the guarantees at June 30, 1982

Company	Capital (in Dollars)	Debts (million)	Pledged assets
Manic	45 million	157	48,000 shares Banca del Gottardo 3.7 million shares Banco Ambrosiano
Zitropo Holding	27.5 million	45	172 million shares Pacchetti
Astolfine (ex-Nordeurop)	10,000	486	2.1 million shares Banco Ambrosiano
Bellatrix	10,000	184	567,000 shares in Rizzoli
Laramie	10,000	26	2 million shares Vianini SpA
Erin	10,000	37	4.5 million shares Credito Varesino
Worldwide Trading	10,000	40	520 shares TV Sorrisi e Canzoni
Belrosa	10,000	88	Shares in Capitalfin International; 100 shares in Montreal Holding Corporation; 19,470 shares, Banca del Gottardo

Index

259

résumé, 16; background, 46; and
Vatican, 46, 48; and Banco Financeiro,
46, 112, 144; and P-2, 47; and Latin
America, 47, 109; and Rizzoli group,
75, 79, 132, 133; and Ambrosiano
money, 235, 236
Ossola, Rinaldo, 243
Ottone, Piero, 79

P-2 freemasons' lodge (main references),
93, 203, 238; outlawed (1981), 20, 133;
finances of, 21; RC joins 44; nature of,
45, 47, 48; membership lists, 45, 47, 114,
134, 136; Latin American links, 47, 236;
American links, 47; and Rizzoli group,
73, 75, 78; and Genghini group, 93, 125;
repercussions of discovery, 152; and De
Benedetti, 158; and RC's death, 199;
and Corriere, 224–5
Paccheti, 60, 61–2, 63, 69, 71, 84, 105,
111, 112, 234
Padalino, Giulio, 90, 94, 95, 96, 106, 159,
221
Paese Sera, 72, 124
Pahlevis, 172
Palazzini, Cardinal, 177
Pandolfi, Filippo Maria, 101, 103
Paribas, 32
Parlato, Giuseppe, 38
Pasargiklian, Vahan, 69
Paul, Dr David, 200
Paul VI, Pope, 28, 40, 51, 52, 53, 55, 60,
91, 177, 212
Pazienza, Francesco (main references),
résumé, 16; background, 140; meets
RC, 141; as "international adviser",
141; arrogant behaviour, 148, 158, 174;
pressurizes RC, 161, 244; and Vianini,
171, 232–3; consortium idea, 172–3,
179; in London, 193, 195; payment of,
236
Pecorelli, Mino, 101
Pellicani, Emilio, 181, 182, 238
Permaflex, 46
Peron, Juan, 46
Pertini, President, 228
Pesenti, Carlo, 16, 41, 57, 66, 90, 99, 124,
166, 167, 180, 186, 224
Petromin, 114
Piazzesi, Gianfranco, 48
Piccoli, Flaminio, 141, 158, 201
Pirelli, 42
Pisanu, Giuseppe, 239
Pius XI, Pope, 28, 243
Pius XII, Pope, 55, 209
Prefecture for Economic Affairs, 55
Prima Linea, 97

Prisco, Giuseppe, 165, 180
"Proletarian Autonomy", 108
Propaganda Lodge, 45
Propaganda-2, see P-2 freemasons' lodge
Puzo, Mario, 44

Radicals, 134
Ratti, Achille see Pius XI, Pope
Ratti, Franco, 28, 29
Razza Padrona (Scalfari and Turani), 67
Recioto account, Zurich, 137, 235
Red Brigades, 91, 97, 103, 105, 186
Rekofinanz, 70, 252, 253
Republicans, 15, 113, 139, 210
Rizzoli, Alberto, 223
Rizzoli, Andrea, 74, 75, 76
Rizzoli, Angelo, 74
Rizzoli, Angelo, Jnr, 16, 74, 75, 133, 135,
136, 139, 153, 159, 222, 223, 224
Rizzoli publishing group (main
references), 112, 141, 188, 235–6; and
P-2, 73, 75, 78, 235; and Corriere, 73,
74–5, 76, 78, 132–3; 150, 219; origins,
74; plans for, 79; debts of, 132, 222–3;
rescue plans, 135–7, 139; Bank of Italy
forces sale, 150, 153, 160; arrest of
Rizzolis, 223
Rosone, Roberto (main references),
résumé, 16; and foreign banks, 143;
background, 147–8; tries to remove RC,
148; becomes deputy chairman, 149;
shot in legs, 175, 203, 239, 241; acting
chairman, 184, 187; and IOR, 187–8,
190; Power struggle, 190; and severance
pay, 240–41
Rossi, Guido, 17, 130–32, 161, 186, 219,
220
Rothschild, Evelyn de, 43, 61
Rothschild Bank, 186, 235
Rovelli, Nino, 88, 98, 100
Royal Bank of Canada, 178
Rueta, Silva, 109

SACE, 121
SGI (Società Generale Immobiliare), 40,
41, 42, 54, 65
SIR, 88, 90, 98, 100
STET, 209
"St Peter's Pence", 53, 55, 229, 233
Sandinistas, 95, 109, 236, 244
Sansinvest, 70, 252
Sapi, 70, 82, 252
Sarcinelli, Mario, 17, 89, 90, 95, 96, 98,
99, 100, 101, 102, 103, 105, 106, 111,
125, 130, 148, 208, 245
Saudi, Abdullah, 127
Savignano, Aristide, 243

262